Youth Subcultures

OTHER TITLES IN THE LONGMAN TOPICS READER SERIES

Translating Tradition
Karen E. Beardslee

City Life
Patrick Bruch and Richard Marback

Diversity: Strength and Struggle
Joseph Calabrese and Susan Tchudi

Legends, Lore, and Lies: A Skeptic's Stance
Joseph Calabrese

Citizenship Now
Jon Ford and Marjorie Ford

The Changing World of Work
Marjorie Ford

Issues of Gender
Ellen G. Friedman and Jennifer D. Marshall

Youth Subcultures: Exploring Underground America
Arielle Greenberg

International Views: America and the Rest of the World
Keith Gumery

Listening to Earth: A Reader
Christopher Hallowell and Walter Levy

Body and Culture
Greg Lyons

Writing Places
Paula Mathieu, George Grattan, Tim Lindgren, and Staci Shulty

Peace, War, and Terrorism
Denis Okerstrom

The World of the Image
Trudy Smoke and Alan Robbins

Hip Hop Reader
Tim Strode and Tim Wood

The Counterculture Reader
E. A. Swingrover

Discovering Popular Culture
Anna Tomasino

Music and Culture
Anna Tomasino

Ethics in the 21ˢᵗ Century
Mary Alice Trent

Considering Culture Difference
Pauline Uchmanowicz

Language and Prejudice
Tamara M. Valentine

CyberReader, Abridged Edition
Victor J. Vitanza

A LONGMAN TOPICS READER

Youth Subcultures

Exploring Underground America

ARIELLE GREENBERG
Columbia College Chicago

PEARSON
Longman

New York   San Francisco   Boston
London   Toronto   Sydney   Tokyo   Singapore   Madrid
Mexico City   Munich   Paris   Cape Town   Hong Kong   Montreal

Acquisitions Editor: Lauren A. Finn
Senior Marketing Manager: Sandra McGuire
Production Manager: Donna DeBenedictis
Project Coordination, Text Design Adaption, Art Rendering, and
    Electronic Page Makeup: Carlisle Publishing Services
Cover Designer/Manager: Wendy Ann Fredericks
Cover Photo: © Getty/Photodisc
Manufacturing Manager: Mary Fischer

For permission to use copyrighted material, grateful acknowledgment
is made to the copyright holders on pp. 234–235, which are hereby
made part of this copyright page.

Library of Congress Cataloging-in-Publication Data
Greenberg, Arielle.
    Youth subcultures: exploring underground America / Arielle
Greenberg.
        p. cm.
    Includes bibliographical references.
    ISBN 0-321-24194-0
    1. Subculture—United States. 2. Youth—United States. I. Title.

HM646.G74 2007
05.2350973—dc23

                                        2006050697

Please visit us at www.ablongman.com

ISBN 0-321-24194-0

CONTENTS

Rhetorical Contents   *vii*
Thematic Contents   *xiii*
Preface   *xv*

INTRODUCTION   1

CHAPTER 1   Roots and Origins   5

Michael Dennis, Youth Activism in the 1990s   5
Catherine Walsh, The Rainbow Family Gathering   18
G. Beato, The Lords of Dogtown   21
*Yoly A. Carrillo and Arielle Greenberg, Norteña
    Slang Dictionary   36
Deena Weinstein, Heavy Metal's Proud Pariahs   38

CHAPTER 2   Fitting in and Coming Together   53

Sasha Vliet, The Bboy Style on the Eastside   53
Rob Maitra, The Homeless Community of the Piers   64
Mimi Nguyen, Thoughts on the Movie *Afro-Punk*   72
*Heidi Schubert, Where We Belong: A Report on
    Anime Central 2004   77
Kylie Lee, My Life as an Enterprise Slash Writer   86

CHAPTER 3   Myths and Truths   98

Amy Wilkins, From Geeks to Freaks:
    Goth and the Middle Class   99
J. Patrick Williams, How the Internet Is
    Changing Straightedge   104
*Sarah Norton, My Night as a Wiccan:
    Dusting Away the Stereotypes   116

*The asterisk indicates essays written by undergraduate students.

Natalie Porter, She Rips When She Skates: Female
  Skateboarders as Active Subcultural Participants   121

Zhi Zhu, A Different View of Hackers   136

CHAPTER 4   Merchandise, Commercialism, and Co-opting the Scene   148

Adrienne Lai, Towards a Critical Understanding
  of "Asian Cute Culture"   149

Emily Lamison, So Emo It Hurts   160

Christina Robinson, Economic Status and Raving   170

Robert Rundquist, Street Skateboarding and the
  Government Stamp of Approval   179

CHAPTER 5   Dropping Out and Dropping Back In   190

Jerry Adler, The Graying of Aquarius   191

Johanna M. Hoadley, Growing Up and Out
  of the Rave Scene   196

Melissa McCray Pattacini, Deadheads
  Yesterday and Today: An Audience Study   203

John Lennon, Too Dirty to Be a Hobo?   212

Robert T. Wood, A Straightedger's Journey   223

Credits   234

Rhetorical Contents

Narration

Catherine Walsh, The Rainbow Family Gathering   18

G. Beato, The Lords of Dogtown   21

Sasha Vliet, The Bboy Style on the Eastside   53

Rob Maitra, The Homeless Community of the Piers   64

Heidi Schubert, A Report on Anime Central 2004   77

Sarah Norton, My Night as a Wiccan   116

Johanna M. Hoadley, Growing Up and
    Out of the Rave Scene   196

John Lennon, Too Dirty to Be a Hobo?   212

Robert T. Wood, A Straightedger's Journey   223

Description

Michael Dennis, Youth Activism in the 1990s   5

Catherine Walsh, The Rainbow Family Gathering   18

G. Beato, The Lords of Dogtown   21

Deena Weinstein, Heavy Metal's Proud Pariahs   38

Sasha Vliet, The Bboy Style on the Eastside   53

Rob Maitra, The Homeless Community of the Piers   64

Mimi Nguyen, Thoughts on the Movie *Afro-Punk*   72

Heidi Schubert, A Report on Anime Central 2004   77

Kylie Lee, My Life as an Enterprise Slash Writer   86

Amy Wilkins, From Geeks to Freaks:
    Goth and the Middle Class   99

J. Patrick Williams, How the Internet is Changing
    Straightedge   104

Sarah Norton, My Night as a Wiccan   116

Natalie Porter, She Rips When She Skates   121

Zhi Zhu, A Different View of Hackers   136

Adrienne Lai, Towards a Critical Understanding of
    "Asian Cute Culture"   149

Emily Lamison, So Emo It Hurts   160

Christina Robinson, Economic Status and Raving   170

Robert Rundquist, Street Skateboarding and the Government
    Stamp of Approval   179
Jerry Adler, The Graying of Aquarius   191
Johanna Hoadley, Growing Up and Out of the Rave Scene   196
John Lennon, Too Dirty to Be a Hobo?   212

Analysis

Michael Dennis, Youth Activism in the 1990s   5
Catherine Walsh, The Rainbow Family Gathering   18
G. Beato, The Lords of Dogtown   21
Deena Weinstein, Heavy Metal's Proud Pariahs   38
Sasha Vliet, The Bboy Style on the Eastside   53
Rob Maitra, The Homeless Community of the Piers   64
Mimi Nguyen, Thoughts on the Movie *Afro-Punk*   72
Heidi Schubert, A Report on Anime Central 2004   77
Kylie Lee, My Life as an Enterprise Slash Writer   86
Amy Wilkins, From Geeks to Freaks:
    Goths and the Middle Class   99
J. Patrick Williams, How the Internet Is
    Changing Straightedge   104
Natalie Porter, She Rips When She Skates   121
Zhi Zhu, A Different View of Hackers   136
Adrienne Lai, Towards a Critical Understanding of
    "Asian Cute Culture"   149
Emily Lamison, So Emo It Hurts   160
Christina Robinson, Economic Status and Raving   170
Robert Rundquist, Street Skateboarding and the
    Government Stamp of Approval   179
Jerry Adler, The Graying of Aquarius   191
Melissa McCray Pattacini, Deadheads Yesterday and Today:
    An Audience Study   203
John Lennon, Too Dirty to Be a Hobo?   212

Comparison and Contrast

Michael Dennis, Youth Activism in the 1990s   5
Catherine Walsh, The Rainbow Family Gathering   18
Deena Weinstein, Heavy Metal's Proud Pariahs   38
Amy Wilkins, From Geeks to Freaks:
    Goths and the Middle Class   99

Natalie Porter, She Rips When She Skates   121
Adrienne Lai, Towards a Critical Understanding of
    "Asian Cute Culture"   149
Emily Lamison, So Emo It Hurts   160
Jerry Adler, The Graying of Aquarius   191
Melissa McCray Pattacini, Deadheads Yesterday and Today:
    An Audience Study   203
John Lennon, Too Dirty to Be a Hobo?   212
Robert T. Wood, A Straightedger's Journey   223

Definition

Michael Dennis, Youth Activism in the 1990s   5
Catherine Walsh, The Rainbow Family Gathering   18
G. Beato, The Lords of Dogtown   21
Yoly A, Carillo and Arielle Greenberg. Norteña Slang,
    Dictionary   36
Deena Weinstein, Heavy Metal's Proud Pariahs   38
Sasha Vliet, The Bboy Style on the Eastside   53
Rob Maitra, The Homeless Community of the Piers   64
Mimi Nguyen, Thoughts on the Movie *Afro-Punk*   72
Heidi Schubert, A Report on Anime Central 2004   77
Kylie Lee, My Life as an Enterprise Slash Writer   86
Amy Wilkins, From Geeks to Freaks:
    Goths and the Middle Class   99
J. Patrick Williams, How the Internet Is Changing
    Straightedge   104
Sarah Norton, My Night as a Wiccan   116
Natalie Porter, She Rips When She Skates   121
Zhi Zhu, A Different View of Hackers   136
Adrienne Lai, Towards a Critical Understanding of
    "Asian Cute Culture"   149
Emily Lamison, So Emo It Hurts   160
Christina Robinson, Economic Status and Raving   170
Jerry Adler, The Graying of Aquarius   191
Johanna Hoadley, Growing Up and Out of the Rave Scene   196
Melissa McCray Pattacini, Deadheads Yesterday
    and Today: An Audience Study   203
John Lennon, Too Dirty to Be a Hobo?   212

Argument and Persuasion

Michael Dennis, Youth Activism in the 1990s 5

Sasha Vliet, The Bboy Style on the Eastside 53

Rob Maitra, The Homeless Community of the Piers 64

Amy Wilkins, From Geeks to Freaks:
Goths and the Middle Class 99

Natalie Porter, She Rips When She Skates 121

Zhi Zhu, A Different View of Hackers 136

Adrienne Lai, Towards a Critical Understanding of
"Asian Cute Culture" 149

Robert Rundquist, Street Skateboarding and the
Government Stamp of Approval 179

Memoir

Sasha Vliet, The Bboy Style on the Eastside 53

Heidi Schubert, A Report on Anime Central 2004 77

Kylie Lee, My Life as an Enterprise Slash Writer 86

Johanna Hoadley, Growing Up and Out of the Rave Scene 196

Ethnography

Catherine Walsh, The Rainbow Family Gathering 18

G. Beato, The Lords of Dogtown 21

Deena Weinstein, Heavy Metal's Proud Pariahs 38

Sasha Vliet, The Bboy Style on the Eastside 53

Rob Maitra, The Homeless Community of the Piers 64

Heidi Schubert, A Report on Anime Central 2004 77

Amy Wilkins, From Geeks to Freaks:
Goths and the Middle Class 99

J. Patrick Williams, How the Internet Is Changing
Straightedge 104

Sarah Norton, My Night as a Wiccan 116

Natalie Porter, She Rips When She Skates 121

Emily Lamison, So Emo It Hurts 160

Jerry Adler, The Graying of Aquarius 191

Johanna M. Hoadley, Growing Up and Out of the Rave Scene 196

Melissa McCray Pattacini, Deadheads Yesterday and
Today: An Audience Study 203

John Lennon, Too Dirty to Be a Hobo? 212

Interview

Sasha Vliet, The Bboy Style on the Eastside   53
Natalie Porter, She Rips When She Skates   121
Melissa McCray Pattacini, Deadheads Yesterday and
     Today: An Audience Study   203
Robert T. Wood, A Straightedger's Journey   223

Profile

G. Beato, The Lords of Dogtown   21
Sasha Vliet, The Bboy Style on the Eastside   53
John Lennon, Too Dirty to Be a Hobo?   212
Robert T. Wood, A Straightedger's Journey   223

Journalism and Reportage

Catherine Walsh, The Rainbow Family Gathering   18
G. Beato, The Lords of Dogtown   21
Sasha Vliet, The Bboy Style on the Eastside   53
Mimi Nguyen, Thoughts on the Movie *Afro-Punk*   72
Heidi Schubert, A Report on Anime Central 2004   77
Christina Robinson, Economic Status and Raving   170
Jerry Adler, The Graying of Aquarius   191

THEMATIC CONTENTS

Issues of Race and Ethnicity

Yoly A. Carillo and Arielle Greenberg, Norteña Slang
    Dictionary   36
Deena Weinstein, Heavy Metal's Proud Pariahs   38
Sasha Vliet, The Bboy Style on the Eastside   53
Rob Maitra, The Homeless Community of the Piers   64
Mimi Nguyen, Thoughts on the Movie *Afro-Punk*   72
Adrienne Lai, Towards a Critical Understanding of
    "Asian Cute Culture"   149

Issues of Gender and Sexuality

Deena Weinstein, Heavy Metal's Proud Pariahs   38
Rob Maitra, The Homeless Community of the Piers   64
Kylie Lee, My Life as an Enterprise Slash Writer   86
Sarah Norton, My Night as a Wiccan   116
Natalie Porter, She Rips When She Skates   121
Adrienne Lai, Towards a Critical Understanding of
    "Asian Cute Culture"   149
John Lennon, Too Dirty to Be a Hobo?   212

Issues of Class

G. Beato, The Lords of Dogtown   21
Deena Weinstein, Heavy Metal's Proud Pariahs   38
Sasha Vliet, The Bboy Style on the Eastside   53
Rob Maitra, The Homeless Community of the Piers   64
Amy Wilkins, From Geeks to Freaks:
    Goths and the Middle Class   99
Christina Robinson, Economic Status and Raving   170
John Lennon, Too Dirty to Be a Hobo?   212

Subcultures and Technology

Heidi Schubert, A Report on Anime Central 2004   77
Kylie Lee, My Life as an Enterprise Slash Writer   86
J. Patrick Williams, How the Internet
    Is Changing Straightedge   104

Zhi Zhu, A Different View of Hackers   136

Melissa McCray Pattacini, Deadheads Yesterday and Today:
An Audience Study   203

Music Subcultures

Yoly A. Carillo and Arielle Greenberg,
Norteña Slang Dictionary   36

Deena Weinstein, Heavy Metal's Proud Pariahs   38

Mimi Nguyen, Thoughts on the Movie *Afro-Punk*   72

Amy Wilkins, From Geeks to Freaks:
Goths and the Middle Class   99

Emily Lamison, So Emo It Hurts   160

Christina Robinson, Economic Status and Raving   170

Johanna Hoadley, Growing Up and Out of the Rave Scene   196

Melissa McCray Pattacini, Deadheads Yesterday
and Today: An Audience Study   203

Robert T. Wood, A Straightedger's Journey   223

Sports Subcultures

G. Beato, The Lords of Dogtown   21

Sasha Vliet, The Bboy Style on the Eastside   53

Robert Rundquist, Street Skateboarding and the
Government Stamp of Approval   179

Hippie Subcultures

Catherine Walsh, The Rainbow Family Gathering   18

Jerry Adler, The Graying of Aquarius   191

Melissa McCray Pattacini, Deadheads Yesterday
and Today: An Audience Study   203

Punk Subcultures

Mimi Nguyen, Thoughts on the Movie *Afro-Punk*   72

Amy Wilkins, From Geeks to Freaks:
Goths and the Middle Class   99

J. Patrick Williams, How the Internet
Is Changing Straightedge   104

Emily Lamison, So Emo It Hurts   160

Robert T. Wood, A Straightedger's Journey   223

PREFACE

As a college professor, I begin each semester eager to meet my new students for the first time, knowing that the mix of people in the classroom will create the chemistry for the course. As my students fill the seats on that first day of class, there are assumptions I can make about them before they even tell me their names. For instance, I can guess as to whether or not I have any athletes in the class, or sports fans. I can usually tell if I have students who participate in the Greek system, or students who are visual artists or actors. I can often tell which parts of the country my students are from, or if they like hip-hop music. Am I psychic? No, of course not. I am simply doing what we all do: "reading" the signs and symbols of our culture to help me make sense of my surroundings. Elements of our outward appearance—our clothing, accessories, body language, and hairstyles—broadcast important, though sometimes erroneous, information about ourselves, and we learn to interpret those messages as a means to decoding others and determining how to negotiate and communicate with those around us.

While some of the essays in this book do discuss clothing style, this is not a book about personal appearance. Rather, it is a book that explores the many methods we humans use to find our way in society. Over the course of each day, we interact with people of different ages, genders, races, religions, ethnicities, and lifestyles. In order to accomplish tasks both large and small, we make connections with other human beings. To make these many interactions easier, we form smaller units within the culture at large; these units support and encourage us, and may be comprised of relatives, friends, or others. Without our interdependence on these smaller units, we could probably not handle this enormous world: humans, like many other animals, form packs, small groups that work together within the species to survive.

When we are young, our pack consists primarily of our families, and maybe the other kids in the neighborhood or at our schools. As we mature, we begin to forge our own identities—the teenage years are a peak time for this process. One of the ways American teenagers negotiate identity development is to reject certain small communities and join others, based on who shares their interests and passions. These personality-derived packs could include amateur rock bands, sports teams, religious youth groups, community service clubs, or simply small numbers of like-minded friends. We've all heard of "cliques," and the recent film *Mean Girls* illustrates the pack mentality of the clique when the main character imagines the cliques in her high school behaving like wild jungle animals, sniffing around their territories.

One kind of pack is a subculture, a group of people that band together based on a shared set of values or beliefs that *deny, resist, or stray from* those commonly held by the mainstream culture overall. Some of the most noticeable subcultures that have teenage members include punks, Goths, and Deadheads (who, now that the Grateful Dead no longer exists, are hippie-style followers of another jam band). These kids choose to stand out in the larger culture in order to fit in within their smaller one.

This book is a collection of essays about people who populate these subcultures. In some cases, it may be about what these people do when they get together, or what they wear, or what they buy, or what they talk about, but it's always about them: the subculture members. In this way, the emphasis of this book is very different than many other books about subcultures, which analyze the stuff the subculture produces—such as magazines or fashions—or consumes—such as rock lyrics or motorcycles. Here, we're fascinated with the people themselves.

Questions and theories as to the whys and wherefores of specific subcultures are the substance of this book, so I will not discuss them further here. Suffice it to say that subcultures seem to be increasingly popular and varied in the United States in the 21st century, and that many subcultures are centered around or even exclusive to adolescents—we will have ample opportunity to explore *why* later. But because they seem to be growing, and because they are so often generated for and by young people, when I began to teach college, I thought that subcultures would make the perfect topic for study by undergraduate students.

One of the things I teach is composition, and one of the challenges of designing the classes, which are often required, is finding ways to keep student writers engaged and invested in their chosen topics. I believe that good writing happens when the writer is excited about the subject matter, and when the outcome of the paper has the potential to impact more than just the student's grade, so the best subjects are those that *need* to be written about, concepts that have yet to be fully explored. This is difficult, because many of the more obscure or complex topics are also out of reach for the average undergraduate, requiring advanced knowledge in specialized fields. Subcultures, however, are both in need of serious study and accessible to young adults. In fact, they are perhaps better studied by college students than by any other population, because college-age people make up the majority of these cultures, and so college students are often already experts in the field.

One of the tantalizing things about subcultures is that they are somewhat "underground," meaning that the members attempt to keep some aspects of the culture to themselves, out of the public eye, so that the subculture can maintain an air of mystery and foreignness to nonmembers. So while many reporters and scholars have tried to write about various subcultures and how and why they exist, as mainstream adults, these writers are often too far removed to be able to report with open-minded accuracy, or to obtain total access to the subculture itself. As a result, much of what is written about subcultures seems phony, exploitative, or off base to subculture members. But college students often own a "backstage pass" to one or more subcultures.

HOW TO USE THIS BOOK

This book is organized into five chapters, each with its own way of addressing the notion of subcultures. Each chapter begins with an **Overview** of the essays included—a brief introduction to the themes, concepts, and topics presented in the chapter's pieces—and after each essay you'll find a **Notebook** section of ideas for further study, writing exercises, activities, and discussion questions. You'll notice that some subcultures are only addressed once, while others are tackled a couple of times.

There are several different ways to move through *Youth Subcultures*. I've suggested some groupings by style and theme in the preceding **Rhetorical Contents** and **Thematic Contents** lists. You can also pay attention to the differences and similarities between the essays written by professionals—scholars and teachers and journalists—and those by undergraduate students.

But before you jump into the essays themselves, I would suggest that you look at the **Introduction**, which explores what subcultures are, why we might choose to study them, and what it means to approach subcultures through cultural studies. Finally, you may want to pay attention to the biographical notes provided by each writer. In them, you'll learn something about who the other writers in this book are and what interests them, and this may help you understand their individual strengths and weaknesses, as well as their approaches and arguments.

ACKNOWLEDGMENTS

All uncredited pieces of writing in this book are my own, but many of the ancillary materials were prepared in collaboration with students from Bentley College and Columbia College Chicago, and I am very grateful for their commitment, hard work, good attitudes, and insights. My thanks to my Bentley students, who first tested much of this material and wrote some amazing essays that we did not have room for here: Kira Abraham, Brett Bell, Jumari Calderon, Jeffrey Hart, Marc A. Marrocco, Coreen Melville, and Kristin Pomeroy. Special thanks to the Bentley students whose work is included here, and who have stayed in touch with me to make this happen: Sarah Norton, Christina Robsinon, and Zhi Zhu. I also want to thank members of my Columbia College subcultures textbook class, many of whom wrote and researched incredible material, some of which did not make it into this final version of the book—Dave Davison, Haydee Franco, Nadia Hayek, Keith M. Judge, Brittney Nini, Ian Tomele, Luis Valadez, and John West—along with those whose essays appear in this book, Yoly Carillo and Heidi Schubert. This book would not exist without my students.

Nor would it exist, of course, without my other contributors and the editors and staff at the journals and presses that first published them. My gratitude to them all, and to the writers who composed original pieces for this book, and who participated in rounds of revision, process interviews, and title changes. Although I haven't yet met them, my contributors form the community of this book, and I hope its publication is as gratifying for them as it is for me.

I first taught college under the auspices of the Syracuse University Writing Program while I was a graduate student in the Creative Writing Program in the English Department. My thanks to the colleagues and professors—especially my professor Michael Burkard, my department chair Bob Gates, and my officemate and friend Jenn Nichols—who served as role models, mentors, and collaborators. Additional thanks to the Pop Culture Institute, where my colleagues introduced me to cultural studies, first when I was a student in their summer class on teaching with popular culture, and then when I was a teaching assistant for the same class later on.

At Bentley College, where I was a full-time lecturer, Bruce Herzberg was a supportive and wise chair, and allowed me to develop the composition courses that spawned this project.

My thanks to him, and to my other friends in the English department and on the Gender Issues Council and at the Spiritual Life Center. While at Bentley, I taught in the Contractual Admissions Program, a diversity initiative aimed at students of color, and teaching those students was one of the most exciting and rewarding experiences I've had. Thanks to the "CAPies" who taught me so much.

I feel very lucky to be teaching now at Columbia College Chicago. Special thanks to my former chair, Garnett Kilberg-Cohen, who was helpful in my transition to this wonderful institution, and to my fellow faculty and friends who empathized and helped while this book was in process: Tony Trigilio, David Trinidad, Jean Petrolle, Suzanne Blum-Malley, Amy Hawkins, and others.

Special thanks also to a couple other Columbia College students in particular: Marguerite Harrold, a graduate student in poetry and skilled instructor, who helped me think through the teaching of this book and contributed to it in many ways, most notably by developing many of the Notebook questions and activities here; and Natalie Hill, who sat on the floor on my office with me to put together photocopied pages.

My gratitude to my family and friends who stood by me while I completed this project. Rob Morris is one of the funniest, smartest, kindest people I know, and I could not have gone through this process without him. Everyone should have such a partner.

At Pearson Longman, I am indebted to Lauren Finn, whom I met when she was selling books at Bentley and asked, "What book do you *wish* we would publish?" I told her, "What I'd really like is a reader on American youth subcultures." She said, "Sounds cool—why don't you write one for us?" . . . and went on to become my editor. There would be no book without her initial enthusiasm and her support and guidance throughout. We have come full circle together.

The book has since been carried through by the capable hands and sage counsel of my editors, including Eben Ludlow, and my reviewers: Andrew Alexander, Pennsylvania State University; Jessica Barros, Bristol Community College; Anne Bliss, University of Colorado Boulder; Patric Cullinan, Truckee Meadows Community College; Angelique M. Davi, Bentley College; Sharon Delmendo, St. John Fisher College; Mark DiPaolo, Drew University; Kathy Fedorko, Middlesex County College; Ramiza S. Koya, SUNY Purchase; Tim Melnarik, California State, San Bernardino; Joyce Marie Miller, Collin County Community College; James Murphy,

Southern Illinois University, Edwardsville; John Panza, Cuyahoga Community College, East; Elizabeth Swingrover, University of Nevada, Reno; Steven Walton-Illadlock, De Anza College; Brownyn T. Williams, University of Louisville. My deepest thanks to them.

ARIELLE GREENBERG

Introduction

First, let's define our terms. What exactly *is* a subculture? The term *subculture* means different things to different people, but is always used to describe a subset of the larger culture—thus, subculture. You are probably part of a subculture: an ethnic or religious heritage, a sports team, a hobby. You may be a Buddhist, soccer-playing swing dancer. You may be a vegan, a surfer, a slam poet. In the broadest definition of the term, each of those interests or traits is its own subculture.

But when we talk about subcultures as scholars, we define the term more narrowly than that. Until recently, social scientists used the word *subcultures* to categorize groups of "deviants," so youth subcultures were roughly equivalent to specific types of juvenile delinquents. But this definition has changed. For the last couple decades, social scientists have defined subcultures as communities of people who share specific interests—interests that, while bringing them together, set them apart from the mainstream culture. This is the definition of subcultures we'll be using: self-identified cultures that are united by shared interests, beliefs, rituals, traditions, and values that oppose or at least challenge the dominant ideology.

Remember that just because something is mainstream does not mean it's good or bad. The mainstream culture isn't necessarily moral: For a long time, this country thought it was fine to force black people to drink from a separate water fountain. And the mainstream culture doesn't always represent the majority culture: Most of the dolls available in your local toy store are probably blond and blue-eyed, even if most of the people in your town aren't.

Likewise, although subcultures are known to be "edgy," they aren't necessarily criminal (although some are). For example,

1

if the mainstream culture condones something like drinking alcohol, a subculture may take an opposing view. Drinking alcohol is not only popular for young adults in this culture right now, it's also cheerfully promoted in mainstream movies, television shows, and social situations. So the fact that straightedge punks choose *not* to drink alcohol makes them unusual in this case—even though at other points in history, alcohol has been illegal or frowned upon by the mainstream culture. Which gets to another point: Cultures are constantly changing, and what's unusual now may well be mainstream in a few years.

Ideologies are another way to talk about cultures. While tastes and beliefs differ from person to person, in any group, community, society, or nation there is a dominant ideology: the network of beliefs, customs, and tastes that are so supported by the systems and institutions of that culture that they take precedence over other ideologies. Just because an ideology is dominant doesn't mean it's objectively good—consider the example of segregation. Also, despite the fact that Americans live in a democracy, the majority does not always rule when it comes to our dominant ideology: Despite the fact that the numbers of women and men in this country are roughly equal, and even though many years have passed since women were given the right to vote and other civil rights, men still far outnumber women in holding positions of power. The dominant ideology is upheld by a complex and somewhat unconscious network of systems, and systems can take a long time to reflect change.

Another key point about the dominant ideology is this: It dominates. It has power. It tells us something about who gets to have power, who is kept from power, and what power means. Cultural studies scholars, those who analyze the stuff of the culture, examine power—and ideology—partly as an expression of difference: differences of race, class, gender, ethnicity, sexual orientation, ability, age. Most scholars suggest that America's current dominant ideology favors those who are adult, white, professional and wealthy, male, Anglo-Saxon protestant, straight, and able-bodied. Most Americans do not fit that profile; cultural studies asks us to think about why, then, it is able to stay in place, and what impact it has on us all.

For every dominant ideology, there are individuals or groups who struggle against it. This tension keeps culture dynamic. In fact, culture is a constant game of imitation and comparison; it's fluid, a dialog between every member of the culture. The members of subcultures choose to be part of the subculture; they are self-defined as actively resisting some part of the dominant ideology that would have them live otherwise.

We assume that subcultures must have some separation from mainstream ideals. Consider two ostensible subcultures: tennis players and skateboarders. Tennis players share a particular interest, but we wouldn't call them a subculture: Their activities and behaviors are completely accepted by the dominant ideology of mainstream America. Skateboarders, like tennis players, share an interest and play a sport that, like tennis, requires athletic skills and talents and specific equipment and culminates in competitive challenges and tournaments. Yet most would agree that skateboarding is a subculture. Why?

The answer has to do with politics, power, and difference. What do skateboarders represent that tennis players do not? What are the differences between people who play tennis and people who skateboard? Do these differences have something to do with systems of power—with class, for instance? With race or age? Cultural studies scholars would say: of course. And they would consider the various aspects of skateboarding—its history, rituals, stereotypes—along with its relationship to issues of race, class, or age in order to make sense of its place in the culture.

You can read essays that do exactly that in the chapters ahead. In this book, we'll try to understand American subcultures: Why do people join them? How do they join them? What's involved in being in them? Why do people leave them? Why are they more popular among youth than any other age group?

This book features work from a wide range of writers: student papers along with previously published essays by graduate students, professors, and journalists. It includes writing from a wide range of genres: interviews, informal blog articles, memoirs, and other nontraditional essays, along with argumentative papers, thesis-driven essays, and research projects. You'll see that there are plenty of different ways to approach any given subject.

There are many issues that students can write about passionately and knowledgably. For instance: the technique of headspinning with or without a hat on. That's a breakdancing term that a lot of professional adults have probably never heard. But there are 17-year-old kids who not only know what it means, they know how to do it. They are, in fact, experts in breakdancing. So as you discuss and explore American youth subcultures, perhaps you can begin to look at yourselves in the same regard—as experts. Your real-life experiences are stories worth telling. The subject encompassed by this book gives us a chance to speak of our shared experience in a scholarly context.

I hope this has given you enough of a sense of the book so that you'll want to jump right in: to read essays by college students, graduate students, professors, journalists, and other writers about subjects like punk rock, skateboarding, and anime fans. I hope you'll find these subjects as fascinating and relevant and worthy of study as I do. You have a role to play here, as a reader and a scholar of American youth subcultures. You could document and analyze something that has never been studied before. But where do you start?

Think for a moment of different social groups with which you're familiar. If you are a college student, you may already consider yourself an expert on many of the cultural nuances of college life and of your campus in particular. There are undoubtedly a number of groups you could write a few pages of stories about: people who use the gym weight room at six in the morning; your sorority or fraternity; the Asian Student Alliance; the kids who vandalize the school mascot; the fencing club. Each of these groups is a culture unto itself. How would you write about it? What are its rituals, its traditions, its costumes and artifacts? How has it changed over time? What do many of its members share in common?

If you take a step away from your local community and start to think about how these groups identify themselves and work across the culture at large, you can adjust your thinking to envision the kinds of subcultures included in this book: those that in some way buck against the mainstream culture, in which the members self-identify, in which the culture has a distinct personality and way of life.

CHAPTER 1

Roots and Origins

OVERVIEW

In this chapter, you will read essays that are written about subcultures through the lens of history. These essays consider how subcultures are created from something else that is happening in the culture: economic conditions, the impact of a war, racism and fears, the desire to assimilate or blend in, or even the legacy of a previous subculture. They also look at how subcultures change over time, transforming as their memberships change, expand, or contract.

Every subculture examined in this book is the product of its times—the laws, events, media, tastes, values, and customs that make an era unique. The pieces in this chapter make the study of those historical roots into the foundation of their research questions, but the same questions can be asked of any subculture you can name. Which of the subcultures in this book already seem dated, defunct, or different to you? How do you think the current historical moment, in terms of politics, trends, and events, is impacting the subcultures you see around you?

Youth Activism in the 1990s
MICHAEL DENNIS

In this essay, Michael Dennis looks at the cultural moment that defined "alternative" youth in the early 1990s, and how a sense of grunge apathy got transformed into a community-oriented activist subculture in time for the massive protests against the World Trade

Organization in Seattle in 1999. Michael Dennis is an associate professor in the department of history and classics at Acadia University in Canada, and his area of focus is the history of organized labor and the movement for social democracy in America. He holds a Ph.D. from Queen's University in Ontario.

─────────── ✦ ───────────

Interviewing a handful of privileged university students for a book about the 1990s, journalist Haynes Johnson asked them to define their generation. Some suggested that the technological revolution with its hyper-speed connections, instant access, and auto-didactic possibilities set them apart from their predecessors. Yet the information revolution was as much a source of uncertainty as vehicle of personal liberation. "There's nothing that's uniting us, or defining a movement for us," confessed one woman. "I wish we had something to fight for," added another. Expressing a longing for something more profound than the images on her computer screen, another student observed, "I do feel like I missed out on something in the Sixties. Not that I would have wanted to live in that time, but there was something that so united everyone."

Despite the romanticization of 1960s activism, the comments reflected the predicament of middle class youth in the late 20th century. Confronted by shrinking career prospects (even while people were becoming internet millionaires), buffeted by an economy of downsized corporations, frustrated by the inability to approximate the achievements of their elders, and deluged by a consumer ethos, young, middle-class Americans found themselves suspended in what sociologist Ryan Moore characterized as a web of "nihilism, cynicism, and cultural exhaustion."

At the same time that most young Americans confronted a world of diminished opportunities and suburban meaninglessness, some found channels of political expression that restored a sense of control over their lives. Joining environmental groups, anti-sweatshop campaigns, and corporate accountability initiatives, young Americans began to turn the tide against post-modern drift. This renewed enthusiasm for democratic participation and social engagement culminated at the fabled Battle of Seattle in 1999. Using the tactics of civil disobedience and street theater borrowed from an earlier generation of American activists, the youth formed an oppositional subculture that exalted community interests over the 90s ethic of fulfilment through individual consumption. As historian Kevin Mattson suggested in "Did Punk Really Matter?," an article published in the *Journal of American Studies*, this new subculture, grounded in participatory democracy and direct action, represented a break with a youth subculture defined more by its *style* of personal protest than by its commitment to political action. While body piercing, hairstyles, clothing, and music distinguished a youth subculture of personal autonomy in the 1980s, collective decision-making, organized protest, and critical thinking about a global economy characterized the young people who faced rain and rubber bullets in Seattle.

More than computers, MTV, skateboarding, and hip-hop—a musical genre that crossed the persistent racial divide in America— economic insecurity dominated the lives of this post-industrial generation. According to the U.S. Bureau of the Census, child poverty increased from 15 percent in 1970 to 20 percent in 1990, at precisely the same time that the poverty index was declining for the elderly. Over one in five people under the age of 18 lives in poverty, a statistic that some experts expect will increase to one out of every four by 2021. More than escalating poverty and declining social insurance, Generation X and their Y protégés faced a working world that offered few opportunities for gratifying, stable employment. Part time, temporary jobs in retail outlets, fast food restaurants, and other service sector companies promised low wages, limited benefits, and uncertainty for the children of America's most prosperous generation, the Baby Boomers.

And it wasn't just the service sector that challenged the middle-class myth of upward mobility through education and hard work. Managerial and administrative positions in the white-collar sector evaporated as companies merged or shed employees through "downsizing." Those who did work found themselves wedged into jobs offering fewer hours, fewer benefits, and little security. Middle- and working-class young people also suffered from higher rates of obesity, mental illness, suicide, drug use, and depression than their elders. At the political level, leaders embraced a conservative philosophy of minimal government and maximum freedom for corporations, which whittled away the protections built up since the 1930s for the poor, unemployed, disadvantaged, young, unskilled, and non-white. This same philosophy of ruthless economic competition offered young people little comfort in their struggle to make sense of living in a prosperous, consumer-driven society while being told to accept the reality of making seven or eight career changes throughout their working lives and earning considerably less than their parents. Add to this the escalating cost of college education and the realization that it would not guarantee them a steady job, and middle-class youths had every reason to feel what Ryan Moore describes in a chapter for *Generations of Youth: Youth Cultures and History in Twentieth Century America* as a "sense of betrayal, the suspicion of failure, the resentment of more fortunate generations." For young middle-class whites, the sense of isolation and despair bred by these dislocating changes was reflected in their music, particularly grunge rock. Put out by independent record labels that embodied the anti-corporate, punk subculture of the 1980s, grunge encapsulated the sense of dislocation portrayed in films such as *Slackers* and *Clerks*. Grunge was also the self-conscious antithesis of the love and peace vibe that permeated the Sixties' counterculture. As Kim Thayil, from the grunge band Soundgarden, exclaimed, "[Yuppies are] this ultimate white-bread suburban upper-middle-class group that were spoiled little fuckers as kids 'cause they were all children of Dr. Spock, and then they were stupid stinky hippies, and then they were spoiled yuppie materialists." Focusing their discontent on the Baby Boomers, Thayil, Kurt Cobain, and the other purveyors of "alternative" rock ignored the impact of race and class on one's position in the American social order: the problem became sell-out yuppies, and the solution, an introverted search for healing. Nirvana, Soundgarden, Pearl Jam, and the Stone Temple Pilots offered what cultural critic Hal Foster described as "an aesthetic of indifference that went beyond a pose of boredom to a desire to be done with it all."

Alongside grunge, fledgling radicals crafted a subculture fuelled by punk music, alternative zines, and a commitment to independent cultural production. Devotees of this subculture read *Maximum RocknRoll*, recorded at studios such as SubPop Records (the Nirvana label), and extolled the virtues of music freed from the grip of corporate parasites. In an era of conservative ascendancy, as President Ronald Reagan forged a coalition of Christian evangelicals and anti-tax activists to dismantle an allegedly bloated welfare state, the impulse to oppose the status quo grew strong. It grew stronger as Reagan ratcheted up the Cold War, stockpiling nuclear warheads, testing cruise missiles, and laying plans for the "Star Wars" anti-ballistic missile system. Beyond the clubs and the record stores, the alternative culture gathered around single issues such as nuclear weapons proliferation, welfare reform, gay rights, and American meddling in Central America.

These activists abandoned the traditional marches for a style of protest defined by direct action. Anti-nuclear activists experimented with "die-ins" at the headquarters of companies manufacturing weaponry and "Punk Percussion Protests" against apartheid outside the South African embassy in Washington. Experimenting in direct action tactics that had enjoyed considerable currency during the 1960s, young activists challenged the ethic of "spectatorship," as Kevin Mattson describes it, the media-induced posture in which life becomes a series of discrete and disconnected experiences. Despite the impact on public consciousness, the protests were too sporadic to affect public policy or develop into a widespread social movement. Prosperity and the continuing Cold War saga also muted public protest against corporate dominance. Moreover, members of the punk subculture opted for a version of dissent based more on style than ideas, withdrawing into a world defined by clothes, and posture. Personal accessorizing—Mohawk haircuts, safety pins in leather jackets, all-black ensembles—became the signifiers of the "alternative" subculture, offering an edgy but marketable (think Billy Idol) alternative to the button-down preppie look.

At this point, one might conclude that the urban, predominantly white, punk and hardcore listening crowd of the 1980s exalted style over substance. But the radicals of the 1990s sported their *own* inimitable fashion: hemp-spun ponchos, retro-hippie Birkenstocks, dreadlocks, bandanas, army fatigues, and just about anything that might have appealed to a countercultural enthusiast in 1968. Yet the 1990s did see the emergence of a new youth subculture, one grounded in the ideals of democratic inclusion and social responsibility. More than a new protest fashion, this subculture responded directly to the social climate that consumer capitalism generated in the late 20th century.

Through grass-roots initiatives, young people challenged the ideology of individualism that dominated American society in the late 20th century. According to Shannon Service, an organizer of the Direct Action Network that played a key role in coordinating the anti-WTO campaign in Seattle, "Growing up with Generation X meant growing up in a world where everything was for sale. . . . Everywhere I turned, I was encouraged to consume my identity and even my liberation in the form of this new computer or that new SUV." By contrast, her decision to challenge the materialist consensus proved truly liberating. Hanging an anti-WTO banner above a freeway during the Seattle campaign, she embraced "a life that was a little freer, more profound, and fun."

Author Naomi Klein echoed Service's yearning for authenticity. As Janet Thomas reports in her book *The Battle in Seattle: The Story Behind and Beyond the WTO Demonstrations*, Klein's anti-corporate manifesto No Logo was an expression of the "deep craving for metaphorical space: release, escape, some kind of open-ended freedom." Abandoning isolated introspection for co-operative action, young Americans restored a sense of personal engagement dulled by the culture of consumption. At the same time, they revived the practice of democratic community that lay dormant at least since the 1960s.

The growing determination to live a life defined by more than purchasing the latest style of khakis led young, white, middle-class Americans into a variety of social causes. Students from across the United States and Canada joined environmental action outfits such as Greenpeace, Earth First!, the Rainforest Action Network, and community action groups such as Public Interest Research Groups (PIRGS) that sprung up in the 1970s. What they shared was a veneration of the environment, a search for truth in the green spaces threatened by industrial polluting and corporate globalization. Deprived of the kind of spiritual framework that organized religion once provided, young people sought it in nature. Examining a seashell on a trip to the beach, Shannon Service "realized very clearly, in a moment, that the delicate and beautiful sea form in my hand was considered valueless in our market economy" (quoted in *Global Uprising: Confronting the Tyrannies of the 21st Century*). This epiphany probably occurred to dozens of young Americans throughout the 1990s.

Environmentalists translated their quasi-spiritual convictions into action. From obstructing logging routes to sitting in trees destined for the wood chipper to raising consciousness about global warming, college students challenged the sense of entitlement that underlay private industry's exploitation of nature. Dwindling water supplies, declining forest stocks, and evaporating ozone layers were not isolated issues, nor were they the inevitable byproducts of progress. Instead, they were the consequences of decisions made by first world entrepreneurs and leaders to privilege industrial growth over ecological stability. Activists found a cause that expressed their impulse for purity over materialism, and through organizing began to articulate a critique of consumer capitalism that reached far beyond the efforts of their 1980s predecessors.

This impulse to organize, to overcome the social isolation of modern life manifested itself powerfully in the campaign against third world sweatshop labor. Galvanized by journalistic exposes of Nike Corporation's exploitive practices in Indonesia, by the revelation that celebrity Kathy Lee Gifford's company paid Honduran girls working 31 cents an hour to work under sweatshop conditions, and by an AFL-CIO "Union Summer" campaign that recruited a cadre of "Students Against Sweatshops," young activists transformed more than 20 university campuses into sites of corporate resistance. Students traveled, sometimes at considerable risk, to investigate working conditions in El Salvador and other nations sponsoring corporate sweatshops. By 2000, 150 branches of United Students Against Sweatshops had emerged on college campuses across the United States.

Ted Hargrave of YES! (Youth for Environmental Sanity) celebrated the community-building features of JAMS!, the group's youth leadership conferences: "We have found again and again, that there is power in coming together to do nothing but hang out and build relationships." More than love-ins, though, Hargrave identified the larger political implications of community formation: "It's covert activism. It's building deep foundations. It's pausing to let the roots of our activism sink into the deeper waters that will sustain us." The sentiment was classically American: idealistic, principled, slightly naïve, but sincere. Here was an activist searching, much like his 1960s predecessors, for individual fulfillment through collective action. That search for belonging led thousands to the streets of Seattle.

Of course, the protest against the World Trade Organization (WTO) meeting in November 1999 was not the first site of struggle against international corporate influence. Earlier protests in Venezuela, South Korea, Brazil, and Berlin targeted at the International Monetary Fund, the World Bank, and the WTO mobilized young people in defense of personal and national autonomy. But those were largely adult fights. For young people, the Seattle demonstration signaled a turning point in their struggle. As Barbara Epstein explained, "many of the young people who participated in direct action belonged to a youth subculture that opposes corporate power, and capitalism generally, because it has created a society in which virtually everything has become a commodity."

A legion of political pundits and academics weighed in to explain why the WTO had to be abolished, reformed, or defended. But the focus here is in what young people *themselves* thought about the protest in Seattle. First, though, a word or two is necessary about the WTO.

The WTO was formed in 1995 out of the framework of the General Agreement on Tariffs and Trade, which American policymakers formed in 1947 to facilitate international exchange after the devastation of World War II. Unlike the GATT, though, the WTO's rulings are binding, meaning that participating nations are expected to subordinate domestic laws to the dictates of the WTO.

As *Time Magazine* described it, The WTO is "both traffic cop and top court of the global economy." Since its inception, the organization has issued over 175 rulings, many of which have been condemned for favoring corporate interests over that of workers, the environment, small businesses and farmers, human rights, and national sovereignty. Committed to expanding the boundaries of corporate trade, the WTO opposes the public management of education, health care, and municipal utilities, services that have traditionally benefited the most marginal. Behind closed doors, the WTO operated as the representative of international corporations. The fewer the barriers to international trade, WTO defenders argue, the easier it is to exchange goods and services throughout the world, creating in the process a higher standard of living throughout the western industrialized and developing world. For proponents of the WTO, free trade equaled global prosperity.

But this was hardly the vision of the global village that protesters brought to Seattle in November 1999. According to Sarah Jay Staude, a college student in Portland at the time of the protest, her willingness to protest was an expression of "a common sentiment among people my age," the sentiment of those privileged enough to study and challenge injustice. "The poor people who are being exploited don't have the time to think about the global situation because they're just trying to survive. We have enough money, or scholarships, or whatever, to be going to a small liberal arts school and discuss and debate and get outraged." Mixing liberal guilt with social obligation, the themes that underlay the Progressive Movement in the early 20th century, Staude joined the direct action protesters who shut down the WTO meeting. Despite the "dizzying array" of issues that motivated participants, a protestor identified as "Jason" believed that "most people seemed genuinely united by the idea [that] the WTO is quietly effecting a global corporate free-for-all where massive companies force countries to vie for the weakest environmental laws and labor standards, and where corporate lawyers have the right to overturn decisions of democratically-elected local governments that are deemed 'restrictive to trade.'" Far from celebrating the lawyer as the role model for the young and upwardly mobile, Jason defended local democracy against corporate encroachments. For young people like Jason, cooperation and the principled commitment to social change became an alternative to a life of stylish consumption.

College students from across the country were enthusiastic about the possibility of having some impact on the debate, but they came equipped with more than passion. Most had studied the

WTO's decisions and arrived willing to learn from others through teach-ins and seminars. They were also prepared to take nonviolent action. As participant Janet Thomas observed, "There were thousands of students in the streets of Seattle on N30. Most of them knew the issues, did the training, and made conscious, committed decision to participate in direct action." This doesn't mean that the protesters were "right" and the WTO representatives were misguided. What it does suggest is that at the root of the Seattle event lay conflicting *ideas* about how to govern global society, distribute its goods, and promote social improvement. What Seattle highlighted was an emerging debate about the meaning of democracy and the preservation of civil society. Most protestors understood the benefits that flowed from entrepreneurial capitalism, but they sought to balance them against values that could not be reduced to commercial exchange. Ideas, not style, separated the 50,000 protesters from the power brokers inside the Convention Center. Far from an antiauthoritarian jamboree, the WTO protest offered a chance for young people to respond to the seemingly uncontrollable forces that governed their lives.

And what exactly happened in Seattle? Why was it significant and what made this protest different? Perhaps most importantly, what did it mean to those who participated? More impressive than the individual events was the sheer diversity and magnitude of the action in Seattle. First, over 700 organizations, ranging from the Alliance for Democracy to the Students from Everywhere to the Raging Grannies to the Rainforest Action Network, took part in the protests. Second, the participants were overwhelmingly, but not exclusively, white and privileged. As Jason noted after the demonstration, "There were . . . radical environmentalists, aging anti-nuke activists, Tibetan monks, and locked-out steelworkers" shoulder-to-shoulder with "Salvadoran campesinos and a contingent of Falun Gong adherents meditating as the tear gas rolled over them." Gay rights activists, Latino and African American anti-poverty activists, African trade unionists, Native American groups, and dozens of women's advocacy groups joined this kaleidoscope of democratic protest.

The diversity of the protest tactics mirrored the diversity of the participants. Marches, sit-ins, teach-ins, stadium-sized assemblies, and "lock-downs," in which protesters would chain themselves together using bicycle locks or PVC pipes, were all part of the Direct Action repertoire. Young activists affiliated with the group Art and Revolution constructed elaborate puppets to illustrate the grievances that protesters brought to Seattle. As Art and Revolution founder Alli Starr described it, "collaborative creativity," the opposite of aggression and violence, played a key role in derailing the first day of WTO meetings. Activists hoisted a huge condom promoting "safe trade" while the Radical Cheerleaders jumped and twirled for justice. Street dancers, musicians, banner bearers ("Today We Shut Down the Evil Empire,") cardboard turtles (people protesting the needless slaughter of sea turtles by shrimp trawlers that refused to carry Turtle Exclusion Devices), and participants in the "Boston WTeaO Party," which ceremoniously dumped the shrimp caught in the offending nets while demanding "no globalization with representation," testified to the versatility of direct action tactics.

The guerilla street theater and the puppets were not new, nor were the direct action and non-violent civil disobedience tactics. Each harkened back to the civil rights movement, the anti-Vietnam War movement, and the New Left of the 1960s. What was new was the sheer determination to use these tactics to reclaim public space from private, corporate control. As Naomi Klein suggests in "Reclaiming the Commons," an article published in *New Left Review*, street protest was not so much about condemning state corruption as about insisting that the streets, sidewalks, and public parks belonged to them rather than corporate sponsors determined to "brand" young people into consumer passivity. Against a culture that sought to transform every public space into a marketing vehicle, young protesters asserted the right to use it as a forum for citizenship.

Youth protesters also signaled their departure from protesters of the 60s and 70s by aligning with labor and more conventional environmentalists. As Audrey Vanderford observed, "Teamster president James Hoffa sharing a stage with student anti-sweatshop activists, of Earth First!ers marching with Sierra Clubbers, and a chain of barebreasted BGH-free Lesbian Avengers weaving through a crowd of machinists" marked the carnival of participatory democracy that the WTO protest became. What began to form, even briefly, in the streets of Seattle was a coalition of people on the economic periphery. And unlike earlier coalitions, this one reflected the increasingly boundary-less world in which they lived. Generation Xers and their younger counterparts began to see, through the smoke of the tear gas canisters lobbed at them in November 1999, that they were not alone.

The majority of direct action protesters organized themselves into "affinity groups" of five to twenty people that invited maximum participation, permitted dissent, arrived at a consensus, and protected members involved in vulnerable lock-down positions. "Flying groups" circulated throughout the downtown area reinforcing protesters under fire, while affinity groups divided themselves into those who were "arrestable" and those who were not. In contrast to the hierarchical, bureaucratic, and unrepresentative organizations they opposed, the students—and the vast majority of direct action protesters were students—functioned on the basis of participatory democracy, that lofty ideal that the Students for a Democratic Society contributed to the cultural ferment of the 1960s. Through the sit-ins, the brutal police retaliation, and the mass arrests, young activists exercised a determination to hold the group together. As protester Jason described it,

> When the smoke cleared the blockades reformed on either side of the path the police had blazed. . . . Someone in the front row was holding an American flag, and another person began singing the Star Spangled Banner. Soon, the whole crowd took it up, and many people saluted. The rain dripped down the face masks of the police as we sang of "the land of the free, and the home of the brave." "Whose streets?" someone shouted. "Our streets!" came the reply from 500 people. "Whose democracy?" "Our democracy." Then the police started shooting tear gas again.

It was this sense of collective purpose that resonated among the young militants in Seattle. Exhilarated by the experience, university student Jesus Sepulveda reported that "We were just one energy of common sense and solidarity and dignity and integrity." Wesleyan student Sarah Norr joined a group of 50 protesters who formed a human chain that shut down one of the intersections close to the Convention Center where the WTO delegates planned to meet. When police announced that they would use "pain compliance techniques" to clear the intersection, the student protesters faced their moment of truth. "[Staying there] was a hard decision to make," Norr later commented. "Some people, including me, thought there was no point in staying around. . . . But then some people said, 'We're staying,' and then other people did not want to leave them behind."

The exhilarating feeling of unity, the determination to act democratically, and the willingness to build alliances stemmed from the realization that people find themselves through what Aristotle called the "polis," the community. Through community, selfishness and indifference is transformed into concern and respect for the interests of others. In the streets of Seattle, and through the organizations that activists had built since the early 1990s, students tasted this kind of community. That doesn't mean that every protestor was magically transformed into some kind of virtuous supercitizen; more than a handful came for the street party atmosphere.

Others kicked over trash containers and broke store windows. But for most, the Seattle protest became something more than the political equivalent of bungee jumping and snowboarding. Those communities solidified the convictions that had brought them to Seattle, but which their elders—not to mention their professors— had insisted belonged only to an earlier generation of peace freaks.

Yet, as student activists reveled in a newfound sense of community, they excluded a huge swath of their contemporaries from the experience. Protesters were overwhelmingly young and white. Why, at a time when young African Americans and Latinos suffered the highest rates of youth mortality, the highest likelihood of imprisonment, the highest probability of being unemployed, and the highest chance of police harassment, did they not join the protests? As Van Jones of the Ella Baker Center for Human Rights put it, "structural adjustment" (the lessening of debt to developing countries) seems remote at best to people "who are getting our asses kicked daily." Environmental protection and an end to sweatshops might be important to privileged whites, but ending police brutality, reducing unemployment, and exposing the racial discrimination that continues to influence the criminal justice system seemed like more urgent issues to African American activists. For young blacks all too familiar with the limits of police tolerance, courting arrest and jail seemed like a recipe for disaster. As Andrew Hsiao noted in an article for *The Battle of Seattle: The New Challenge to Corporate Globalization,* anarchists displayed a remarkable ignorance of the historical relationship between the federal government and American blacks. Moreover, those persons of color who did participate came away feeling that the global democracy movement fostered what Hsiao described as "an insider's culture of privileged militancy" that failed to include those who didn't look and sound the same. The erosion of environmental standards abroad and the decline of social assistance at home were not unrelated issues, but the failure to make the connection undermined the credibility of the Seattle protests among America's minority groups.

Its strengths and weaknesses, then, were typically American. Strong in their commitment to a brand of participatory democracy inherited from the New Left of the 1960s, young activists were largely indifferent to the persistence of racial inequality in their own society. Concentrating on the poverty of those in the developing world, they overlooked the chronic insecurity that millions of Americans endured from part-time, low-wage, service-industry jobs. They did not offer a thorough critique of anti-labor practices in the

United States, even while these devastated the ranks of the unionized workers who marched beside them. Idealistically committed to direct action protest, they ignored the tendency of this strategy to attract an angry youth crowd that undermined their credibility as peaceful protestors. Failing to separate themselves from trash can-throwing anarchists, they suffered the same public censure.

Despite their limitations, the protesters who took to the streets in Seattle accelerated the democratic youth subculture that became an undercurrent of the 1990s. They reawakened the yearnings of the 1960s counterculture to overcome the alienation of a suburban, consumer society. Like the young activists who formed the Students for a Democratic Society in the 1960s, they wanted to transform dehumanizing institutions according to humane ideals.

At the same time, they echoed the democratic strains of an even earlier generation. In the late nineteenth century, as industrial capitalism transformed American society, small farmers, skilled workers, and middle-class reformers bonded together in protest. Like the WTO protestors, they believed that American government had fallen into the hands of corporate interests. They too believed that average Americans had lost control of the institutions governing their lives. They launched what was known as the Populist Movement. Although it burned brightly in the 1890s, the movement collapsed when it failed to win the presidency through an alliance with the Democrats in 1896. Even so, the Populists imparted to a later generation of reformers the idea that government had to restrain industrial capitalism and protect working people, young and old alike. As Michael Kazin notes in his December 7, 1999 *Seattle Post-Intelligencer* article "Battle of Seattle Echoes Similar Cries from 1890s," in identifying the danger that unrestricted corporate behavior posed to American liberty, the youth who gathered in Seattle in November 1999 harkened back to the Populist Movement. In alerting Americans to the threat of concentrated power, both political and economic, the young activists tapped into a stream of democratic protest stretching back to the founding of the Republic.

Notebook

1.   In this essay, Michael Dennis considers the economic factors that caused some youth in the 1990s to become politically active. How have current conditions changed, and how have they stayed the same, for you right now? How do these conditions factor into the activist subculture, and other subcultures, you see happening around you?

2.   In small groups, try to tell the future. Thinking about the economic and
cultural realities that your generation is currently experiencing, predict some
of the subcultures that might arise in coming years. What will they be working to oppose? What might define them? Using your psychic abilities, sketch
possible outfits for these subculture members, and make up slang for them.
3.   Youth activism has been around for a long time. Do some research into
previous generations. How are the youth activists of today similar to those
of the 1940s, or 1960s, or 1990s?
4.   Try your own hand at the kind of "street theater" described in this essay. As a class, identify some hot issues on your college campus, and come up
with ways to educate about or protest them through creative demonstration.
5.   How do you feel about activists like the ones discussed in this article?
How did hearing their own voices, through the quotes included in this piece,
change or confirm your attitude? Do you think this piece would have been
more effective with more quotations from actual activists involved, or with
less?

The Rainbow Family Gathering
CATHERINE WALSH

*In this article, Catherine Walsh reports from an annual event for hip-
pies new and old. She asks a "tribe elder" to shed some light on the
purpose of the event, and tries to get a sense of whether the Rainbowgoers meet their goal of peace and harmonious living. Catherine
Walsh is a journalist who wrote this piece for* America *magazine.*

──────────── ✦ ────────────

Robert Calvin Gordon 3d, Princeton '67, was one of more than
17,000 people at the Rainbow Family of Living Light gathering
near Taos, N.M., over the July 4 weekend. "Princeton teaches you
how to think and that is plenty O.K.," he said. "Unfortunately, it
doesn't teach you how to love." As a brief summer rain drummed
on his tepee, Robbie—as he likes to be called—built a fire in the
tepee's center and told me his life story. A one-time hippie who
never went back to mainstream society, he has been a regular at
Rainbow Family gatherings since 1980.

Anyone who has a navel belongs to the Rainbow Family, adherents like to say. But if you don't have a navel, an exception will
be made for you. And how do you exercise your Rainbow Family

membership? Well, the ideal is to treat everyone as your brother or sister and work for world peace. One of the best ways to learn how to do this, Rainbow regulars say, is to attend the annual gathering during the first week of July. Ever since the first gathering was organized in 1972 by peace activists and Vietnam veterans, Rainbowgoers have come together for a 1960's-style, peace-and-love fest on different national forest lands throughout the country. Because I was only eight years old when the 60's ended, I was intrigued by the Rainbow Family. As a freelance reporter for the *Santa Fe New Mexican*, I made several trips to the gathering site—a series of high-mountain meadows dotted with dozens of tepees and thousands of brightly colored tents—and camped out with the Rainbow Family over Independence Day.

On the first day of the gathering, I watched dozens of young people pound drums and hundreds more dance in half-naked or fully naked abandon. There were quite a few 60's wannabe's here, who looked like they had been born around 1975, and lots of graying, long-haired folks in their late 40's. A sari-clad group went past, moving rhythmically to the chant of "Hari Krishna, Hari Krishna." Nearby an evangelical Christian group served tea from a tent. Everyone is accepted at the Rainbow Family gathering, I was told again and again; the goal is to be a family, an all-inclusive tribe.

Cries of "Welcome home, brother" and "Welcome home, sister" rang through the camp as newcomers poured in by the minute. The four-mile-long trail into the gathering felt like a crowded escalator. I visited a quiet campfire called Dreamer's Den—"where you sit by the fire and dream"—cut through the "Ship of Love" kitchen and checked out the "Children's Camp," where hundreds of tie-dye clad kids played under the eyes of watchful adults. In an effort to understand what I was seeing, I sought out Rainbow Family "elders" like Robbie Gordon.

Robbie is from a "fine old Pittsburgh family" that once employed people like my grandparents—Irish domestics just off the boat. He was the third generation of his family to attend Princeton, where he studied physics and Russian literature. "I smoked a lot of weed while I was there, too," he said. He lived in a commune near Taos for a while after graduation and recently moved back to the area. His business card identifies him as a "minstrel, apothecary, mystic fool, laborer, sorcerer, librarian, Libra, Russian expert. . . ."

Puffing on a pipe filled with marijuana leaves, which he calls a "sacred herb," Robbie told me that the Rainbow Family "is about the conscious and positive evolution of humankind. It's about world peace and healing our poor, damaged Mother Earth. It's about making us into better people. It happens like a miracle—it's just love, all these wounded, strange, crazy people learning how to love one another." Jesus, he said, would feel at home at the gathering.

When I asked Robbie what he wanted the human race to evolve into, he responded: "The ideal is what the Lakota Nation, the Cherokee Nation, the Taos Nation and other Indian nations have. That kind of unity with diversity. The ability to know who you are in a society and on the earth. Knowing that you are related to every human being you may come across." Loving and sharing, he said, are at the heart of so-called "primitive" societies.

Robbie hoped that lots of local Taos Indians would come to the gathering, but I didn't see any. (Local Hispanics had protested the event, saying they had not invited thousands of hippies to camp out on their forest lands.) The handful of Native Americans who were present seemed comfortable with the gathering's use of Indian rituals and symbols. But I had mixed feelings. I know Native Americans who are deeply concerned about the usurping of elements of their culture by needy middle-class white people.

Observing the gathering, I was struck by what a lost tribe Americans are. A rootless society, we are constantly looking for and inventing new forms of community. The Rainbow Family rejects much of American culture—often referred to within the gathering as "Babylon"—but its ideal of a cooperative, family-based society doesn't seem realistic. Real tribes and families are complicated, painful entities made up not only of "brothers and sisters" but also mothers and fathers and other imperfect authority figures. Still, it felt great to join hands with 17,000 Rainbow people at noon on July 4 and pray for world peace. So this is what the 60's felt like!

Notebook

1.   Think about your own participation in subcultures, or in a group of any kind. Freewrite about what you know of the roots and origins of that group. Do you know who founded it, and when? What was it reacting to in the larger culture?

2.   What historical and political events seem to have shaped the Rainbow Family Gathering? How does geography—the landscape, the location—impact the roots and mission of this subculture?

3.   Research an American subculture that no longer exists, such as the flapper culture of the 1920s or the Beatniks of the 1950s. Present the class with

a fashion show or dance demonstration or other show-and-tell presentation from that extinct subculture.

4. Interview someone older than yourself about the subcultures that existed when he or she was a teenager. Ask about the slang, the costumes, and the rituals and values. Then do some research to come up with a list of historical reasons why that subculture might have existed when it did.

5. For more on the Rainbow Family, check out *People of the Rainbow: a Nomadic Utopia* by Michael I. Niman (University of Tennessee Press, 1999).

The Lords of Dogtown
G. BEATO

In an article that led to at least two movies and a resurgence in interest in the roots of skateboard culture, G. Beato considers the origins of skateboarding and its rise from goofy novelty to gritty street sport to hyper-cool phenomenon and finally to a commercialized, widely popular industry. Greg Beato is a freelance journalist who has written for SPIN, Reason, LA Weekly, *and dozens of other publications. His work has also been anthologized in the book* Best Music Writing 2003 *(Da Capo Press).*

◆

Twenty years ago, you did not drop in on Tony Alva.

Twenty years ago, if you found yourself standing next to the volatile, gravity-defying Alva at some crowded backyard pool in the Valley, and he was planning to take the next run—even though he'd just taken the last one—it was best to not even look at him.

Tonight, however, such ancient protocols are no longer in effect. Alva, 41 now, bearded and dreadlocked, has come to The Block, a theme park-size mall in Orange, California, to skate the new Vans Skatepark, an indoor, 46,000-square-foot skateboarding Oz located between a Virgin Megastore and a brewpub. Hundreds of skaters and spectators are here celebrating the park's opening. As a dozen or so mostly teenage skaters stand in an informal line, waiting for their chance to try out the smaller one of the park's two cement pools, they seem wholly oblivious to Alva. To them he's just another skateboarder in baggy jeans and a scuffed yellow helmet. Somewhat older, perhaps, but of no readily apparent significance.

True, a handful of old-school types approach Alva as he waits, tapping his shoulder, talking briefly, paying their respects. But

so the banks were really smooth and pristine—just these huge, glassy waves."

Throughout the '60s, surfing had always taken precedence over skateboarding in Dogtown. Skating was mostly just a means of transportation, or something to do if the waves weren't breaking. By 1970, the sport had reached a particularly desultory stage. "No one was skateboarding back then. You couldn't even buy a skateboard in the store," says Stacy Peralta, another Dogtown local. Kids would often have to construct their own from spare pieces of household furniture and repurposed roller skate parts.

But after the Dogtown kids discovered Paul Revere and other schoolyard skate spots like Bellagio and Kenter Canyon, the inadequacies of their equipment seemed incidental. The schoolyards' asphalt "waves" broke beautifully every single day, all year round, creating entirely new possibilities for the sport. The Dogtown kids started applying their surfing techniques to concrete, riding low to the ground with their arms outstretched for balance, skating with such intensity that they often destroyed their homemade boards in a single session.

"We were just trying to emulate our favorite Australian surfers," Alva says, explaining the genesis of their new low-slung, super-aggressive style. "They were doing all this crazy stuff that we were still trying to figure out in the water—but on skateboards, we could do it."

Three years later, the introduction of urethane wheels resurrected interest in skateboarding. By then, the Dogtown kids had developed an approach to skating that was far more evolved than what anyone was doing at the time. "No one else had that same surf-skate style, because they didn't have banks like that anywhere else," Alva says. "We had this tradition that was unique to our area."

THE IMPORTANCE OF CUSTOMER SERVICE

Outside the Jeff Ho & Zephyr Productions Surf Shop, in front of a wall-size mural of co-owner Jeff Ho surfing a wave that was almost pornographic in its perfect, arcing glassiness, Alva and Adams and a few other Dogtown kids were skateboarding back and forth, cutting off cars, catcalling passing girls, staring down all the pedestrians who failed to avoid them—like the two guys who had just rolled in from Van Nuys or wherever, more jock than surfer (but trying hard with their Vans and Hang Ten shirts), who tried to enter the shop's front door. It was locked. They looked at their watches. It was 3 p.m.

Inside, Skip Engblom, one of the shop's owners, sat in a rocking chair, drinking vodka and papaya juice and watching the scene play out. This was one of his favorite pastimes. "Hey!" cried one of the Van Nuys guys, finally noticing him. "Open up. This door's locked." "What the fuck do you want?" Engblom yelled back. "I want to look around." "If you want to come in here, you've got to give me some money first," Engblom said. "If you just want to look around, go to the fucking library." "I've got fucking money," the guy said, pulling a twenty out of his wallet and waving it in front of the window. "Let me in and I'll spend it!"

It was an innovative approach to customer service, characteristic of Ho and Engblom's general approach to commerce. The pair had formed their partnership in 1968, when both men were still in their late teens. Ho was a gypsy surfboard shaper living in the back of his '48 Chevy panel truck; Engblom was a vagabond surfer who'd been traveling around the world in an effort to avoid the draft.

Their goal was to be a completely self-contained entity, reliant on no one. To this end, they designed, manufactured, and sold their own surfboards; they created their own clothing line; they produced their own advertising and promotional movies. Sometimes, however, they would sell other people's merchandise. "We did a lot of stuff that would be considered illegal," allows Engblom. Various wholesalers sold them an impressive array of surfing lifestyle accessories, like 15,000 Quaaludes or vast amounts of fireworks. "Once, we ended up buying a quarter of a barge of firecrackers," says Engblom. "We didn't know how much that was exactly. But the price sounded really cheap."

For the local Dogtown kids, the shop served as a second home. They used to help Ho shape and repair boards in the shop's backrooms in exchange for discounts or free merchandise. At night, the place turned into a kind of speakeasy, over which the charismatic Ho—wearing rainbow-tinted glasses, four-inch platform shoes, and striped velveteen pants—presided. Local bands performed, and drugs were dispensed with typical '70s largesse.

With his shop, Ho tried to provide the same sense of family and community that he'd found at the beach as a kid growing up. "I was a loner, this geeky little Chinese runt kid who couldn't play sports until I discovered surfing. And then I saw these other kids, growing up the same way. I mean, who's going to be hanging out all day at the beach? The kids who don't want to be hanging out at home. So, to them, I would say, 'Check it out, this is surfing. If you use your talents, you can make something of yourself.'"

To this end, Ho sponsored two surf teams: one for the area's best surfers, guys who were in their late teens and early 20s, and, in a move that was fairly unusual at the time, one for the younger kids, who were destined to become the next wave of stars. As skateboarding's popularity increased, the junior surf team, which had included Tony Alva, Jay Adams, Shogo Kubo, and Stacy Peralta, evolved into the Zephyr Competition Skate Team—a 12-member group of the best skaters in Dogtown. Ho gave them team T-shirts. "We wanted to give them colors, something to be a part of."

"To wear the team shirt was just unreal," says Peralta. "We were all middle- and lower-class kids, and it wasn't like we had a lot of opportunities. We weren't the kids who were going to graduate as valedictorians or the guys from Palisades driving BMWs to the beach. So to be chosen to be a part of something like that was just the hottest thing that could happen to a kid in that area."

A FUNKY, FUNKY LOOK

The Bahne-Cadillac Skateboard Championship, held in the summer of 1975, was the largest competition that skating's revival had yet inspired. The two-day event featured downhill, slalom, and freestyle competitions. The organizers had built a 150-foot-long wooden ramp especially for the competition. More than 400 enthusiasts traveled to Del Mar, California, to attend the championship. "It was the first major contest where skaters from all over the country came together," says Peralta. "We came in not knowing anything about the outside world—who else was skating, what their style was like. It was as if we'd evolved in this Galapagos Island vacuum."

The Zephyr team wore uniforms, sort of—matching Vans deck shoes and blue T- shirts emblazoned with their team name. Even so, the Z-Boys, as they would come to be known, seemed wild-looking compared to the other competitors. Their shoes were torn and scuffed, and their jeans were missing back pockets, the inevitable result of low-altitude power-slides. "Our hair was so long and fluffy that we'd all chopped our bangs off two inches over our eyebrows," says Alva. "It was just a funky, funky look." In addition, they carried themselves with an aggressive, streetwise swagger. "We were pretty hard-core when it came to anybody trying to compete with us," he says. "We kind of psyched out everyone there before we even started skating against them."

Skip Engblom, who had dressed for the occasion in his finest beachfront pimp-wear (a long-sleeved purple Hawaiian-print shirt, a snap-brim fedora, vanilla-white dress shoes, dark sunglasses, a black briefcase), led the team toward the registration table. "We all went up to the table together, shoving people out of the way—a bunch of poor kids with something to prove," he says. "When we finally made it up to the front, everyone was staring at us. 'There's our entries and there's our check,' I told them. 'Where's our trophies?' "

In the competition's first event, the freestyle preliminaries, contestants had two minutes in which to impress a panel of judges with their most creative skateboard skills. At that time, state-of-the-art freestyle was a static, tricks-oriented endeavor: Competitors performed nose wheelies while rolling in perfect circles, popped handstands on their boards, or did as many consecutive 360s as they could manage.

The Z-Boys thought that kind of stick-man, tick-tack style was pathetic. And Jay Adams, the team's first member to ride, immediately demonstrated their contempt. Pushing hard across the platform that had been set up for the event, Adams picked up speed quickly, carving back and forth to generate more forward momentum. As he neared the platform's far end, he crouched low, lower than most of the people who were sitting in the bleachers had ever seen anyone get on a skateboard.

The crowd started shouting as Adams pushed closer to the platform's edge—he looked as if he were about to shoot right off. But then he lowered his body even more and pulled a hard, extremely fast turn. The maneuver left his body fully extended, hovering just inches above the platform, with his right arm thrust out for balance and his left hand, palm down, planted on the platform, serving as his pivot. In an instant, he spun 180 degrees and began rolling in the opposite direction, even faster than he was before launching into the turn. The bleachers erupted with enthusiastic, disbelieving cheers. "All the kids just went ballistic, completely out of their minds," says Peralta. "They'd never seen that kind of speed and aggressive style before."

In slightly under two minutes, Adams's explosive performance was over. He hadn't done a single handstand or kickflip. For the rest of the day, while their competitors rolled around the platform like ridiculous, slow-motion, runaway gymnasts, every other Z-Boy proceeded to dazzle the audience. "It was like Ferrari's versus Model-T's," says team member Nathan Pratt.

And it wasn't just the crowd that sensed the discrepancy. For the first time, the Z-Boys themselves began to realize that what had become commonplace to them was actually a revelation to everyone else. "After competing against other skaters, we knew straight out we were a step above," Alva says. "Our whole approach to the deal was different." The Zephyr team's routines were so unprecedented the judges didn't even know how to score them.

A GUNFIGHT EVERY AFTERNOON

News traveled fast. Within a week of the contest, kids from all over the state were showing up at the shop to see if they could best the Z-Boys. "It was like a gunfight every afternoon of the week," says Engblom. "And the more guys that Tony and Jay and Stacy blew out, the more would show up. One bunch of guys came all the way from Arizona."

Around town, the team's blue Zephyr Competition jerseys turned to gold. Team members called them their "get-laid" shirts. Other kids tried to buy them, and when that didn't work, they tried to steal them. *Skateboarder* magazine started publishing articles about the Z-Boys and Dogtown; photographers became a standard feature of even their most informal skate sessions. Competitions were proliferating, thousands of kids all over the country were buying boards, and suddenly people who weren't particularly interested in skateboarding itself were interested in skateboarders.

"I remember this one girl, she was like, 'I can give the best head in Dogtown!' " Adams says. "But I was just embarrassed by all that fame. Like after I started getting in the magazines, I'd be in a 7-Eleven in the Valley somewhere, and kids would be like, 'Are you Jay Adams?' And I was like, 'Nah, nah, that's not me.' "

Alva started hiding his skateboard in the bushes before going to high school every morning. He didn't want to deal with the hype that was developing around him or skateboarding. "I was kind of in my own little world at that point," says Alva. After his early-morning surf sessions, his fingers would be so cold that he could barely hold a pencil during his first-period class. After school, he tried working as a busboy for a while, but hated all the rules. "At that point, I didn't really have time for anything else. I was just trying to stay focused on what was important to me—and that was every day, every minute, every instant, just surfing and skating."

FLYING LESSONS

"Skaters by their very nature are urban guerrillas," wrote Craig Stecyk, an artist friend of Ho and Engblom who maintained a small studio at the shop. Stecyk documented, and in large part, defined the emerging Dogtown ethos, via the photographs and articles he submitted to *Skateboarder* magazine. "The skater makes everyday use of the useless artifacts of the technological burden. The skating urban anarchist employs [structures] in a thousand ways that the original architects could never dream of." This was a radical notion; before the Z-Boys, few people had ever thought to skate anything but the street.

In the summer of 1976, the useless artifact that the Dogtown boys employed most often could be found in the bone-dry backyards of rich SoCal homeowners. The state was in the midst of its worst drought in recorded history, and all over Los Angeles, there were empty pools—in Brentwood backyards, at the secluded outer reaches of Malibu estates, in the hills of Bel Air, where recent fires had leveled million-dollar houses but left the pools intact.

"Almost immediately after we discovered that you could skate these things, a network of kids developed," says Peralta. "It was like how people will use drugs to attract famous people. These kids would call up the shop and say 'Hey, we got a pool,' because they wanted us to come out there and skate with them."

Every week brought a new pool. There was O. J. Simpson's football-shaped pool in Pacific Palisades, a magician's rabbit-shaped pool in Santa Monica. When a pool grew too crowded or the neighbors started calling the cops too often, they simply found another. Hunting for pools was almost as important as skating them, and the Dogtown boys became obsessed with finding new ones. "I would drive my VW squareback really slowly down these alleys in Beverly Hills, and Jay would be standing on the roof, looking over fences," says Peralta. They consulted the local real estate listings in the hope of finding unoccupied homes with pools in the back. Out in the Valley, they staked out a fireman's house until they learned his schedule; when he left one night for his 24-hour shift they used gas-powered pumps to drain his pool, then returned the next morning to skate it. Once, Jay and another Dogtown kid named Shogo Kubo paid $40 to a pilot at the Santa Monica airport for a one-hour ride. "You were supposed to be listening to this guy's pitch for flying lessons, but we spent the whole time looking for pools," he says.

"It became this big, secret cat-and-mouse-type deal," Jim Muir, one of the most avid Dogtown pool-skaters, explains. "You'd be sneaking around from your friends, because you didn't want them to know about a new pool because then it'd get too crowded. You'd be sneaking around from the property owners, sneaking around from the cops." They kept lookouts posted at strategic vantage points. If the cops rolled up in front of the house, they simply ran out the back. If the cops came from the back as well, then the Dogtowners went sideways, over fences. Soon, as many as four or five police cars were responding to calls. "The one place where we did get harassed constantly was this abandoned estate in Santa Monica Canyon across the street from [Mission Impossible star] Peter Graves' place," says Peralta. "He'd call the cops on us and we'd climb up into the trees and hide—and they'd be right below us, searching, not seeing us while we were up there. As soon as they left, we'd climb down and start skating again."

When the cops did catch them, they were usually let off with a warning. On occasion, they were arrested for trespassing. That only made them more committed. "The adrenaline rush of jumping over a fence and actually skating in someone's backyard and getting out of there before they came home—that was totally crazy," Alva says. "You can't jump over people's fences in Beverly Hills nowadays. You'd get eaten by a Doberman, shot by a security guy."

Like the schoolyard banks, pools offered a controlled vertical enviroment that led to rapid innovation—including the first documented aerials. "There's a lot of pool-skaters from San Diego who say that Dogtown wasn't that trend-setting, that it was just what the media hyped as the epicenter," says Alva. "I'm biased when it comes to that, but I still think my boys and I were the first ones to get out of the pool. And we were the ones that affected the entire skateboarding world with it."

Aerials, Alva recounts, came from surviving, from hitting the pool's lip so hard that eventually he was popping out of the pool and grabbing his board in the air. "It was something instinctive. Either you made it or you ended up on the bottom of pool, a bloody mess. It happened by total spontaneous combustion. Then we realized that there was an endless array of things we could do."

Photographers like Craig Stecyk and Glen E. Friedman (who was 13 at the time) started capturing these unprecedented, mindblowing moves on film and suddenly, all across America, kids were ripping out the pages of *Skateboarder* magazine and hanging photos of the Dogtowners on their walls. Tony Alva, flipping off the camera while hanging sideways in mid-air. Jay Adams, his face twisted into a look of the most primal juvenile-delinquent disdain, grinding the edge of a pool so hard he actually knocks its coping out of place.

"Rebels have always been popular—but really obnoxious, fucked up rebels?" says Friedman, assessing the appeal of these overnight teenage icons. "When girls used to ask Jay for his autograph, he'd draw swastikas on their breasts. He wasn't a Nazi, he just did it to be fucked up. What the Sex Pistols started doing in 1976, Jay and Tony were doing a year earlier."

"EVERYONE WANTED TO MAKE THEIR MILLIONS"

In the beginning, free equipment and the get-laid utility of the Zephyr Competition T-shirts had been reward enough for the team's members. By 1976, however, skateboarding was on the verge of becoming a $400 million industry. The Z-Boys were getting older; they were graduating from high school and starting to wonder about what bigger, better deals might be out there for them. Complicating matters were the shop's own growing pains. Ho and Engblom had entered into a partnership with Jay Adams's stepfather, Kent Sherwood, to produce a line of Zephyr-Flex fiberglass skateboards, and the new partners began to have disagreements. "Basically, Kent decided we weren't selling the boards fast enough, so things got kind of weird and crazy," says Ho. "Selling skateboards fucked things up."

"We were still basically kids ourselves," says Engblom. "But all the sudden we were getting orders for 10,000 skateboards, and it was like, 'How do we produce this?'"

Ultimately, Sherwood ended his partnership with the pair and started his own company called Z-Flex. As a consequence, Adams and several others team members left Zephyr and began riding for the new company.

In the aftermath of that exodus, Ho began trying to put together a sponsorship deal that would keep the rest of the team together, but he wasn't able to pull it off. Alva left for Logan Earth Ski; Peralta signed a deal with Gordon & Smith. "I tried to get them to see the value of starting as a unit, and ending as a unit," says Ho. "But everyone had decided that they wanted to make their millions."

INTRODUCING TONY BLUETILE

One day, the Dogtown boys were sneaking into movie star pools; the next, they were appearing in movies. Tony Alva landed a role in the film *Skateboard* as "Tony Bluetile," a farting, beer-drinking, *Playboy*-reading skate-thug who ends up losing the big race to teen idol Leif Garrett. Stacy Peralta, who at 17 was suddenly earning $5,000 a month from his sponsorship deal with G&S, starred in

Freewheelin', a low-budget, cheesy skateboarder romance released in 1976. "I was so embarrassed at the premiere," says Peralta, "that I hid behind a curtain the whole time." While the executive director of the International Skateboard Association primly told *People* magazine that Tony Alva represented "everything that is vile in the sport," the new Dogtown style was in high demand all across the country. For kids who couldn't quite match Alva's radical athleticism or Jay Adams's spontaneous irreverence, a skateboard or helmet bearing their signatures was the next best thing.

But could you really package the ungovernable energy of a guy like Jay Adams? Could you really turn a kid who barreled down the streets of West Los Angeles plucking wigs from the heads of old ladies into your corporate spokesdude? Often you couldn't. In Mexico, where Adams, Alva, and several other Dogtowners had traveled to attend the opening of a new skatepark, the kids who had once emulated their favorite Australian surf heroes now began to resemble rock stars.

"When we got there, this guy told us that if we wanted to score any pot or anything, that they would set us up," says Alva. "It ended up being the cops who brought it to us, this big trash bag full of weed." In the daytime they skated, and at night they partied with groupies and trashed their hotel rooms. At a local brothel, a fat, lactating prostitute ardently pursued the 16-year-old Adams. "She just kept chasing him around the room, shooting milk out of her tits at him," says Alva. "We were these full-on little rats in surf trunks who got wild and raised hell, and [skate promoters] just fed off our energy. It was almost like being on tour with Metallica."

As Alva's notoriety increased, he started hanging out with rock stars and wearing white suits and wide-brimmed, pimp-style fedoras. When he and his new friend Bunker Spreckels, a playboy millionaire heir to a sugar fortune and the stepson of Clark Gable, went in search of new pools to skate in Beverly Hills, they hired limousines to chauffeur them.

By 1977, all of the Dogtown boys were prospering. Alva won the World Pro Championship that year. Soon after, he left Logan Earth Ski, and, with the help of an entrepreneur named Pete Zehnder, created his own line of skateboards. (The company's slogan: "No matter how big your ego, my boards will blow your mind.") Peralta left his sponsor to become a partner in Powell Skateboards, which subsequently became known as Powell-Peralta. Jim Muir and another Dogtown local, Wes Humpston—who used to draw on his homemade boards to pass the time while traveling to various skate spots—trademarked the Dogtown name and produced the first line of skateboards to feature elaborate graphics on the underside of their decks. Jay Adams had his signature Z-Flex board and a helmet called the Flyaway. "I made good money off that for a while," he says. "But that only lasted about a year."

"A ROLLING BALL OF CHAOS"

In the mid-'70s, Adams and Alva were a step ahead of everyone, pioneers of skating's hardcore approach to life in general. But in the late '70s, the punks caught up. "Black Flag, Circle Jerks, Descendents, Bad Religion, Suicidal Tendencies. We picked up on all the music that was happening in L.A. at that time," says Alva. "There was so much energy at those shows. Skate and punk fed off each other because they were both total outlets for aggression."

Punk replaced Ted Nugent and Jimi Hendrix as the soundtrack for skate sessions; the music paralleled the sessions themselves, which had been turning more and more violent as the Dogtowners' hard-core reputations preceded them. "A lot of people were gunning for us, because they'd read about us in the magazines," Alva says. "We were like a rolling ball of chaos, this mobile gang on a recon mission. We'd show up at a skatepark somewhere, and there'd be guys who'd come up to us and get in our faces, telling us we weren't so hard-core." Naturally, a fight would ensue.

At night, after going to shows for local bands like Suicidal Tendencies (whose lead singer was Jim Muir's younger brother Mike), things got even more violent. "We'd go to parties, take Quaaludes, get in fights with bats and stuff," says Adams.

Drugs and alcohol were starting to exact a toll. Alva's friend Bunker O.D.'d from a combination of sedatives and alcohol, while trying to kick a heroin habit. "We definitely lost soldiers because of drugs," says Alva. "Coke, heroin, downers. People started losing track of what was most important—the skating." Alva was nearly a casualty himself: "I did a lot of coke at that time."

Yet in the early '80s, when bands like Black Flag and the Adolescents were on the ascent, the skateboarding industry was collapsing. Skateparks that had opened just a couple years earlier were already starting to close, unable to obtain insurance or attract enough patrons on a regular basis. The kids who'd taken up the sport in the '70s were growing older and giving it up. Making things worse, America slipped into a recession.

Skateboard sales dropped overnight. Stacy Peralta's signature board, which had once sold more than 5,000 units per month, was

which were epitomized by the images of the outlaw biker gang. This hybrid youth subculture, a melding of hippie and biker, began to appear in the late 1960s, but it was unorganized and had no unique forms of self-expression. It was a nondistinctive part of the scene.

At the same time that a blue-collar variant of the youth culture was forming, psychedelic music was getting harder. Indeed, according to *FLIP Magazine*, the manager of Blue Cheer, one of the hardest psychedelic groups, was a former Hell's Angel; straddling two worlds, this manager's career demonstrates that a hybrid subculture was crystallizing on the level of its music in the late 1960s. As the broad 1960s youth culture collapsed and fragmented at the turn of the new decade, both the blue-collar long-hairs and the psychedelic bands were left stranded. Eventually they found each other with the help of the music industry and the result was a heavy metal subculture, in which both audience and music became essential to one another's definition. The music became the prime representation or emblem of the youth group's identity because it cohered with the life-styles and mythologies of that group. The important thing to note here is that the subculture was not a fabrication of the popular-culture industry, but existed, in germ, before heavy metal music as a distinctive genre erupted.

The heavy metal subculture, then, is a legitimate offspring of the 1960s youth culture, inheriting and preserving some of its central symbols, attitudes, practices, and fashions, and carrying them forward into the next historical period. Thus, the heavy metal subculture basically represents a preservationist and conservative tendency, the first 1960s nostalgia movement, arising amidst the decay of the 1960s youth culture. Why a segment of white, blue-collar, and male youth should find an ideological home in a nostalgic utopia is partly explained as a response to declining economic opportunities for that group, whose members faced increasing disadvantages in their lives. They were ripe for a rock-and-roll fantasy rooted in the high times of the recent past. Also, as the general youth culture, which was dominated by white males, fell apart, white, male, and heterosexual youth became socioculturally de-centered by emerging movements of women, gays, and nonwhites. Nostalgia for centricity, then, also had its part in the metal subculture's conservation of the 1960s.

Considered from the viewpoint of historical sociology, heavy metal music is the master emblem of the subculture of a well-defined segment of youth. Not all those who form the audience for metal are white, male, blue-collar youth. Not all white, male, blue-collar youth are members of the metal subculture. But the core of the metal audience is a subculture whose members have those demographic characteristics, not by chance, but because heavy metal music came to express the utopian desires, the life-style, and the discontents of a structurally defined segment of youth. There could have been no heavy metal music if there had been no incipient subculture ready to guide and embrace it.

As an expression of a distinctive segment of youth, the metal subculture valorizes the demographics of its membership. Masculinity, blue-collar sentiments, youthfulness, and, to a lesser extent, "whiteness" are values shared and upheld by the metal audience. Moreover, many of the other features of the heavy metal subculture are strongly related to or implicated in these demographically derived values.

It is difficult to determine which of the four demographic factors is the most important in determining the subculture. Together they describe a social position that should be understood as a whole, not analyzed into its components. There are also interrelationships among the factors. Yet there is a general order of importance, moving from maleness, through youthfulness, to whiteness, to blue-collar sentiments.

MALE

Heavy metal is a form of rock music, sharing with that larger category an array of features. Various authors have commented on the male orientation of rock culture in general. Although it is most evident in metal, as John Street points out in *Rebel Rock*, "Rock's following tends to be male; pop fans tend to be younger and female." Simon Frith and Howard Horne argue that in Britain rock was a predominantly male interest because, in part, the leading British rock musicians of the 1960s had an art-school background. In their book *Art into Pop*, they theorize that the romantic ideology that was rampant in these schools stressed a bohemian ideal, which was both masculine and somewhat misogynistic. Heavy metal artists did not come from the art schools but were, like their fans, steeped in the rock ideology. In some sense metal is the Ur-rock practice, taking to an extreme many of the ideals of 1960s rock.

Not merely rock, but youth culture as such, tends to be male-oriented. In his comparative study of adolescent culture in the United States, Canada, and Britain, Michael Brake concluded that it is "male dominated and predominantly heterosexual, thus celebrating masculinity and excluding girls to the periphery." And in "Genre and Gender in the Structure of Music Preferences," P. G. Christenson and J. B. Peterson note two different adolescent cultures, distinguished by gender, "each with its own distinctive characteristics, style, and world view, in which boys are encouraged to settle career and personal identity issues first and foremost, whereas girls are taught that their primary developmental task is to attract a husband and prepare for caring for a family."

One can go even further, arguing that males, in contrast to females, tend to form bonding groups with members of their own sex. Writing in 1963, Jules Henry observed in *Culture Against Man* that in the United States "Boys flock. . . . Boys are dependent on masculine solidarity within a relatively large group. In boys' groups the emphasis is on masculine unity; in girls' cliques the purpose is to shut out other girls." Male culture, for Henry, was centered around sports: "The faithfulness of boys to sports is a striking characteristic of American life. There is a total, almost a religious, community of sport among boys, in which maleness, masculine solidarity, and the rules of the game are validated, year in and year out." His observations—if one substitutes "watching" for "playing"—also apply to male adults. Substitute "music" for "sport" and one gets an idea of the intensity of the heavy metal subculture.

"That the audience for heavy-metal music is heavily male-dominated is generally acknowledged, and statistically confirmed," wrote Straw in "Characterizing Music Cultures." But the heavy metal audience is more than just male; it is masculinist. That is, the heavy metal subculture, as a community with shared values, norms, and behaviors, highly esteems masculinity. Whereas other youth cultures and audiences, such as the early 1970s glam rock following that coalesced around David Bowie, and the mid-1980s pop audience for Culture Club and Michael Jackson, countenanced play with gender, heavy metal fans are deadly earnest about the value of male identity. Masculinity is understood in the metal subculture to be the binary opposite of femininity. Much like the religious fundamentalism that denounces heavy metal, the metal subculture holds that gender differences are rooted in the order of things: it is perilous even to question, let alone play with or breach, the boundaries.

Influenced in part by the British biker subculture and the related, though more diffuse, American "greasers," the masculinist model predated metal. Paul Willis's analysis of the motor-bike boys in *Profane Culture* defines the model: "Their appearance was aggressively masculine. The motorcycle gear both looked tough, with its leather, studs and denim, and by association with the motorbike, took over some of the intimidating quality of the machine. Hair was worn long. . . . Tattoos on the hands, arms and chest were extremely common."

Insofar as male youths have a different set of problems than their female counterparts, expressive activities such as music mean different things to each gender group. Women are part of the problem for males, not only because they are objects of lust but because they symbolize repressive authority in the persons of the mother and the teacher. Young males are, at a minimum, ambivalent regarding women, seeking to escape from maternal and other forms of female authority and fearful of being viewed as "mama's boys," and yet attracted to women sexually. Childhood socialization patterns, in which boys are allowed freer rein than girls, make the transition from youth to adulthood more difficult for males than for females. The expected adult role in Western industrialized society is closer to the female pattern of low aggression, stricter conformity to the "rules," and supervision by adults, such as spouses. It is my theory that heavy metal music celebrates the very qualities that boys must sacrifice in order to become adult members of society.

The male chauvinism and misogyny that characterize the metal subculture are tempered by its sense of community. Females who do not flaunt their femininity, that is, who dress in jeans and black T-shirts, and who even more importantly display a love of the music, are often welcomed and treated as equals at such events as concerts. Open hostility of various sorts is displayed toward females who do not conform to the dress and behavior codes. Women who dress in "provocative" attire, such as miniskirts and high heels, are either denounced as sluts waiting to have sex with the band or are ogled as obnoxiously as they might be by the most chauvinistic construction workers. The distinction made by the metal subculture between women who dress and behave according to the masculine code and those who fit feminine stereotypes indicates that it is the culture of masculinity, not biological differences, that is of greatest significance.

The masculinist element in metal subculture is not merely relevant to the attitudes toward and treatment of women. There is also an attitude of extreme intolerance toward male homosexuality. As Philip Bashe describes in *Heavy Metal Thunder*, heavy metal fans "are often vehemently opposed to other forms of music and to acts that display the slightest hint of ambisexuality. Headbangers are notoriously homophobic and generally regard any act that does not go in for metal's much-macho posturing as beneath contempt."

According to John Clarke's "The Skinheads & the Magical Recovery of Community," during the 1970s the British Skinheads carried the animus against homosexuality into the activity of "Queer

Bashing." The metal subculture did not incorporate this violent practice, but expressed its abhorrence for gays by means of more acceptable cultural practices, such as an impassioned loathing for disco music. The relevance of and hostility toward homosexuality in the heavy metal subculture is in some sense a reaction of resistance by masculinist interests against the change in dominant values. The gay culture, the source of the mass popularity of disco and disco fashion, came to be admired in the 1970s by the hip culture mavens. At that time, too, the gay rights movement came into its own. Gays "coming out" of the closet were seen by many traditional males as flaunting their "gay culture."

The masculine mystique that characterizes the metal subculture has many roots, the most important of which is simply the general sexist bias of modern and more generally human culture, which is intensified by the special insecurities of youth. This general tendency is fortified in a historically specific way by the social, cultural, and economic marginalization of white, blue-collar males in the post-1960s era. The heavy metal subculture is usefully interpreted as a defensive reaction of members of this group as their standing and security declined.

YOUTH

The metal subculture is also characterized by the midadolescent age grouping of its membership. That metal's audience is overwhelmingly young is not surprising. Audiences for rock music traditionally have been teenagers. For example, the study "Rock Music and the Socialization of Moral Values in Early Adolescence" by James S. Leming published in 1984, looked at 1500 twelve to eighteen year olds who were representative of the national population and "found that almost 81% of the students cited music as an important part of their lives. Music was the sample's fourth highest ranked hobby."

Rock music in general responds to the ambivalence of youth. As I wrote in "Rock: Youth and Its Music," "Caught between the moment of suspended freedom and the transition from dependency to responsibility, the typical dualistic consciousness of youth is modified by the counter-tendencies to sink back into childhood and to advance towards adulthood." Stuart Hall and Paddy Whannel write in their book *Popular Arts*, "Teenage culture is, in part, an authentic response to this situation, an area of common symbols and meanings, shared in part or in whole by a generation, in which they can work out or work through not only the natural tensions of adolescence, but the special tensions of being an adolescent in our kind of society." People seem to become members of youth subcultures at a structurally meaningful time, as Mike Brake writes in *Comparative Youth Culture*: "[Membership] occurs in the period between, or near to, the end of the school career, usually at a point when education is perceived as meaningless in terms of a young person's work prospects, and lasts until marriage."

Heavy metal's subculture emerged from the wreckage of the youth counter(sub)culture of the 1960s. The great consensus following World War II was shattered in the United States by the civil rights movement and then the antiwar movement. The youth subculture, an amalgam of the so-called hippie movement and the free speech movement on college campuses, and a wide assortment of commercial and community-based groupings, emerged in the second half of the 1960s. It spread around the world, including Britain, where it merged with class-based youth subcultures. Symbolized by the audience at the Woodstock Festival in 1969 and by terms such as "the generation gap," the youth culture was never as all-encompassing as the media, always eager to woo baby boomers nostalgic for their lost youth, would have one believe. But it was a genuine cultural phenomenon that, as it broke apart, released a host of related social and cultural movements, including heavy metal.

A series of events beginning in 1968, some of which were meant to repress the counterculture, shattered its fragile unity. The litany for the United States includes the police riot at the Democratic National Convention in Chicago in 1968, the deaths and disorder at the Altamont Concert in 1969, the National Guard's shooting of students at Kent State University in 1970, and the end of the draft. Cultural icons died too. As George Lipsitz writes in *Time Passages*, "The hippie counter-culture confronted its own demise most dramatically in the deaths of Hendrix and Joplin. With the break-up of the Beatles, the murder of a participant in the 1969 Altamont Rock festival . . . the degeneration into drug-ravaged slums of . . . Haight-Ashbury and New York's East Village, it became clear even to its adherents that 'the dream' was over."

The ensuing fragmentation, which led to what Tom Wolfe mischaracterized as the "me decade," was the environment in which the metal subculture surfaced. Lloyd Grossman, in his social history of rock music, characterizes heavy metal, which he calls "downer rock," as a response to the antiyouth crusade. "It appeared that society had formally declared war against the young and Heavy Rock brought forth Downer Rock, a particularly appropriate genre for the times."

At least as serious as the undoing of the youth counterculture, and concurrent with it, was the radical change in the meaning of the term "youth" in social discourse. Beyond and indeed in place of its use in referring to a biological or a social group, "youth" became a cultural signifier, referring to a style and a spirit. Through the 1960s the notion of "youth" was anchored to its biological and social definitions; that is, the youth culture belonged to that group in the population that was undergoing adolescent maturation and was moving socially from childhood to adulthood. But then the youth culture got co-opted into the general leisure culture and lost its moorings in a particular age group.

Youth in the sense of young people in a special biological and social predicament became marginal to "youth" as a cultural code of beliefs, values, sentiments, and practices. Young people responded to the extortion of "youth" in a variety of ways. Mainly they merged into the youthful leisure culture as its distinctive representatives. Others, reacting in the manner of tribal peoples who have become deracinated, dropped out of society into depression, becoming heavy users of alcohol and other drugs, and sometimes committing suicide. Some entered cults and authoritarian sects, which set themselves sharply off from the general culture. Still others formed subcultures that raised the symbolic stakes too high for the general leisure culture easily to co-opt them.

The heavy metal and punk subcultures are the two dominant examples of youth attempting to create and hold onto their own distinctive and unassimilable culture. The significance in both subcultures of hairstyles demonstrates the raising of symbolic stakes. E. Ellis Cashmore argues in "Shades of Black, Shades of White" that punk's major feature was the valorization of youth: "Punks decried anyone or anything connected with the established social order as boring old farts (BOFs). They regurgitated the impulse behind the mod slogan of the 1960s, 'I hope I die before I get old.'" Although dissimilar on the surface, the heavy metal and punk styles were united at their core by the desire to constitute themselves as unacceptable to the respectable world. They could not be modified, in the way that clothes can, to allow for weekend warriors. Metal and punk required permanent stigmata. The subculture was inscribed on the body.

Both the metal and punk subcultures borrowed heavily from prior youth cultures. In a highly oversimplified summary, punk took a rave-up beat from early rock and roll, and cobbled it together with inverted features of art-rock conventions. Metal appropriated musical, visual, and performance elements from the hard-rock/biker and the psychedelic musical subcultures. Whereas punk's transformations were understood, internally and by the critics, as progressive, metal's appropriations were interpreted, from within and especially from without, as retrograde. Indeed, the heavy metal subculture initially was a movement to preserve the best of the youth counterculture even as it died. Beyond the musical components, heavy metal perpetuated the sense of community, the use of marijuana, and the visual element of performances, among other values and practices. The conservativism of the metal subculture, so abhorred by the critics, is rooted here: "there are few things as conservative and hidebound as a crazed Heavy Metal fan," as Mike Cobley notes in "Again & Again." The metal subculture selected only a small portion of the 1960s youth culture to preserve, but what it chose was genuine. Perhaps the critics of metal simply do not like to be reminded that the 1960s contained both more and less than they wish it did.

What happens to heavy metal fans when they become adults? The metal subculture does not fully include those metal fans who are no longer in their teens. The editors of *Rock of Ages: The Rolling Stone History of Rock n' Roll* contend that "Heavy metal was consumed by one generation of teenagers after another; attending a concert, one would rarely find anyone over the age of eighteen or nineteen. Heavy metal, with its deafening volume and proud hostility to cultural and aesthetic niceties, is the primary music of teenage rebellion and, almost by definition, something a listener outgrows."

Not everyone seems to outgrow it fully, but evidence of adult metal fans is hard to come by. Adults are not studied as an audience for rock music, except as potential players in the marketplace. It is the high school and college students, who are easily and cheaply available to researchers, whose preferences are measured by sociologists. However, observation of the audience at classic metal concerts in the late 1980s (Ozzy, the regrouped Deep Purple, and Motorhead, among others), revealed a few people who were well past their youth. The rest of the audience not only tolerated these generational oddities, but saw their presence as an affirmation of the metal culture itself. The same is not true of audiences for lite metal groups, such as Poison and Ratt, nor for speed and thrash metal groups such as Anthrax, Slayer, and Nuclear Assault. Lite and thrash metal audiences tend to be uniformly adolescent.

The adults who continue to appreciate metal rarely use the metal media, except for playing their old albums. They do not attend many, if any, concerts; do not buy new metal releases or metal magazines; and do not call in requests on the radio. Many do not even play their albums all that much, but they have not thrown them out either. Once part of the metal subculture, they are now like wistful emigrants, living a continent away in another world than their own.

WHITE

The members of the metal subculture are predominantly white, except in countries with overwhelmingly nonwhite populations, such as Japan and Brazil. The performers of metal music are also overwhelmingly white. As was the case for maleness, "whiteness" is not merely a demographic category but has a cultural significance. That significance is not overtly or even necessarily covertly racist. Indeed, it is less an affirmation of "whiteness" than it is an absence—an obtrusive absence—of blacks.

Heavy metal emerged at a time when the position of blacks in Anglo-American society was undergoing massive changes. The black power movement in the United States, with its separatist, white-rejecting strains, was in full flower. At the same time, civil rights legislation started to have an impact in housing, in schools, and in the workplace. This, coupled with the severe downturn in the economy, led to a strong sense of resentment against blacks by marginal whites.

One could look over the vast sea of thousands of faces at a heavy metal concert and fail to find one black person. By the mid-1980s, when a few brave blacks started to enter the arena, they were in the company of their white buddies. I recall speaking with a black college student, an avid metal guitarist. His favorite band, Rush, was coming to town, and although he would have loved to have seen them, he was too intimidated to go. (He did get to attend their concert the next year and reported no problems.)

The experience of this black fan points up the fact, already noted in the section on maleness, that the metal subculture tends to be tolerant of those outside its core demographic base who follow its codes of dress, appearance, and behavior, and who show devotion to the music. Neither sexist, ageist, nor racist on principle, the metal subculture is exclusivist, insistent upon upholding the codes of its core membership. Hispanics rarely joined the heavy metal subculture until the late 1980s. The fragmentation of the youth subculture in the early 1970s, which had integrated some elements of Hispanic music (for example, Santana), led to the emergence of a new wave of separate Hispanic music. Salsa and its variants were the musical base of the Hispanic youth subculture. There was nothing in the metal subculture that symbolically excluded Hispanics. Indeed, a number of symbols found in some segments of metal were present in some Hispanic cultures, especially the symbolism of death. In communities in the United States where Mexican youth are in the majority, notably in south Texas, the audience for heavy metal is rapidly growing and the metal subculture is taking root.

Although the white demographic base was not given cultural expression primarily as a racial value, either in the prowhite or the antiblack sense, metal has been associated with a strong ethnocentrism bordering on xenophobia. Many of the symbols, especially the visual ones, of heavy metal are derived from medieval northern Europe, ancient Anglo-Saxon, and Nordic mythologies. Thus the heavy metal subculture is less a racially based than a cultural grouping, drawing on the symbols of particular ethnic traditions. Emerging at the time of a "discovering and celebrating one's roots" mania among racial and ethnic groups, particularly in the United States, the valorization of "white" into heavy metal subculture can be interpreted as the creation of the semblance of an ethnic group for individuals who were perceived to be nonethnics in the Anglo-American context. Jon Epstein, studying a group of junior high school students in 1990 in North Carolina, found that their musical preferences were closely allied with race. Blacks preferred rap, whites metal.

BLUE COLLAR

It is generally accepted that the members of the metal subculture are predominantly male, young, and white. Mike Brake adds that they also tend to come from working-class/blue-collar backgrounds. This observation is more accurate concerning England than the United States; youth subcultures that are related, in part, to leisure culture, are more class-based in Britain than they are in the United States. But in a cultural sense, heavy metal has a class signification wherever it appears. For the United States, it might be most accurate to say that metal partakes of a blue-collar ethos. Blue-collar mythologies replace the romance of black culture in metal's syllabus of rebellion.

During the 1970s the working class(es) in the West were under siege. The fierce economic "stagflation," caused in part by the OPEC oil cartel, seriously hurt those working at manufacturing jobs. Working-class youths could no longer expect to follow their fathers and uncles into the nearby factories. In addition to suffering

straightened economic conditions, the working class was culturally threatened by the growing hegemony of a middle-class/
mass-culture life-style in the mass media. In the United States
many blue-collar families migrated from their "rust belt" surroundings, dislocating the sense of community that had existed
there for several generations. Mike Brake argues that "Subcultures
try to retrieve the lost, socially cohesive elements in the parent culture; they attempt to relocate 'in an imaginary relation' the real
relations which those in subcultures cannot transcend." Thus, just
as the heavy metal subculture was a response to the collapse of the
1960s youth culture, it was also a response to the cultural marginalization of the working class.

In terms of many of its values and mythologies, the heavy
metal subculture is blue collar. Brake writes that the expectations
for blue-collar young males is that they will sow their wild oats in
a "period of intense emotion, colour, and excitement during the
brief respite between school and the insecurities of the early days
of working and settling down into marriage and adulthood."

The heavy metal audience was never exclusively working class.
The older metal fans, those in their late teens and early twenties, were
more likely to be blue-collar workers, but a significant portion of high
school-aged adherents came from middle-class families. Nonetheless, blue-collar culture permeated the heavy metal subculture. The
separation of the sexes, the boisterous, beer-swilling, male cama-
raderie, among other features, are rooted in blue-collar folkways.
Hebdige interprets part of the heavy metal subculture as a "football
terrace machismo," a distinctly male, working-class culture.

By the 1970s the blue-collar romance had the same appeal for
middle-class youth that the black fantasia had for an earlier cohort
in the 1950s. Blue-collar culture was disreputable. American youth
cultures, succeeding one another over decades and embracing a
variety of styles, all rebel against the bourgeois culture. The
process has been aptly characterized by George Lipsitz as "pres-
tige from below." The middle-class kids who embraced metal were
not from the upper reaches of their class. They were centered in
the lower middle class, whose members are the most insecure in
their standing. There could be few things more threatening for
lower-middle-class parents than to witness their sons aping blue-
collar manners and espousing blue-collar values.

The class composition of the core metal audience is working
and middle class, but the metal subculture is steeped in the blue-
collar ethos. Ethos, however, need not and does not translate
in this case into a political stance. According to Cashmore, the

members of the metal subculture normally do not have the sense of themselves as political actors in the way that the punks did. This is a major reason why they are not admired by the graduates of the counterculture who became the dominant popular music critics. In the metal subculture, blue-collar style and sentiments are tied to political attitudes, but these are not progressive in any conventional sense, basically amounting to a cynical animosity toward those in positions of governmental authority. There is a strongly shared antibourgeois sentiment, but this is a remnant of the youth counterculture. For fans, perhaps the worst thing that can be said about a heavy metal band is that it has "gone commercial."

The demographic unity of the metal subculture shifted in the mid-1980s. The differentiation of heavy metal into rather distinctive subgenres, especially in the United States, paralleled these demographic changes. Overall, the heavy metal audience became de-differentiated. The age group widened on both ends of the mid-teen norm and wider ranges of the middle class became involved. In addition, nonwhite, especially Latin American, groups entered the audience; and evangelical Christian youth got their own subgenre of metal. Chicago has even given birth to a Gay Metal Society, which might seem to deconstruct the subculture altogether. Most importantly, females became a significant segment of metal fans. This has led in the Chicago area to the formation of the Chicago Women's Rock Club the motto of which is "Let 'em know that you're no bimbo." These changes in the demographics of the audience did not impact on each of the metal subgenres uniformly. The audiences for classic metal, which continued traditional heavy metal, lite or pop metal, and speed/thrash metal were as differentiated as the distinctive forms of music that they appreciated.

The classic metal audience maintained the demographics described above for the heavy metal subculture, but not as strictly. The audience for thrash/speed metal, particularly those examples of it that integrated many punk elements, became exclusively male and concentrated at the lower end of the age group. Lite metal audiences became almost undistinguishable demographically from pop-rock audiences: they were teenaged, middle class, and included significant percentages of females. Indeed, males were in the minority of the audiences for some groups, such as Ratt, Poison, and White Lion. As the group Bon Jovi was seen to be the major innovator of lite metal, creating a music which, while specifically aimed at a female audience, did not fully alienate the males.

Despite the demographic changes of the 1980s, the original makeup of the heavy metal audience—male, midteen, white, and blue collar—left a deep trace on the metal subculture(s). As a valorization and culturalization of demographic categories, the metal subculture is a child of its time. In a world in which all groups have been de-centered, marginalization tends to become a universal condition. The metal subculture follows the black and Chicano movements in making a strong sense of negative marginality a badge of honor by taking as its name an epithet hurled against it. It is a cultural defense for maleness, a ghetto for youth when "youth" no longer signifies the young, a white preserve by default, and a stylization of blue-collar leisure culture. It is the reproduction of a world that never was, but in constituting itself as this yearned-for world it has become a real force in the lives of individuals and even in the environing society. It cannot make the world at large over, but it provides that world with some of its significance and meaning.

Notebook

1. Which of the subcultures in this chapter most appeal to you? Which do you feel most negatively about? Where do you think your attitudes come from?

2. Check out some metal bands and think about how their lyrics reflect some of the cultural concerns Weinstein claims are important for the fans. Some of the most famous American groups include Queensryche, Anthrax, and Slayer, but there are metal bands all over the world, such as Havok from Italy, Necrost from Russia, and Dezember from Thailand. What metal bands are popular where you are right now? If you don't know, how could you find out?

3. Watch the film *Heavy Metal Parking Lot*, a documentary looking at heavy metal fans. How does the film seem to want to portray the fans? In what ways do the people interviewed uphold the theories Weinstein puts forth here? In what ways do they contradict her theories?

4. This essay breaks down the subculture of heavy metal fans into demographic categories of race, class, age, and gender. Try to perform a similar analysis of the subculture you will be studying, paying special attention to the origin of the subculture and its influence on these demographics. What are the advantages of writing an essay that is divided into these sorts of sections? What are the disadvantages?

CHAPTER 2

Fitting in and Coming Together

OVERVIEW

The essays in this chapter look at what happens when members of a subculture join forces, whether for an event such as a fan convention or a rock show that is held in a specific space, or online in a virtual community. The elements that draw in the members of a subculture—a common interest, a shared activity, or the need for support—tell a great deal about what makes the subculture tick. By looking at the reasons why and places where subculture members gather, we can learn something about what they bring to the subculture and what they take from it. When you observe subcultures around you, consider the places and moments—both virtual and physical—where the subculture seems to come alive. What is it about a particular space, or a particular event, that defines or shapes the subculture? Look beyond subcultures to consider how and why the places we go and the activities we do influence and inform our behavior and beliefs. What is the culture at your local coffeehouse? At a school sports game? In an online chatroom you frequent? How do you feel yourself change when you enter these different spaces?

The Bboy Style on the Eastside
SASHA VLIET

In this personal essay, Sasha Vliet looks at what is important to a group of young breakdancers in Texas—not only their dance moves and clothing, but also their shared value system, which Vliet observes at work during a local competition. Vliet grew up in Kansas, where she worked in family restaurants and explored the family farm. She attended Oberlin College and afterward became a high school teacher in the public schools of Dorchester, Massachusetts, and Austin, Texas. She has traveled extensively and has taught in Mexico and Latin America. She is currently a novelist, teacher, and Ph.D. candidate at the University of Texas at Austin, where she is completing doctoral work in American Studies.

———————————— ✦ ————————————

ELEMENTS OF EXPRESSION

Spring, 1999. I am in the school gym at lunchtime. The break-dancers have finished with their chips and Big Red and are now stretching their bodies in preparation for a practice session. Rafael and Nando sit facing each other, their legs spread out in wide Vs, their hands locked together. They take turns pulling each other forward so that their heads come down, close to the ground. Wizard stands near the wall, his hand out for balance, and pulls his right foot up behind him in a quadriceps stretch. Gabe is running circles around the gym, lifting his knees up high with each stride. Nando bites his fingernails. Mike repeatedly runs his hands through his hair and then shakes his arms and legs out, like a runner on the line. I know enough by now, about these practice sessions, to understand that each boy wants to do better than he did the day before. The boys have told me about what takes place during these sessions, inside the practice circle. Each boy anticipates finally landing that power move he has worked so hard to master. He visualizes himself on the floor, picturing new moves and poses, forcing, in his mind's eye, his limbs into arches and streaks of motion. Each boy imagines himself surprising the group. But he is also careful not to picture too much. "It's about being spontaneous," Gabe has told me. "It's about letting yourself do whatever it is your body wants to do. You can't plan it too much, because if you do, you might fall out. And then you'd have to bail."

I am thinking of spontaneity as Daniel, the designated DJ, starts the music and the boys form their circle. For several minutes, no one moves. The boys wait, relaxing into themselves, until the first brave soul is ready to move into the center.

Finally, Nando steps forward and starts with power. He leans into the empty space the boys have created for him and throws himself into a barrel roll so that his entire body revolves in the air, horizontally. He lands on his feet and pauses for half a beat, and then he throws another barrel roll. He slides into several windmills on the floor. He rolls from one shoulder, across his chest, onto the other shoulder, while his legs spread out like the wooden blades of a ceiling-fan. And then he pushes himself up into a handstand and spins on the palm of one hand. The rest of the boys applaud and smile and shout out their approval. "Starting out with the big shit, huh?" "Go Nando. You landed that. Badass!"

Other boys take their turns and I watch them interact with one another. They yell out pointers to the person in the center when he cannot land his move. They offer suggestions. They tease. They collaborate. They back off. They applaud. They laugh. They celebrate. There is a knock on the back door of the gym and Mike runs from the circle to see who it is. I know they are hoping for Dario, who has dropped out of high school but will still stop by, once in a while, to practice with his friends. I am hoping for him, too. It is a treat to see him; he brings an energy to the circle.

Mike opens the door and we see that grin. It is Dario. The boys step away and rather than stand in the circle, they sit on the floor, giving Dario all the room he needs. He stretches for a minute and then asks Daniel to switch the music. "Gimme something I can get hyped on," he says. The boys like this request, knowing it means Dario is ready to knock out something really raw. "Miss V.," Dario says looking my way, "what'll be?" I ask him to give us something we haven't seen. He does. Dario creates poses without pause and then recreates them before we have time to appreciate all that each pose was. He manipulates his body, repeatedly, into unimaginable positions. He is freestyling (the impromptu "jazz" of break-dancing, when the dancer comes up with moves spontaneously, without rehearsing), and bends and distorts his body in ways that no other dancer is able to replicate. This is how he gains the respect of the other breakdancers. They are all good, but he is extraordinary—no one can copy his style.

When he has tired himself out, Dario steps away from the open space and sits next to Rafael, his childhood friend. They talk and watch the others, who have now been recharged. Time is short, during these lunchtime practices, so the last ten minutes are hectic and the dancing becomes frenzied. The boys rush to get in their final turns and the circle disappears. Dario, now in his instructor role, rushes from friend to friend, counseling on the details of a power move or freeze. "Try holding your leg up like this," he says to Mike. "Yeah. Like that. It looks dope." Gabe is trying out a barrel roll and lands on the ground with a thud. Dario smiles as he watches. "You'll get it. After you practice enough you won't wanna fall out anymore." Gabe rolls his eyes. "Hurts like a mother, though, right now," he says, rubbing his elbow.

   Then it's over. The final lunch bell rings and I watch Dario as he says goodbye to his friends, making sure to bump each of their fists with his own, making sure to give Rafael a one-armed hug, making sure to throw me the peace sign before he leaves. "I'm outy," he says, the back door clicking shut behind him.

BBOY STYLE

During my time with these particular bboys I recognized a desire, on their parts, to present their "ultimate" identities to me, the set of characteristics by which they can be definitively recognized. While searching for different ways to present their "ideal" selves, the boys gave me a chance to see their uncompromised egos. Ralph Cintron, who explores boy culture and masculinity in his work *Angel's Town*, suggests that the ego is "a kind of aura (that) frames the body, and (that) certain artifacts expand the ego's presence in public space . . . allowing the ego to occupy ever-increasing amounts of public space." For the boys, these artifacts (such as the clothing, wristbands, hats, helmets, earrings, performance spaces, and even battle-dancing scars) not only expand the ego's presence, but also define the ways in which the boys gain respect. Additionally, these artifacts, and the ways in which they are used, are themselves modes of expression. John Clarke, in his work "Style," explains that "objects, the 'gear' used to assemble a new subcultural style must not only already exist, but must also carry meanings organized into a system coherent enough for their relocation and transformation."

  In this way then, the boys transform objects and redefine their functions. Performance space is no longer an elevated stage, separate from public space. It is the floor of a gym, a hallway in a school cafeteria, a portion of a crowded street. A wristband is not a piece of cloth worn around the arm for collecting moisture—it is a piece of soft fabric to place under the hand for extending the length of hand-spins. The boys alter the original function of these items and expand on their potential function. As Clarke notes, "there is no point in it (the artifact), if the new assemblage looks exactly like, carries exactly the same message as, that previously existing."

However, what is most interesting to me about the bboy identity is the way in which it is created in and expressed through an opposition to the status quo, to prescribed behaviors encouraged by the school or by the boys' peers, to what is expected of them by teachers, parents, the community outside of the Eastside. It is an identity that is rooted in dance, and in an opposition to mainstream dance/music that was created in the Bronx, during the late 1970s, by young Black and Puerto Rican boys.

In the 1970s Bronx, the bboy identity was a response to the monotony of Disco music and dance, and was, as Tricia Rose explains in her seminal work on Hip Hop expression, *Black Noise*, a dance that "imitated the rupture in rhythmic continuity as it was highlighted in the musical break." And today, the bboy identity is an extension of that opposition, a new form of an old expression. The Eastside bboys adapt and borrow old elements of the original breakdancing forms and incorporate new elements into their individual and group styles. They use the inherent rebellious nature of the breakdancing identity to speak out against the expectations others have of them, to elicit recognition and respect, and to solidify their sense of self as individual dancers with a personal style and as members of a bboy community. I saw that the respect the boys gained through their talents and skills as bboys as being, to them, the most valuable praises they received.

Because this desire for recognition and the quest for attention from their peers are of such significance for the bboys, much of the bboy identity is centered on who each individual is on the dance floor. Gabe, one of the most naturally gifted dancers of the group, said:

> One of the things I like about breakdancing is to know that I am better than someone else. And if they do a move that's better than me, that just gets me hyped up. Makes me just wanna practice that move even more. I like to show off. I like when you know you got skill. Breakdancing is all about style, creativity, not just power.

Much of this creativity is expressed through an assembling of old and new breakdancing styles, of personal twists on shared forms, of innovative moves that define the essence of an individual's particular breakdancing flavor. Because the expression of "style," both individual and shared, is such an integral part of the bboy identity, it is important to explore what I recognize as the elements of the bboy dance style: borrowing, the fear of "biting," and "busting" new moves.

BORROWING AND THE FEAR OF BITING

In the early days of breakdancing, there was a "breaking down" of dance forms and a rupturing of hegemonic norms as the boys took to the streets and made public space their own. The boys broke apart elements of 1970s contemporary dance and then threw the pieces together to create a new articulation. In this way, breakdancing, as a form of public expression and opposition, borrows elements of a variety of oppositional dance forms, including early Black American dance.

Eric Lott, in his text, *Love and Theft*, mentions a testimony of the tradition of "break-down" (exhibited in Black dance of this particular era in American cultural history), in which a Black dancer displays his skill by breaking down a jig into an essence of rhythm and strength, balance and endurance. It is with this idea of "breaking down" a structural norm that I see a long historical tie between black and working class communities that is manifested in elements of dance, riot, and music.

One can follow this tie to the breakdancing phenonmenon, during the early years by way of the Black and Puerto Rican street kids, and now, in this resurgence among urban kids (specifically black and Mexican) in Texas. During its first wave of popularity, breakdancers centered their performances around the "freeze," a moment when the dancer stops all movement and creates a break in the rhythm of their dance. Rose calls this "freeze" a moment when the dancers execute moves that "imitated the rupture in rhythmic continuity." However, in its new phase, dancers are more focused on "flow" and "style" moves, when there is no break in the execution of the move or in the transition from one move to the next.

Through their moves, the Eastside bboys resist assimilation into the mainstream culture, and, even though they share a larger bboy style, are adamant about remaining unique and independent within the breakdancing circle—that fear of "biting." Latino and Black youth dance side by side, borrowing cultural elements from one another, sharing trends and styles: the Latino boys latch on to the "booty-dancing" style that is popular with the Black boys, and the Black boys have incorporated elements of Latin dance into their free-style sessions. Both groups incorporate elements of Afro-Brazilian martial arts. But they have not lost the elements of their own cultural backgrounds in the process of borrowing from one another, nor have they lost their desire to maintain what makes their moves *their own*. The boys rupture many of the racial expectations of the dominant class, which are rooted in separation and marginalization, and create a power and unity that pushes away tension and difference.

Because many of the Eastside bboys come from working class homes, they also contend with and respond to class dynamics and have ultimately found a way to gain recognition, to participate in a subcultural leisure activity that is generated through hard work, determination, struggle, trial and error, and small successes. Additionally, these working class boys have used the art of "collage" to create a style and expression of their own. Dick Hebdige, in his *Subculture: The Meaning of Style*, uses the anthropological term *bricolage* as a way of defining the borrowing and then transforming of styles into new meanings by working class youth in 1970s Great Britain. This same type of stylistic transformation is evident in the manifestations of the Eastside bboys' dances. While much of what the bboys learn about dancing comes from their peers and the bboy culture, they have also learned to borrow and incorporate bits and pieces of past dance forms, as Tricia Rose describes, such as the lindy-hop, the Charleston, the cakewalk, the jitterbug, double dutch, black fraternity and sorority stepping, Asian martial arts moves, and recent hip hop dance moves.

However, although breakdancing involves the incorporation of shared moves, popular dance forms, and historical dance expression, each bboy recognizes the fine line between borrowing and theft, and understands, precisely, where and how one must include his own ideas into his breakdancing. During one interview, Gabe offered an explanation of the dynamics of personal style and how each bboy must be careful not to "borrow" too much:

> Style is the way you throw your moves. Your own moves. The way you make your moves look. It's your own *unique* style you make up as you go. As you keep putting more effort into it, you find that you make up new moves. If you bite another person's style then people look at you as a biter. And that's no good. You don't want to be known as a biter. You want your own style.

WHERE THE INNOVATION IS BORN—BUSTING NEW MOVES

A Battle—Bboy City, 2000. In a gym on the Eastside, bboys from across the country—Texas, Georgia, Oklahoma, California,

Colorado—have gathered for an annual competition, a battle, in which bboys and bgirls compete against one another in front of excited fans, friends and family, crew members, and interested new-comers. It is the final night of a long weekend of competition, and Nando, Dario, and Wizard have all advanced to this final round. The lights are low and the music is loud, heavy, pulsing. There are small breakdancing circles in the corners of the gym as competitors practice and prepare with their crewmates and friends. In these smaller circles, the boys are safe, and they unwind and stretch, protected by the circle of familiarity and support. The competitors exchange bits of advice and observations about the other crews and individual dancers.

I stand on the perimeter of one small circle, watching a group from Houston. Several of the boys look across the gym, nervously, at the corner where the Eastside bboys are practicing. "They were tough, last year," one of the Houston boys mutters. "Yeah, that dude with the orange hair, he's wrong. That dude's just wrong," says another, eyeing Dario and shaking his head in disbelief. "He's got style." I, too, look at Dario and watch him move across the floor, his bright orange shirt and hair popping out from the darkness, his arms and legs and torso all lines and curves and spirals. The MC gives the five-minute warning. The final battle is about to begin.

In a battle of this size and importance, one can see the culmination of a year's worth of hard work. Throughout the weekend, I had watched Dario, Gabe, Nando, Rafael, Wizard, Mike and others, as they performed the moves they had been perfecting in preparation for facing last year's competition, bboys such as Night Hawk and Baby Boy,* as well as bboys they didn't know. They had all performed well. Gabe was recognized during the "freeze" competition and Raphael had finally landed the complicated series of power moves he had been practicing for months.

But it is this final round that matters most. Even the boys who have not advanced are anxious, hoping that their friends will represent the group well. The boys bump their fists together and then Gabe leans in to whisper to Nando, and then to Wizard, making them laugh, too, offering, some light-hearted words of encouragement.

The music starts again and the MC calls the first group to the center for the final competition. One boy uses humor as his weapon. He repeats some of the same moves the previous

---

*These are variations on the names of actual bboys.

Houston boy had executed, mocking him with exaggeration. He then embellishes each move, adding his personal style and creativity, expanding on what the Houston boy had expressed, "booty dancing" to excite the crowd. The Houston boy stands off to the side, nodding and smiling, clapping when his opponent has impressed him. The boys take turns and dance until they are exhausted. At the end of their battle, they fall into each other for a hug and then move off, outside of the circle, to join their friends.

At last, after both Nando and Wizard have competed and won cheers and shouts from the crowd, it is Dario's turn. He steps into the circle and his opponent, Bgroove, from Atlanta, sticks out his hand and they shake. The beats start, and Bgroove falls to the floor, catching himself in a push up, holding himself just a hair above the floor and begins to move. Dario is getting antsy. He claps and begins his footwork, stepping from side to side and moving into the music—a hint that he is ready to respond. Bgroove finishes his turn with a few more floor moves and then steps out of the circle, bowing to Dario with a wink. I feel a pat on my back and I turn to see Wizard, jumping up and down. "Eastside," he shouts. He looks at me, "Get ready, Yo, he's about to blow this place up!" And he is right. It is hard to make out the separate movements, he is breaking so quickly and so fluidly, but I can see that, at once, Dario is a martial artist, a bboy from the early days in the Bronx, a Hip Hop booty dancer, a lindy hopper, a competitor, an artist, a dancer, an athlete . . . but most of all, he is Dario. He is borrower and innovator. He is old school. He is fresh. He is an Eastside bboy.

Both Bgroove and Dario take several turns in the center and the crowd begs for more, knowing that what they are seeing will not last. Bgroove offers up a series of standard power moves, but lands them faster, more connectedly, than anyone I have seen. Dario answers back, with a series of his own, adding complicated freezes in between each move, his body shaking in each pose. The Eastside boys cheer. Dario exits and the MC announces the last round. Bgroove takes his turn, moving a little more slowly now, and ends with a flourish of creativity, free-styling for the audience, one last time. Dario looks exhausted. He squats down at the edge of the circle, catching his breath, and then looks our way and winks. He jumps to his feet and runs to the center, throwing his body into a barrel roll and landing in the splits. He swings one leg out and starts a series of windmills and then stops in a freeze. He ends with a bit of free-styling, doing his signature moves—dancing "goofy legged," as Gabe calls it— letting his legs bend and hinge like awkward folding chairs,

*wobbling around on the inner and outer edges of his feet. The
crowd cheers and he takes off a wristband and flings it towards
our group. Gabe catches it and yells out, "Eastside!"*

AMERICAN EXPRESSION?

American dance and competition have had a long relationship and
have often been expressed, together, as a form of rebellion. In his
piece, "The Death of James Johnson," Shane White describes the
dance competitions between members of the first generation of free
blacks in New York City. As White describes it, "dancers brought
their own shingles—wide springy boards of about six feet in
length—and on these confined spaces engaged in spectacular break-
down contests, to the beat of other blacks patting juba. The dancers
who best pleased their racially-mixed audience were rewarded with
money, fish, and eels." In much the same way, the early breakdancers in the Bronx brought cardboard squares and spread them
out on the sidewalks and streets of New York, and danced, on these
small stages, for onlookers and in competition with their peers.

Nelson George, Black music critic and Hip Hop writer, has said
that it was the Latinos who made breakdancing competitive and
notes that in the early battles it "was a highly stylized from of combat that echoed the kung fu moves of Bruce Lee and the rituals of
martial arts." But what I have seen in this new wave of breakdancing, especially through my interactions with the Eastside bboys, is a
breakdancing community that is supportive and progressive. The
battles, while competitive and tense at times, are also filled with humor, elegant creativity, precision, and respect. The bboys are less
combative, less concerned with turf wars and street pride (although
there is an evident identification with where one is from and who one
represents, in terms of neighborhood and crew), and are more interested in the movements and the dancing itself, more focused on the
creativity that is born through the battle. While there is still the
boasting that has been a part of the bboy identity since the early days,
and is interwoven into much of the Hip Hop expression, it is now less
of an expression of self that is gained through the belittling of others,
and is more of an affirmation of self, gained through creativity and
innovation, brought out from the margins of society, into the open.

It is in Texas where we can see the results of what Jose Limon,
anthroplogist and ethnographer, calls the "scene of Greater Mexican and African-American . . . speech and body play." Limon writes
of the ways in which these two sectors in Texas, "mount their
own alternative or counter-discourse against . . . forces of cultural

hegemony of the dominant groups." This counter-discourse is evident within the breakdancing community, specifically on the Eastside, where urban Black and Latino youth have come together to form a subculture based on speaking out against traditional dance modes and styles, and where theirs is a discourse that is rooted in sharing and personal growth and invention. The Eastside bboys learn from one another, practicing and building strength together, participating in an exchange of ideas that leads to an internal, personal discovery of new moves and combinations.

Is this tradition of making a public space a personal stage of expression a uniquely American one? There is the actual circle to consider—the circle, as a safe place for bodily expression. It is within the circle, both in practice and during competitions, that the boys are able to at once, identify with the bboy culture and express themselves as individuals with definitive styles. It seems to me that the traits of this circle— borrowing, the fear of biting, and busting new moves—are the traits of a uniquely American expression.

Notebook

1. Sasha Vliet talks a bit about how the bboys redefine public space, much in the way that the skateboarders did in the essay about Dogtown. What do you see as the similarities and differences between these two athletic subcultures? What other subcultures redefine public space? Both skaters and breakdancers also redefined specific activities—surfing and dancing—to fit their own needs and styles. What other elements of the culture can be redefined by subcultures?

2. This essay begins with an anecdote, and has other descriptive, observation-based passages throughout. How do these sections help support her argument? Did you find yourself avoiding or looking forward to these sections? How did they compare for you, as a reader, to the more research-based sections? Practice writing your own small stories for use within your research, focusing on vivid, descriptive imagery and plenty of action.

3. As a class, come up with a project to redefine a public space, either on campus on in the larger community. While some people participate in an event or acticvity that uses the space in a way it has never been used before, give others the role of observing what happens—how the redefinition seems to make onlookers feel.

4. Research the history of breakdancing. Vliet suggests that it has its roots and origins in a variety of other American dance cultures—what more can you discover about these earlier dances? When was the heyday of breakdancing, and why? How is breakdancing resurfacing in the culture today? You may want to start with the book *Yes Yes Y'All: The Experience Music Project Oral History of Hip-Hop's First Decade* (Da Capo Press, 2002).

The Homeless Community of the Piers

ROB MAITRA

As in many of the essays in the next chapter, Rob Maitra uses his essay as a means to push beyond stereotypes. By spending time with homeless queer teenagers who hang out in a certain section of New York City and observing them, he understands how these teens forge a community that models itself on a family structure that offers more acceptance than they are able to find in their actual families. Maitra is a doctoral student in Cultural Studies and Education at Columbia University, and lives in New York City.

———————— ✦ ————————

Their lives have been depicted in books such as John Rechy's *City of Night* (1963) and Iceberg Slim's *Black Widow Mama* (1996) and in movies like *Johns* (1996) and *Paris Is Burning* (1990), but how accurate is this depiction of the homeless queer teenagers living on the fringes of America's gay ghettos? Are their lives defined solely by drugs and prostitution? Are they mostly runaways who wind up in big cities living on the street, or do they sometimes create new communities that have meaningful styles and practices?

During the final weeks of the summer and early fall of 2001, I interviewed and led focus groups with many homeless GLBT young people in New York City. During this time, I encountered over 25 youths who spent time on the piers and observed many more while walking through their turf. I had opportunities to watch and participate in their daily lives as they roamed the streets of the West Village, stood and waited for "johns" (those soliciting prostitutes), relaxed and slept in the park, played video games and pool at a local porn shop, and socialized along the highway and piers. The conversations I had with these youths focused on their backgrounds and their lives before the piers, in particular their family lives and education, sexuality, ethnicity, and their journey to the pier community.

GETTING THERE

Along the West Side Highway and in the adjoining park, set between the West Village and the Hudson River, hundreds of young homosexuals, bisexuals, and transvestites, predominately black and Latino, congregate daily. The area is known as "the piers," but the actual piers are almost nonexistent now, as new construction and more restrictive policies by the Guiliani administration over the last few years have limited waterfront accessibility to a space no longer than a city block. This process has increased many of the youths' feelings of being discarded and unwelcome by the larger community. As the space along the piers has shrunk, the members have moved further into the Village, mainly along Christopher Street from the highway to Sixth Avenue. But the piers remain the geographic heart of their subculture.

During the day, youths ranging in age from their early teens to early twenties roam the streets, sleep, dance, talk, flirt, argue, sing, and help each other survive in a sometimes harsh and hazardous world. Together they have created a community not unlike many other subcultures that exist on the social fringes of major cities across the U.S. No one knows for sure the population of the pier community, but on busier days upwards of 150 members of the community can be found in the area. Estimates of the total population by its members range from a few hundred to over a thousand. The community is comprised primarily of gay and bisexual males, but there are also smaller groups of lesbians and bisexual women, as well as transsexuals.

These GLBT adolescents escape their homes and participate in the pier community, which satisfies some of the financial, aesthetic, recreational, and social-emotional needs and desires not fulfilled by their former homes or communities. While many of these youths are homeless and sleep "on the streets"—which includes parks, subways, and rooftops—others are "commuters" who flee to this world on a daily basis, only to return at night to their homes in the outer boroughs of New York City or in New Jersey. Some of them, especially those more veteran, have managed to secure apartments of their own but choose to remain active participants in the homeless community. Numerous familial, economic, geographic, and social factors determine a youth's ability to commute or the decision to run away completely to join this world.

Most of the youths I encountered suggested that a friend had introduced them to the scene in the West Village. Before being introduced to the subculture, the person realized that he or she was queer, but typically had trouble finding outlets for these feelings and desires, and risked verbal and physical abuse if they tried acting on them. Being teased and harassed by classmates made the completion of school difficult. Being gay, they felt they could not turn to parents, teachers, or administrators for support. Facing intolerance at home and in school, such a teenager was open to someone similar who could introduce him to an alternative community such as that of the piers. After experiencing the freedom and security of the subculture's environment, many leave their homes and schools permanently. Some, however, while spending a lot of time in the pier community, never completely sever all ties with their homes. I spoke with a number of people who are still active students, and many of them reported that their schools had support structures in place for GLBT students, whether an organized group or just a sympathetic teacher. What's more, these students intended to remain in school until graduation from high school. Conversely, permanent denizens of the pier community reported that they had lacked all support in school. "Most of these [younger] kids would go back home, back to school if they could," suggested one young man, somewhat older (22) and a high school graduate, explaining that they stay because they cannot face the mistreatment they would receive back home.

Upon arriving at the piers one quickly discoverers that one is not alone, that there are others with similar feelings, experiences, and desires. As Richard Troiden observed in his 1988 book, *Gay and Lesbian Identity: A Sociological Analysis*, interaction in a gay subculture contributes to the process of gay identity assumption. New arrivals are able to see "similarities between themselves and those 'labeled' homosexual," and learn to align themselves with the characteristics of the group. The community provides a safe space for behavior, both sexual and nonsexual, that would be deemed inappropriate and intolerable at home or in school. Above all, it creates opportunities for these youths to talk about their sexuality. For many, their first visit to the community represented their first encounter with other self-identified homosexuals their own age— and the first time they could openly pursue someone sexually and engage in sexual activities. Thus begins a process that Troiden calls "sexual socialization," which heterosexuals carry out openly in school but which gay youths must conduct in their own spaces.

When asked about the role of sexuality in the community, everyone I interviewed stressed its importance as the glue that binds the community together. "We are all here because we are gay. That is what this is all about," one late-teen transvestite explained. According to another youth, "We are here because he loves men, she loves women. We believe it's right, so we will flock together. We feel comfort here."

In addition, the community provides opportunities to participate in activities often associated with GLBT culture, such as those involving music, fashion, and dancing. Music and the culture that surrounds it are a central feature of the scene. Throughout the day and evening, music blasts from boom boxes; people dance, vogue, or "runway model," and sing or lip-sync the lyrics. Beats, house, R&B, and hip-hop are the dominant styles. Dancing or "walking," while not for everyone, is a central activity of the community, taking place in numerous small pockets in the park and along the walkway that runs parallel to the Hudson River.

HOUSES AND BALLS

The high point of dancing/walking is the occurrence of the "balls," made famous by Jennie Livingston's movie, *Paris Is Burning*. At the balls numerous "houses"—well-organized groups of youths run by "house mothers" and "house fathers" (usually older and more experienced members of the subculture)—compete against each other in various categories of walking or voguing. Various balls occur throughout the year and involve numerous dance- and fashion-oriented competitions between the houses. The largest event of the year, the Latex Ball, is organized by the Gay Men's Health Crisis and staged at the Roseland Ballroom in Midtown. Popular culture provides the raw material and the inspiration for creative productions involving elaborate dances and fashions. These productions are aspects of a distinctive style that challenges traditional gender roles as well as sexual orientations, and are not merely recreational but symbolically political in their defiance of conventional norms.

Houses are more than associations for staging the balls, as they also have important social and emotional functions for the adolescents. While some of the house members compared them to college fraternities, others compared them to families. Most of these youths have had largely negative experiences with their families at home. Houses in the pier community are not physical structures but rather organizations that substitute for many youths' lack of familial support. The members of houses hold meetings at the piers, in restaurants, in parks, or in someone's apartment. A house mother talks to his or her wards concerning issues that parents talk about—or don't talk about—such as sex, drugs, and the future. "I look out for the kids in my house," one mother claimed, "and help them out when they need it." House mothers and house fathers fulfill many of the needs that traditional parents fulfill. The houses also have negative aspects. The competition between the houses can become fierce at the balls, and this at times prompts its members to steal clothes and prostitute for money for more clothes. There are also those who choose not to be involved with a house, but instead remain independent members of the community.

Although there are some elements of hierarchy in the pier community, all the members I spoke with said they felt welcome and accepted. Different categories of members are recognized, such as "butch queens" and "femme queens," but there's little evidence of discrimination between these groups. One butch queen suggested that he didn't find the more feminine males, whom he also referred to as "faggots," particularly appealing, but he still considered them friends, adding that "we're all in this together." The bonds they created to survive and struggle against the outside culture appeared to be stronger than any differences within the community.

Leadership in the community is conferred upon those who are able to help others. One young man who goes by the name Satan was regarded as a "brother" by many members of the community. In an interview Satan stated: "I talk to the younger kids, and give them money if they need it, even if I don't like them." He has been a part of the community for about five years and now has an apartment of his own. He's viewed as a sort of sage, someone people turn to when they have a problem; and he seems to take pleasure in this role. In general, the more experienced members of the group look out for the younger ones, and sometimes intervene if the latter behave in inappropriate ways. While many older members begin searching for more independence, the younger ones tend to bond very closely, spending more time in the park and more sheltered areas. (Satan's role as an informant was invaluable to the completion of this research.)

RELATIONS WITH PARENTS

While the community helps to fill the void left by the loss of home, the majority of these youths still struggle mightily with parental issues. For those still in contact with their parents, including those living at home, these relationships are often a source of tension. Relationships with one's family—which usually mean only one's mother—can be classified into four categories: functional, deceptive, strained, and separated.

In a functional relationship, the youth is out to his or her parents, who in turn are comfortable with the youth's sexuality. These youths often live at home or in apartments of their own, and they are less likely than others to be involved in drugs or prostitution.

There are also those who are out to their families, but their relationships with them are very strained. Although the parents allow their children to live at home, they often discriminate against them, abuse them physically, sexually, and/or verbally, and in general make them feel unwelcome. This experience is what drives these young people to run away from home, at which point they typically turn to both prostitution and drugs.

The third category involves youths who maintain a relationship with their parents, but a deceptive one, in which information about their lifestyle is withheld. These youths, who fear being thrown out or abused if the truth were to be revealed, may actively deceive their parents about their activities and identities. These relationships also tend to be very strained. Consequently, such youths often spend a great deal of time on the piers looking for friendship, support, and love. Typically they wish they could tell their parents the truth about their sexuality but fear the result would be a complete withdrawal of parental support. All the people I interviewed thought the deceptive relationship was the smartest option unless you were sure your parents would continue to support you after coming out. One homeless youth explained, "I'm living proof. There is nothing here for you. Stay at home and wait till you can live on your own. Then tell them." The dangers of the street, this hustler suggested, outweigh the problems of living at home. On the other hand, upon learning that there's an alternative to staying at home, many youths decide to abandon the closet and come out to their parents, even if this exposes them to the hazards of street life.

The final category of familial relationship involves those who are separated from their families. A large percentage of these youths are homeless, though some find temporary housing by staying with friends. Separation from the family typically occurs in one of two ways: either the youth is thrown out when his parents learn about his sexuality or he runs away to escape the intolerable conditions of home. The homeless youths face the harshest conditions. One youth described his adolescence in this way: "I never had my teenage years. I've been through hell and back and I'm still here. I'm still there." Lacking financial support from one's family, a homeless youth often turns to prostitution or dealing drugs to survive.

PROSTITUTION, DRUGS, AND LEAVING THE LIFE

Prostitution plays a significant role in the lives of these young people, and constitutes their primary connection to the outside world.

Most of those in the pier community remain in the West Village, which is seen as a safe working environment, and avoid venturing out to other neighborhoods, even when business is slow, for fear of being injured or killed. "People take care of each other around here," one youth explained, and there's at least some safety in numbers. Every afternoon and night, johns cruise up and down the streets of the neighborhood, and hustlers make it known that they're available by waving or looking into cars. Other connections are made at the local bars, but that territory is off limits to most members of the community due to their age and lack of proper identification. Hustling in the clubs is viewed as "a step up [from the streets]—up to a buck-fifty [$150] an hour," as a nineteen-year-old street hustler explained. Many of the street prostitutes expect to graduate eventually to the clubs, once they can get ID indicating that they're 21.

The youths began hustling as a way to earn easy money, and many reported that they were "curious" about the sexual experiences. However, as one reported, "after [the curiosity] goes away, it's just the money." All have learned the negative aspects of prostitution, but have found it hard to get away from it. One hustler told me that he had no unpaid sex life at all, believing that "no one would ever want to go out with a prostitute." While turning tricks, he just "want[s] it to be over." Like many of his peers, he felt trapped by his life of prostitution. When asked, the hustlers I interviewed usually could not think of anything else they could do to survive.

A large percentage of those in the pier community use drugs on a regular basis, while virtually all have used drugs at one time or another. Many said that they only became involved with drugs upon coming to the Village. There appears to be a correlation between heavy drug use and prostitution. One eighteen-year-old hustler explained: "I first started smoking [marijuana] after tricks. I wanted to forget what I did. The amount I smoke usually depends on how bad it was. If it was really bad, I will, like, buy a twenty-dollar bag and smoke it all to myself." Prostitutes use drugs to escape the negative aspects of the trade. They ease the grief and self-loathing generated by their hustling.

At a center of gay life in America, just blocks from the Stonewall Inn, most of these youths feel excluded from the mainstream gay society that thrives in the West Village. While this society largely tolerates the youth subculture living in their neighborhood, it provides little assistance or support. Sometimes people call the police on the youths to complain of noise or large crowds. The youths are well aware that the older gay population is uneasy about their subculture, chalking it up to a fear of robbery or violence. But they also detect that this fear is due in part to their race. They believe that any support they do receive comes with a quid pro quo. "The only time they do something nice to you is when they want something," one nineteen-year-old stated. "And they always want the same thing." He said he had often been offered "help" by middle-aged, seemingly well-off West Village gays, but understood this to mean that they would be his "sugar daddy" in exchange for sex. But he always rejected these offers, preferring the freedom of the streets to the security of being a "kept boy."

Most members would leave the pier community if they had the means. The biggest challenge to getting off the street is obtaining legal identification, which is necessary for finding employment. This is hard to obtain without the support of one's parents. Once that hurdle is crossed, many of the more "straight-acting" youths do find jobs, but the transvestites or exceptionally feminine-acting males still have great difficulty.

No one could say for sure what had become of the people who had left the subculture in recent years. Typically someone would just drift away and eventually stop showing up. Maybe he or she found a job, got an apartment, or started hanging out at the clubs. While many members of the West Side Highway community expected to move on, they did not want to abandon the community, and hoped to help the young people who continued to arrive in the community. Unfortunately, financial challenges will probably prevent them from looking back once they've left this world.

While the community provides a much-needed haven for the youths who end up there, it also exposes these young people to the considerable dangers of street life. Social policy should aim at reducing the need for this community by asking how schools, local governments, and families can create a situation in which the needs that are satisfied by this youthful subculture can be met without the attending dangers and risks.

Notebook

1. Being gay does not automatically make someone a part of a subculture, since many different kinds of people with all sorts of interests and values are gay: there are lesbian Republicans, gay baseball fans, transgendered punks, bisexual knitters, and so on. In other words, while being something other than heterosexual does not mean you are part of a subculture, there are certainly subcultures within the gay, lesbian, bisexual, transgendered, and queer communities. Investigate some youth-based GLBTQ subcultures and interview the members to see how they feel about the way they do—or do not—fit into the larger queer community.

2. What, if anything, did you assume about homeless gay teenagers before you read this article? Did this essay make you think differently? Which parts of this essay were surprising to you? Which parts reified—reinforced—what you already believed?

3. As a class, watch the documentary film *Paris Is Burning* (directed by Jennie Livingston) discussed in this essay. What do the subculture participants seem to gain out of belonging to the subculture? What might they lose by participating, if anything?

Thoughts on the Movie *Afro-Punk*
MIMI NGUYEN

Mimi Thi Nguyen maintains a pop-culture punk website called Worse Than Queer and was a columnist for Punk Planet *magazine; this essay, a review of a documentary film on African Americans in the punk scene, was published in both.* Nguyen is an assistant professor of Gender and Women's Studies and Asian American studies at the University of Illinois, Urbana-Champaign and earned her doctorate in Ethnic Studies at the University of California, Berkeley, with a Designated Emphasis on Women, Gender, and Sexuality. She is co-editor with Thuy Linh Tu of Alien Encounters: Pop Culture in Asian America *(forthcoming) and author of multiple essays on Asian American, queer, and punk subcultures; digital technologies, and Vietnamese diasporic culture, published in both academic collections and popular magazines.*

———————— ✦ ————————

October 5, 2003, 10:44 p.m.

In a series of blurred, multiple-exposure photographs, New York City filmmaker James Spooner (with photographer Pauline St. Denis and stylist Christine Baker) recreates iconoclastic punk rock images but replaces their white subjects with black punk rockers from his documentary film *Afro-Punk: The "Rock and Roll Nigger" Experience.* The resulting photographs are not faithful reproductions, and the substitution of black bodies is not a mere corrective or additive. Instead, the fascination lies elsewhere, in the haunting dissonance of seeing these familiar images made unfamiliar. Does the image of a black man, rather than the Clash's Joe Strummer, caught in the act of smashing his guitar, forcefully change the meaning of his rage? If it is a black woman and not a youthful Ian McKaye who holds his head in weariness? Does the hooded figure in the white face paint evoke the skeletal logo of the Misfits, but also black filmmakers the

Hughes brothers' *Dead Presidents*? And the bare-chested black woman, slouching in a white tuxedo jacket, open beer bottle in one hand? Yeah, she belongs to a different world.

The photographs are all cases of mistaken identity. Threatening to unravel the abstractions of punk rock, these photographs call into question the socially coded nature of punk rock's histories, identities, icons, values, and meanings. Sid Vicious' sickly pallor and his appetite for self-destruction written in the track marks and the razor cuts criss-crossing his wasted body, are part of what cemented this image in punk's historical archive. But what often passes in punk (and other avant-gardes, other modernisms) for a romance with danger when a British white boy plays the addict is not available to the black woman in America. The staged photograph of a black female "as" Sid Vicious then is part of a strategy that reveals visual images—like this and the other iconoclastic punk images—to be part of a complex of representations that produce "punk rock" as a contingent identity. That is, these photographs offer a privileged opportunity to examine the subterranean politics of the "original," including the historical racial hegemony of punk rock.

Afro-Punk is James Spooner's 70-minute documentary about blackness and punk rock and, like the photographs he staged for a magazine spread, the film approaches the troubled relationship of race and punk rock with a critical eye for its possibilities and its problematics. Scores of interviews with black punks, filmed over the course of several cross-country road trips, are intercut with photographs and footage of live performances and set to a soundtrack of punk rock. Beginning with a series of origin stories, the kids in the picture (ranging in actual age from teenage to mid-life) tell remarkably similar narratives about their initial forays into punk rock. Many were the only black children growing up in white neighborhoods, and punk—with its contrary aesthetic and attitude—seemed to fit their psychological and corporeal alienation. It answered a need for expression and individuality, for a political framework and social community, and we hear, at least once, "[Punk] saved my life."

But these stories become more complicated and convoluted in the clash of contradictions and underlying tensions involved in turning to a subculture marked by white (boy) hegemony for "community" and other relationships. The feeling of having to prove oneself worthy, to be more punk than the white kids, is echoed here as Spooner's interviewees count on one hand the number of black punks in their local scenes (sometimes all that is required is a thumb). What emerges is a sometimes contradictory, but always complicated, patchwork of emotions—self-loathing, sadness, frustration, anger, resentment, loneliness and conviction. A poignant sequence relating a familiar dilemma for black punk rockers—what to do with hair that does not spike naturally—leaves a deep impression and a series of difficult questions about the racial politics of punk rock aesthetics.

Culled from his interviews, Spooner chose four individuals (all of whom are involved in either performing or promoting) to provide focus in some of the more personal segments and highlight the differences in their responses: Brooklyn's fierce Tamar Kali, easygoing Matt Davis from Iowa City, Long Island's dedicated black revolutionary Moe Mitchell, and quiet Southern Californian Mariko Jones. They represent a range of reactions and approaches to the question of integrating—or not—racial identity with their chosen subcultural affiliation.

Biracial Mariko Jones insists she is glad her friends tell her, "You don't act like a black person, you don't act like an Asian person. You're just Mariko." Because no one has ever called her "nigger" or barred her from a show, she doesn't seem to believe that race or racism has an impact on her interactions in punk, and says, a bit reproachfully, "I feel like the ones complaining are the ones who aren't doing anything." But her sentiments are contradicted in a series of cuts to interviews that powerfully (in both quality and quantity) argue otherwise. A young woman outside a club notes, "A lot of white people put black people in categories, like the safe black person." Laughing, she continues, "A lot of people mistake me for that safe black person." As one subject notes, while punk rock answered for a part of his alienation, it highlighted another aspect—being black in a white-dominated scene. The interviewees testify to the range of racisms reinforcing punk rock silence about race. Many mentioned former friends who believed that every other black person except him or her qualified as a "nigger." With palpable disgust, another targets the color-blindness of righteous punk rockers, "anarchists [who tell me] their politics transcend race and gender." And Chicagoan Rachel sums up this frustration with punk rock's racial politics: "People are not trying to have a dialogue with you, but they do want to tokenize you. People want a multicultural vision of punk rock, and they want to showcase you, 'Look at all the Negros!' But at the same time they don't want to deal with you as a person who experiences race."

In perhaps the film's most pointed scene, Mitchell's band Cipher performs punk rock black power for a cramped room full of white boys. Members of the audience wind-mill, floor-punch, and grab the microphone away from Mitchell to scream incoherently. Spooner draws out the footage of this performance to underscore a swelling sense of discomfort and the hardcore dissonance embedded in its multiple contradictions—Mitchell's lyrics about the historical rape, pillage and enslavement of African peoples by Europeans and Americans, drowned out by the shouts of slamming white punk rockers. (This was the most painful scene for me for other reasons too. Watching these boys "dance" was like watching a primitive tooth extraction or root canal. Give me head-nodding over this machismo.) Interviewed outside the club, a series of white boys admit they don't know what the lyrics were about—slavery, maybe? One offers the vague answer, "I guess they're about their beliefs," but pronounces "their" as if referring to an alien race of beings.

But the film is not only critical of white punks' negligence or unacknowledged privilege. Accused of "trying to be white," the interviewees maintain that much of the animosity and alienation—made worse because of a higher degree of investment both emotional and historical—has come from their families and black peers. There are plenty of stories here about being stuffed into garbage cans, being jumped for wearing punk gear, being spat upon and generally despised by other black kids in high school. And in another of the more powerful sequences here, the interviewees discuss their complicated responses to seeing other black punks at shows or on the streets. Laughing, some of them report feelings that the other black person is "trespassing" on their territory: "I'm supposed to be the only black person here!" Others debate the desire to speak to every other black person at a show *because* of the isolation. And one woman, sitting outside a club in a puff-sleeved shirt, gestures ruefully as she explains her dilemma—excitement at seeing another black person or person of color in the same venue, and a weird shame for being "discovered" in a scene that excitement at such a surprising appearance would be possible. But it is the film's willingness to embrace such contradictions and complexity in mapping the trials and tribulations of being black and being punk (along with the pleasures and the joys) that leaves an imprint, long after the credits have rolled.

Two years in the making, Spooner is clear about his priorities—first and foremost, this is a film about black subculture for black people. Having once sported a mohawk himself, he says, "I wanted to make the movie that I wished I had as a kid." (At the bottom of his list of priorities, is reiterating to white punk rock audiences the critical nature of race and racism in everyday life, and the privileges they maintain even as punks.) The film has garnered some mainstream black press and so far the warm reception has been rewarding. For Spooner, this success confirms the importance of this attempt to make black punk rockers intelligible to black audiences who, as the interviewees relate, might have once scorned these outsiders as "white wannabes," "devil worshippers," or "fags." "The thing that keeps me going," he relates, "is what happens when I go out to promote the film. I always have flyers with me for the film and when I see black kids into something weird, I'll go up to them and talk to them about the documentary. And they get all shy, especially when they're with white people. It's like they think, 'Why are you calling me out? It's taken this long for them to forget that I'm black!' And I think I know what that feels like, so maybe they'll recognize and see themselves in the other people in the film." And as Spooner and most of his black subjects note, rock 'n' roll was an invention of African Americans. Mounting a fierce attack on the belief that rock is a "white thing," the subjects cite a long, semi-buried history of black innovation in guitar-based music being reconstructed by Detroit's Mick Collins (The Gories, The Dirtbombs) and Lisa Kekaula (The Bellrays) and more mainstream black artists like Mos Def and Wyclef Jean. As one interviewee suggests, "Check out Jimi."

Spooner offers no set resolution or fixed relation of race to punk rock, but does suggest that in the final tally, blackness is nonetheless policed in ways that a mohawk is not. An interviewee tells a story familiar to black men in America—being pulled over by police officers while out for a walk. "There's no question, I don't have to say, 'Am I a part of the black community?' I walk out and I figured out all black people are part of the black community. You don't have to do anything, you're black. That was comforting." The film fades to black to the sounds of his wry laughter.

Afro-Punk: The "Rock and Roll Nigger" Experience is screened at independent film festivals and other venues across the North American continent. For more information about filmmaker James Spooner, the film itself, and its upcoming screening schedule, please check: http://www.afropunk.com. There is also a community messageboard at the website for further discussion and dialogue about the issues raised in the film. Unfortunately, Matt Davis, who appears as one of the four main interviewees in the film, died on August 10, 2003. There is an on-line memorial for him at: http://www.tengrand.com. James can be reached at james@afropunk.com, and would love to bring the documentary to a screening near you. He is not as lazy as I am, because I will not be going on tour with the compilation zine *Race Riot* any time soon. Still, you can get a copy of the zine from Pander Zine Distro (http://www.panderzinedistro) and it will come to you. For other resources, check out the article on the history of black punks (1976–1983) in *Roctober* 32, written by James Porter and Jake Austen.

Notebook

1. The failure of the punk culture to adequately address racism, as depicted in this essay on the film *Afro-Punk*, has parallels in other subcultures, like women in skateboarding, for example. Think about which power structures are subverted by the subculture you're studying—and which seem to be upheld, accepted or ignored.

2. As Nguyen and the documentary film she reviews describe, punk is mostly a white subculture. Are there other subcultures primarily made up of one racial group? Could you write about the racial minorities who nonetheless join these subcultures, and what that experience is like for them? What do they gain, and what do they lose? What about subcultures that are made up of people of only one gender, or class, or geographic location? If a subculture is segregated, is it subverting the dominant ideology of our nation?

3. Have you ever been to a punk show? See if there is one coming up that you can attend, and while there, observe and take notes on who seems to make up the audience. Does the subculture in attendance break down into even smaller sub-subcultures?

Where We Belong: a Report on Anime Central 2004

HEIDI SCHUBERT

One rather well-known type of subculture is fandom—fans of a particular sport, musical group, or, in this case, television phenomenon. In this first-person account, Heidi Schubert describes the relief and thrill of being around other anime fans at an annual convention. Heidi Schubert is a student at Columbia College, Chicago. For the past nine years she has been involved in the anime and comic book subcultures, and founded and maintains a fan club for her favorite voice actor, Rachael Lillis. In the mid 1990s she was part of the riot grrl subculture and published in friends' zines. Ms. Schubert is interested in music, Jane Austen's books, the Beat Generation, Harry Potter, *and* Lord of the Rings.

———————— ✦ ————————

S ince the 1960s, children's animation created in Japan has been dubbed into English and shown on television in America, starting with shows such as "Astro Boy" and "Speed Racer," and more recently "Sailor Moon" and "Pokemon." Most Americans who have become anime fans started out watching one of these programs as a kid, only to find out later on that this show is part of something called "anime," Japanese animation in a wide variety of typical cinema genres. Some of these fans then try to find more shows like the one they saw on television. This was the case for me: when it appeared on American television in 1996, I became a huge fan of the anime "Sailor Moon," a show about a clumsy junior high student who finds out via a talking cat that in her past life she was the princess of the moon, and now she and her friends must protect the Earth. I discovered more anime series online and in comic book stores and my collection steadily grew.

The first few years as an anime fan were somewhat lonely: none of my friends were into it, so I could only discus anime with my mom and brother (who were also fans). I felt like there was a big part of myself that I couldn't share with my friends—it wouldn't make any sense to them. So in 2000 when I found out about a yearly anime convention held in my area called "Anime Central," I was thrilled. Finally, an opportunity to meet and make friends with other fans!

Fan conventions got their start in America back in the late 1960s when a group of *Star Trek* fans gathered together and brought in a couple of the actors from the show to sign autographs. Now there seems to be a fan convention for just about every fan group imaginable, ranging from TV shows and comic books to classical literature and sports teams. Although I had never been to an anime convention before, I had been attending comic book conventions for the previous six years, and so I expected Anime Central to include some similar features: a dealer's room, where you can spend hours buying merchandise that fits the convention theme; panels, where people who work in the business answer questions from the audience about upcoming projects; and workshops where the professionals in the field teach attendees some of the tricks of their trade.

The only thing was that I have a fear of crowds and was worried that if the convention was too packed, I'd have to come right back home. It *was* crowded, but the remarkable thing was that I didn't feel worried at all; in fact I felt safer than I did anywhere outside of my home. I think that it is because when I'm at Anime Central, even though most of the people are strangers, I feel connected to them.

Part of this feeling stems from the fact that many attendees of Anime Central come dressed as characters from anime, manga, or Japanese video games. I've noticed that people often view the people in costume (called "cosplayers") as if they *were* the character that they are dressed as. This can lead people to avoid those dressed as menacing villains (or simply characters that aren't liked), but it can also serve as a great incentive to make friends with someone dressed as a character you do like. This is actually how I met my friend Kelly at Anime Central 2001. I attended a panel run by and for fans of the anime series "Slayers," and Kelly was one of the fans moderating it. Kelly was dressed as a character from this series named Amelia. Earlier that afternoon I had bought a pin which I thought was in the shape of Amelia, though my brother thought that it was in the shape of another character. I decided that Kelly, dressed as Amelia, would probably know best, so after the panel I asked her. She agreed with me that it was Amelia, and we chatted a little more. Though we live several states apart, we've kept in touch through emails and chatting online. Through Kelly I've made more friends whom I chat with online frequently and reunite with every year at Anime Central.

The ritual of going to Anime Central begins (for me) several days beforehand when I make sure that I have the cell phone numbers of the friends I'll be meeting up with there. I also have to pack my trusty pink "Hello Kitty" backpack to use as my purse for the convention, though not too full since I'll be stuffing it with merchandise from the dealer's room, and I don't want to lug around a heavy backpack all day. I also set aside time to review the list of programs scheduled for the weekend so I can decide when I want to get there and when to tell my dad to come pick me up.

This year my Anime Central adventure began much as it has in the past: Dad dropped me off at about 11AM on Friday morning, and I made my way to the line for people who preregistered for passes. There was another convention going on in the same building as Anime Central, for Midwestern makers of eyeglasses. During my stay in the preregistration line, a confused elderly woman approached a guy in front of me and asked him what our convention was about. He tried very politely to explain it was for fans of Japanese animation, or anime, but the woman didn't really seem to grasp it.

While shopping in the dealer's room, where stores from across the country have small booths of anime and manga merchandise ranging from DVDs and comic books to replications of jewelry worn by the characters, posters, CDs, and stuffed toys, I ran into Aaron, from a class I had last semester on J. R. R. Tolkien. Something that always amazes me at Anime Central is the wide variety of people there—all different shapes and sizes, races, ages, abilities—and how none of this seems to matter. I have never heard or made a comment on somebody's appearance at Anime Central, other than commenting on costumes. Perhaps this lack of judgmental comments has something to do with a lot of anime fans feeling like they don't fit in "normal" culture and thus being sensitive to what being teased feels like, and not wanting to inflict it on others. Whatever the reason may be, I think it is a wonderful thing to be in a place where everyone is accepted just the way they are. At least half the people at Anime Central come dressed in costume, and in this way it can sometimes feel like being at Disney World. The excitement a child in Disney World feels seeing Cinderella is comparable to how I've felt when I spot someone dressed as a favorite character of mine. If you come to Anime Central in costume, be prepared to be bombarded with people wanting to take your photograph. Though I've never cosplayed before, my friends always do, and it can feel odd to see people asking to take your friends' photographs frequently. In a way, I guess this might be what it is like to be friends with a celebrity. Strangers run up to hug them, or chase them through a room.

Every year I wind up asking a lot of costumed people for photographs, though this year I was a bit apprehensive to mention this project because I didn't want people to think that I was there only as a reporter and not as a fan. I was worried that the people I approached would think that I didn't know anything about anime, that I wasn't part of this subculture. I had a hunch that they wouldn't be very cooperative with me if it wasn't clear that I was a fan first.

Luckily, the people I did approach responded positively and were interested in the book itself. They seemed excited that someone would be publishing an account of our subculture and that a member of the anime subculture would be the one writing it.

Later that afternoon I watched the last half of an anime version of the classic television game show "Press Your Luck." Three contestants were quizzed on anime trivia and at the end, of course, the winner was given anime DVDs as prizes. Other game shows given an anime spin that were featured were "The Price is Right" and "Win, Lose, or Draw." After Anime "Press Your Luck" ended, I joined Kelly, Jennie, and some of their other friends in line for a panel presented by a company called FUNimation who distribute and dub into English a variety of anime titles on DVD and video.

Each year when I reunite with Kelly and Jennie, we just pick up where we left off. When we're together we mainly talk about anime, discussing certain series we like, or don't like, and suggesting new shows to each other. We also talk about stories we've read or written ourselves about characters in anime (fan fiction), or artwork we've seen or drawn of anime characters (fan art). But we do talk about things involving school or work as well.

Anyway, at the panel, a representative of FUNimation told us about their upcoming anime DVD and video releases, and gave us sneak previews of anime titles for which they had just gotten the rights. The representative also urged us to let the company know if there are any anime titles which haven't been brought to America that we'd like to see, if we like or dislike any of the anime they've dubbed, or any other comments and suggestions we have for them. I thought that this was really thoughtful (and smart) of the company to be so interested in what their fans think of their products. Requesting feedback from the fans is something that American comic book companies such as Marvel or DC practice: every issue of their comic books including a letter section, with responses from the editor. But as yet it seems rare in the anime world.

When we were done there, Kelly, Jennie, and I walked around the lobby of the hotel in which part of Anime Central is held, just talking and asking people for their photograph. We made a stop by "Artists' Alley," a conference room where amateur artists rent tables to sell their anime and manga inspired artwork, or be commissioned to draw a picture of pretty much anything you want. On our way back from "Artists' Alley" we saw two guys both dressed as Cloud from the video game "Final Fantasy VII" posing together for a photograph, when a third guy dressed as Krillin from the anime "Dragonball" came running in, carrying a violin (his character does not play violin). This Krillin guy proceeded to play the end of battle victory music from Final Fantasy VII on his violin. It was very amusing.

Friday night was spent watching anime music videos. Each year there is an anime music video contest where people submit music videos they've made and a panel of judges decides which one is the best in each of the categories (comedy, drama, theme, action, and staff), but that's held on Saturday night with the results announced on Sunday. So the music videos that we watched on Friday night were from previous years, though some of them were still new to me and it was fun to watch some old favorites.

A good anime music video takes clips from either a variety of different scenes in an episode, or several different episodes, instead of just showing one scene as it is in the anime, and placing music on top of that. The most important thing, in my opinion, is for the song lyrics (or mood, if the song has no lyrics) match the story or character(s) of the anime. Anime music videos that do this are the ones that move me the most. The only exception to this is in the case of a humorous video where the creator of the video uses a song that is completely the opposite of what the characters would be thinking. I've noticed a big trend in using songs by

"Weird Al" Yankovic. For example, a video set to the "Weird Al" song "Jerry Springer" is edited to look like characters from "Sailor Moon" are on that infamous talk show. Many of the anime music videos, especially those in the comedy division, would make very little sense to people who had not seen the particular anime. Case in point: this year's winner for best comedic video took the opening animation and music sequence for a series called "Cowboy Bebop" and changed the characters in the opening from those actually on "Cowboy Bebop" to those on a radically different anime series called "Neon Genesis Evangeline." Both anime series are very popular within the anime fan community, and it appeared that everyone at the screening understood this inside joke.

Many of the convention goers elect to stay in the hotel (or another nearby hotel) so that they don't miss any of the action. Even those who live close by choose to do this because there are a lot of events that occur after 10 PM, including dances, concerts, and parties that fans throw in their hotel rooms. But I always go back to my house each evening. When I returned on Saturday, the convention was far more packed than it had been the previous day. I spent the first part of my day in the hotel's atrium where a lot of people in costume were posing for pictures.

Something interesting that I've noticed is that if you are cosplaying, complete strangers who are dressed as other characters from the same series will address you in the manner of the relationship between the characters in the anime series. It's a very cool phenomenon. It exemplifies the sense that each person at Anime Central shares a history with you. If two strangers dressed as characters who are friends, it seems only right, if they see one another, to strike up a conversation. My first time at Anime Central, I stood in line next to a girl dressed as one of my favorite characters, so I told her I liked her costume. She responded that I was the only person who'd recognized her, even though there was a guy dressed as the character who is her boyfriend: he had walked right past her without even a smile. This was upsetting to her, though after discussing it, we decided that was actually what the character would have done.

When I stopped for a slice of pizza, I sat at a large communal table with a boy and his mother. The boy's mother began talking to me, telling me that it was their first time at a convention and then asking me all sorts of questions about where different events took place, or why a group of people were standing in a line. Later on I told my friends Kelly and Jennie about the boy and his mom, and they told me that the mom had asked them the same questions. Conventions can be confusing the first time attending them. Maybe

Kelly, Jennie, and I looked like seasoned pros to the boy and his mom?

The FUNimation Company had a booth in the dealers' room, having a contest where if you filled out a consumer survey for them, your name could be drawn and you'd win a prize. I filled out one of the surveys which asked what anime that hasn't been brought to America would you most like to see distributed. The woman who took my survey saw that I had written in an anime called "Kamikaze Kaito Jeanne" and struck up a conversation with me about the series, because she and one of the interns at the company have been bugging all the other staff members to try and get the rights to it.

Finding out about an anime that hasn't been distributed in America can be a tricky matter. The anime series may be based off of a manga, and that manga could be in publication at current time in America. Another way you could find out about an anime that's not in distribution in America is that it may have been made by the same creator (writer, director, artist) as another anime you enjoy, and you read about it in an interview with the creator. Or there might be a Japanese voice actor you like a lot (most anime DVDs have the option of listing to the audio in Japanese, with subtitles) and you heard about a series they do a voice for that hasn't been brought to America. But perhaps one of the most common ways to find out about anime that hasn't been brought to America is through what are called "fan subs," fans who are fluent in Japanese and obtain videotapes of the original Japanese anime, and then use editing equipment to add English subtitles. Fan subbers will tell people about the anime they have fan subbed (often on a website) and then other fans can email them asking for copies of their tapes. There is no money exchanged: you send the fan subber a couple blank tapes, and maybe postage, then they keep one of the blank tapes as payment and send the other one back to you. A fan sub is how I became a fan of "Kamikaze Kaito Jeanne."

As I was wandering around the hotel lobby trying to find my friends, I heard the sounds of a song from one of the Final Fantasy video games. I followed the sound and found it was coming from a keyboard that was set up near the wall on the right side of the lobby. The guy who was playing it was just a teenager, another convention goer like myself, and next to him sat his friend who would occasionally dance along with the music. Shortly thereafter, the guy who was dressed as Krillin the night before came and joined them on his violin. They played really beautifully together. When they played the theme from The Legend of Zelda games, as fate would have it, a girl cosplaying as Link (who's the hero in the games) came walking into the room and looked very surprised and confused that they were playing "her song."

After a while I found Kelly and Jennie, and we went up to their friend Elf's room. Elf has a digital camera, and she hooked it up to the television set to show me the pictures she'd taken so far, as well as a movie of the karaoke held late the previous night after I'd gone home. Elf and a whole bunch of girls, including Kelly and Jennie, sang (and danced) to a hilarious parody one of them had written of the song "Mambo No. 5." The parody was called "Bishonen Mambo" (Bishonen being the Japanese word for pretty boy). I thought this was terribly amusing, though Elf explained that when they finished their song the man in charge of karaoke told their group he hated them. A lot of anime fans, especially male fans, are irritated by "fan girls," fans who fawn over Bishonen characters in the same way that a teen girl would squeal and sigh over, say, actor Orlando Bloom.

When I returned to the lobby later, I found that the keyboardist and violinist from that afternoon were still playing, and were now joined by two guitar players and a singer.

At one point, the band was taking a short break and a guy dressed as Sephiroth, the main villain from Final Fantasy VII, walked over and inquired if he might get his violin and join them. The original violinist asked Sephiroth to play a little something, as an audition, and then agreed to let him join. Because the guy was dressed as this terrible villain, it seemed quite strange to me to see him playing the violin.

By the end of the night the band consisted of a keyboardist, two guitarists, three violinists, and three vocalists. The crowd that had gathered around them reached fifty, not counting the people who looked over the ledges from the atrium at the band, and the people who would walk by and yell out requests or "you rock!" Although these people hadn't known each other before this day, nor had they practiced their music together, it was like they already had a deep history with each other and with us in the audience. There were so many knowing looks exchanged between all of us: although we had not been together when we played the games these songs are from, we knew that each of us had experienced the moments that the songs had played in the games, and we knew the emotions involved in the music. So in a way, we did have a shared history through these games, through the music. This is a feeling that I got throughout the convention: that the whole of Anime Central was a giant inside joke. Not that Anime Central isn't to be taken seriously—I don't mean that at all—but rather that nothing had to be explained, everyone was in on it.

The last song that I got to hear that Saturday night was "Eyes on Me" from Final Fantasy VIII, which is performed at a piano bar in the game itself (though it's played at other times as well). The girl who was singing it had changed her costume for this song so that she was dressed as Julia, the character who sings it in the game. For the few minutes in which the song was performed, it really felt like I was right there at the piano bar in Final Fantasy VIII, and I doubt that I was the only one who felt like that.

I decided to make the most of my time left and attended a fan panel about the anime series "Dual! Parallel Trouble Adventures." Unfortunately, all the moderator of the panel wanted to talk about was how cool the giant robots in the anime were, which isn't something that I particularly care about. I'd much rather have discussed the characters and plot of the story. I wonder if maybe this is because the panel was run by men, and I was one of two girls at the panel, despite "Dual!" being a female dominated show. The pilots of these giant robots (with the exception of one boy) are all females, which is rather unusual in the genre of anime that features giant robots. But not everything at Anime Central can be perfect.

Sunday was the last day of Anime Central for this year, and everyone I saw, myself included, looked glum and appeared to be moving slower than on the previous days. Luggage filled the entryway, friends were hugging, crying, and saying goodbye to one another. It is always hard to leave Anime Central. There is something that happens to me every year when it ends which I've named "Post-Con Depression." Being at Anime Central is such a rush of fun—being with old friends, meeting new people, shopping, going to panels and events—that when it's over, your everyday life feels dull. When I logged on to the Anime Central message boards on Sunday night I saw there was a whole conversation about this very phenomenon, and that was reassuring to me, knowing that I'm not the only one who has a hard time adjusting to everyday life after the convention is over. But after a few days you do get back to your normal routine—and begin planning for next year's Anime Central.

Notebook

1. What makes one group of fans a subculture and another just a group of fans? What have you been a fan of in your life? Have any of your "fandoms" been a subculture?

2. Do you think fictional characters—such as anime characters—can be heros? Why or why not? Whom do you consider a hero? Who are the heros or

heroines of the subculture you're studying, and what do those figures say about that subculture?

3. The popularity of anime has continued to rise since this essay was written. For more on its history, check out the book *Watching Anime, Reading Manga: 25 Years of Essays and Reviews* (Fred Patten, Stone Bridge Press, 2004). What evidence do you see of the fan subculture growing in your area?

4. The convention is its own sort of subcultural phenomenon. Try writing your own first-hand report of whatever group is gathering in your area in the near future—Barbie collectors, Beatlemaniacs, or *Desperate Housewives* fanatics, for example. Or, if you can't get to a convention, watch the documentary films *Trekkies 1 and 2*, about *Star Trek* fans; you might also be interested in the satiric film *Best in Show*, a humorous look at dog show culture. All are available on video.

My Life as an Enterprise Slash Writer

KYLIE LEE

Sometimes members of a fandom are so in love with their subculture that the officially produced stuff—the television show, the movies, the magazine articles—isn't enough to satisfy their enthusiasm. So the fans produce their own material, forming communities to share their homemade tributes and spin-offs. Such a fan is Kylie Lee, who lives on the East Coast and has published books, articles, and reviews about science fiction. Her fanfic is available at http://www. geocities.com/kylielee1000/. Her LiveJournal blog is available at http://www.livejournal.com/users/kylielee1000/. (Disclaimer: As Lee notes, this essay is "rated R": like many of the fanfics it describes, it contains sexually graphic material.)

---------------- ✦ ----------------

Title: Confronting Slash Fan Fiction
Author's pseudonym: Kylie Lee
Author's e-mail: kylielee1000@hotmail.com
Author's URL: http://www.geocities.com/kylielee1000/
Date: September 19, 2005
Length: ~5,000 words
Fandom: *Star Trek Enterprise*
Pairing: None

Rating: R
Summary: A slash writer comes out of the closet and reveals all. Or if not all, some.
Beta: Kim, The Grrrl, and Sarah, as usual. They are flexible in terms of genre.
Disclaimer: The usual. Paramount (http://www.paramount.com/) owns the world, and I adore and worship them, as should we all, in hopes that they won't sue me and all my friends because we feel the urge to write this stuff.

I've never written fiction, really, or had the desire to write fiction. I've never really felt I had that much to say, and in addition, I'm too pragmatic. Were I to write, say, a romance novel, I wouldn't be able to handle the fatal misunderstandings so necessary to drive the plot, and the thought of making up a bunch of characters and throwing them into unlikely situations didn't sound like fun as much as a chore. So it came as a complete surprise to me when, in 2001, after viewing a first-season *Star Trek Enterprise* episode entitled "Silent Enemy," inspiration struck. Frankly, that had never happened before. It was the first time where I felt absolutely compelled to write fiction.

Although I count myself as a fan of the show (which was canceled in 2004 after an embarrassingly short four-season run), I have to admit that it is . . . well, not very good. But with "Silent Enemy," I saw something to redeem the show for me: subtext. I saw, god help me, sexual tension zinging from two of the characters, just begging to be explored. And out of subtext came a piece of fan fiction— fiction written about a television program (or a movie or anime or whatever other kind of mass-culture artifact) featuring the characters in that program. I sat down at my keyboard, and I described the intensity I had seen in terms of a story I had thought of to explain that intensity. There was only one explanation, in my book:

> When Reed took the glass from his hand and set it next to his on the ground near the couch, Tucker did nothing. When Reed took his hand, he let him. When Reed, eyes locking with Tucker's, moved his body to straddle Tucker's seated body, he let him. When Reed leaned in close and brushed his cheek against Tucker's, he let him. And when Reed's mouth gently, persuasively closed on his, he kissed him back.

And let me just say that I didn't stop there. In some detail, I described Tucker and Reed's first sexual encounter, although the story, entitled "Acceptable Risk," does not end with them together as a couple. I posted it on the Internet to an *Enterprise* archive site for fanfic. I got good feedback. I wrote a sequel, then another, and then a bunch more—a total of nine. I wrote an entire backstory, the Acceptable Risk series, to Season 1 of *Enterprise* that was based on the premise that Commander Trip Tucker, *Enterprise's* chief engineer, and the British armory officer, Lieutenant Malcolm Reed, were having an intense secret homosexual relationship. I gave them posttraumatic stress disorder (canon source inspiration for this: "Shuttlepod One"). They admitted their love for each other. Then I broke them up. Thanks to "Desert Crossing," I got Captain Jonathan Archer in on the action. I managed to explain away Tucker and Reed's overt heterosexuality in "Two Days and Two Nights," and I included some Bondage Lite when they got back together.

Oh, yes.

I write slash.

Slash is, for the uninitiated, a genre of fanfic that posits a homoerotic relationship between two characters, usually male. The term "slash" comes from the punctuation (the / symbol) used to separate the initials of the pairing. "Acceptable Risk" is Tucker/Reed slash. The very first slash couple was none other than *Star Trek's* own Kirk/Spock, and according to slash critic Constance Penley, such fanfic dates to 1976. It's mostly written by straight women, although of course plenty of gay men and lesbians read and write it too. And there is a lot of it out there. Before I drafted "Acceptable Risk," I surfed the Internet, and in an hour, I had more *Enterprise* slash than I knew what to do with. In fact, one discussion group, the now-defunct Entslash, was set up as a forum for slash fanfic before the show even aired, in anticipation of slashiness to come.

Although I began the Acceptable Risk series in a vacuum—I hadn't read much *Enterprise* fanfic at that time (April 2002)—the people who wrote me feedback were encouraging and nice. One told me about the Entslash group, a discussion group for *Enterprise* slash. I signed up. Discussion groups are online forums on a particular topic. Yahoo! hosts a number of them (http://groups.yahoo.com/), including Entslash before its demise, and it now hosts another *Enterprise* slash site, EntSTSlash (http://groups.yahoo.com/group/EntSTSlash/), as well as number of discussion groups about *Enterprise* in general and the individual *Enterprise* characters and actors in particular. Before I knew it, I had a tiny fan club of people who liked my writing. I got a few betas (people who read fanfic before it's posted, to make comments and corrections). I became a beta myself. I got feedback, generally positive. I got inquiries to archive my work. And I read a lot of slash. I discovered that The Grrrl writes the best, sexiest PWPs (PWP stands for "Plot? What plot?"), that Macx writes incendiary sex within an emotional context inside an action-adventure story, that MJ writes the kind of plotted story that would be on classic *Star Trek*, that Kalita writes good alternate universes, that Ana just writes damn well, and that Kipli writes hot, playful stories. (*Enterprise* fic is archived at Warp 5, at http://fiction. entstcommunity.org/.)

When the Entslash list went down, the victim of hurt feelings and infighting, I spent two days furiously helping create the new list, EntSTSlash. In just a few months, the slash community had become tremendously important to me, and I hadn't quite been aware of it until that community was threatened. I'm defining the *Enterprise* slash community primarily as expressed through the discussion lists with which I happen to be familiar, but there are of course many other articulations of slash fandom, depending on the media source and the talents of the fans: many people go to conventions (several exist just for slash). Some stories aren't posted but go to print fanzines instead, and there's a whole culture to support this. Many *Enterprise* slashers engage in online role-playing games and write fiction out of the stories generated there. Slash fans have cemented friendships through instant messaging and chat. And recently fandom has moved almost wholesale off the lists and into LiveJournal.com, and Journalfen.net, both blog communities.

Although I did some academic work with slash in the early 1990s and read some Kirk/Spock slash at that time, until I became involved in *Enterprise* fandom, I hadn't really thought much about the genre. Elfin, who writes in a variety of fandoms, writes, "Slash was underground on the net when I became involved—it's become a lot more outspoken, with the slashers being more active in the fandoms than the 'shippers' [worshippers]." I suspect that as communities were built, any residual reluctance or shame at being labeled a slasher couldn't last. There is a kind of anonymity on the Internet that makes writing, posting, and critiquing slash even easier. I write and post under a pseudonym, as do most others. The practice of the use of pseudonyms is not new with the Internet; Henry Jenkins, for instance, in "Welcome to Bisexuality," discusses pseudonyms in fanzine fandom as a kind of clever play, as does Constance Penley in "Feminism, Psychoanalysis, and Popular Culture." Penley directly links the use of pseudonyms to the writers' having "something to hide," remarking, "It's one thing for your co-workers, domestic partners, or children to know you're a 'Trekkie,' it's another to know you're a producer of pornography with gay overtones."

Pseudonyms are also important because of the clandestine nature of slash and fanfic in general: nobody wants to hear from Paramount with a cease-and-desist order, so nobody can make money off her work. Everyone scrupulously includes a disclaimer on their zines, on their fanfic, and on their Web sites. Although some fans are associated with their pseudonyms and their identities are open secrets, others, such as WPAdmirer, one of my questionnaire respondents, are under deep cover. When WPAdmirer went to a convention, for instance, she felt she couldn't reveal herself as a fanfic writer to the other fans, and she felt cut off as a result: she notes, "I wished I could be more open about my involvement. The lack of being able to do that made it less pleasurable." In short, she felt cut off from a supportive community. I myself use a pseudonym to protect my privacy for the sake of my family. I've published under my real name, and I want to keep my slash separate, so that Internet hits on my name for my literary criticism or medical publications won't hit on slash sites. It strikes me as amusing that I do not know the real names of the women I regularly correspond with and whom I consider friends.

This notion of clandenstineness implies that we members of the slash community are doing something weird, perverted, or wrong, and that our product, the fanfics, are things that should be hidden. Critic and science fiction writer Joanna Russ, for instance, notes that her response to Kirk/Spock slash zines was to get "embarrassed (because, I think, the stuff was so female and my response to it so intense)" and she "hid it away—in the closet of all places!" E-mails to me from readers of my work have often spoken of how they had to hide the texts from their children, coworkers, or significant others as they compulsively finished reading a fic. If I'm writing slash and my husband comes in, I flip the computer screen to something else and won't return to it until he leaves, even though my reaction drives him crazy and he says he won't look at it. It's gotten so that when I'm writing slash and I hear his footsteps walking up and down the steps right outside my door, I have to shut the door, for fear that he will stick his head in. I simply can't relax and write when he's lurking.

This notion of secrecy, of slash having to remain hidden, was something I had to overcome before I could write. When I sat down and wrote my very first sex scene, thus moving once and for all into the slashfic camp, I literally paused for a minute before I set my fingers on the keyboard and started typing. It was like I had to take a deep breath, consider it, and then give in. There was a very real moment of decision there. I've loosened up a lot since then. Now I write sex scenes without setting them up, just because I think of a position or a situation I think would be pretty hot, or just because I'm thinking about the boys as I'm doing something else and I just have to stop a minute (well, an hour) and write a 2,000-word graphically sexual depiction of what I'd like to see these guys doing to each other. I file these random sex scenes and embed them in a fic later, editing them to another pairing if needed. Now, there is no hesitation. But slash writers are very aware that what they write is objectionable, that many people are freaked out by it and just don't get it. Slashers who post work online often get flamed; rare is the slasher who has never experienced this. In fact, A. Kite says, "There's only 2 kinds [of slash writers] you know? Them that's been flamed and them that are going to be." So troublesome is the negative reaction to graphic sexuality that the one-stop shop for fan fiction, FanFiction.net, had to ban NC-17 stories, which generated the majority of complaints.

In addition to the loathing of others, there is the loathing of the self that slash engenders. Wendy writes, "When I first discovered my own interest is slash, I felt that it was wrong, or rather that it was a sign of some kind of self hate. I mean, why fantasize about a relationship that downplays the role of, or completely ignores, women? It was a relief to discover this community 2 1/2 years ago shortly after I got a computer. It showed me women who seemed quite happy with themselves and their lives but who still enjoyed m/m." The whole notion of male/male desire as forbidden, and slashers as somehow pathological as a result, is a common point of view, both in the academic treatment of slash and among slashers themselves. Academics who study slash speak of their response to slash: they study texts that they find arousing, and they have to come to terms with that. Joli Jenson, in "Fandom as Pathology," notes that fans themselves are characterized as extreme fanatics, thus implying that fandom as a whole "is seen as excessive, bordering on deranged, behavior." Jenson goes on to argue that by "[stigmatizing] fandom as deviant, we cut ourselves off from understanding how value and meaning are enacted and shared in contemporary life." This notion of deviance is only reinforced when one piles slash, with its graphic depictions of male/male sex, atop fandom. And this notion of deviance is implicit in, for example, fanfic writer Squeaky's understanding of the slash community: "It's a safe, friendly place to discuss the issues that reading/writing slash deal with, and having the community helps to both 'normalize' the love of slash fiction and the acceptance of homosexual relationships. It validates that we are 'righteous, y'all,' and tptb [The Powers That Be—the writers and producers] are wrong and closed-minded. Ergo, the community is empowering to its members and validating about the values we share." In slash fic, homosexuality and homosexual relationships are generally presented as something normal, as something sexy and loving. The slash community takes this as a baseline given. In fact, it's become so normal to me, after years of reading and writing about it, that it's hard for me to understand why people get offended; it's hard to remember that homosexuality is still fraught in our culture, that many perceive it as deeply, morally wrong.

Because of this notion of slash as extreme and wrong, the slash community's biggest role is to provide the simple comfort of dealing with like-minded people. Arctapus sums it up: "I love the sense of total understanding of at least the interest in slash you find there. People get it." It's comforting to be able to talk to people about it without having to first provide context and then justify your interest: The Grrrl speaks for slashers everywhere when she admits of slash, "It really turns me on. Makes me feel warm and squishy inside. Two (or more) hunky men wanting each other, lusting after each other, having sex with each other is just a beautiful thing." WPAdmirer notes, "The function [of the fan community] is to bring together people who enjoy the same sort of things, find the same things (essentially—even if pairings are different) erotic, and have a community in which one is free to enjoy it without feeling strange, or being accused of perversion." Slashers have moved beyond this, but at the same time, we can't exactly have conversations about it with our neighbors or coworkers. To them, we are simply avid *Star Trek* fans. When I tell people I write fanfic, I say, smiling, "I write in a genre called slash," in complete confidence that they have no idea what I'm talking about. Usually, I'm asked if it's violent (apparently the word *slash* brings up violent connotations), and I just say, "No, not really." I haven't shared my pseudonym with many friends, just a few who are particularly close who know my writing in other contexts. Among my family, only my husband knows. Like many slashers, I have real life, and I have slash, and the two don't really meet.

In an interview, Henry Jenkins, an academic who is also a fan, speaks of "confronting" slash and becoming implicated in his own fantasies in relation to slash. He notes, "It was when I confronted slash, when I read slash and found out that I really was getting turned on by this—that this was not just a simple academic object of study—and as I began to rethink fantasy in relation to slash and what it meant to have erotic fantasies and how one relates to one's erotic fantasies, that I began to move away from a theoretical and abstract proposition." Jenkins' interest in slash led to his realization that he was bisexual, and he came out as bi at convention, thus completing his move from the theoretical to the concrete.

Although my own engagement with slash isn't nearly as interesting, one important part of my engagement with slash is desire: desire for pleasure, desire for titillation. I very much enjoy the sexy aspect of slash. Although of course not all slash is sexually explicit, I like the stories that are. I mean, I really, *really* like the stories that are. The physical connection is often a metaphor for the characters' emotional closeness. And much of it is written to arouse. However, for me, writing slash isn't like reading it. When I read it, I devour it: I don't notice technical errors, and I don't pay attention to narrative structure or other formal elements of the story, unless there is something unusual about it—for instance, fanfic is rarely written in the first person, and such stories jump out at me. I read it for the transcendent experience, for the emotional context the writer articulates, for the sex.

But when I write slash, the opposite is true. Unlike many other slash writers, who just sit down and let it flow (some slash writers, like writers everywhere speak of the story writing itself, or the characters hijacking the story and taking over), I approach writing slash formally. When I write, I think about structure, literary devices, symbolism, and the like. I try to fit in canon. I try to involve *Enterprise* characters other than the ones I am slashing. And I try to make all the sex scenes exist for a reason—I try not to write it gratuitously. Sex has to advance the plot or reveal something about the characters. In my header to one story, "Heat," a riff on the canon episode "Desert Crossing," for which I wrote three explicit sex scenes, including an extreme one with elements of dominance and submission, I noted that I couldn't tell whether the sex was hot, but that one beta, The Grrrl, said it definitely was. I got amused responses from people confirming The Grrrl's take on it. Kim said of the story, "The extreme heat of the desert in 'Desert Crossing' comes nowhere near the HOTNESS of this story!" Leah wrote of "Heat," "I also can't get over how brave you are (or seem to be to me, at least) when it comes to the unflinching description in the sex scenes. I still blush when I describe kissing . . . :-)" I don't know about bravery, but I try to write honestly, not metaphorically or poetically. In my writing, sometimes this involves hot sex; sometimes this involves pain; and sometimes this involves power plays. As a writer, I am drawn to characters who are members of a hierarchy—in the military, someone's boss—where one person has legitimate power over another, and then I explore how that power shifts because of the sexual nature of their relationship. I also try to go for realism. I research sexual positions to ensure that they are physically possible, and I've been known to check out gay videos or erotica for insight.

I read "Heat" again a few months after I wrote it and thought, "Oh, my god." It was indeed hot. I didn't remember it being that explicit, and the dominance/submission sex scene between Archer and Reed was pretty extreme, even though I don't write straight-up BDSM. When I reviewed all my fic, I realized that I had escalated. I had become more and more adventurous, more and more playful, more and more graphic. Writing is not easy for me. I write slowly, and stories go through revision after revision. My betas patiently put up with me, and I incorporate their suggestions into my fic without hesitation, only rarely making the authorial decision to override. For the Acceptable Risk series, part of the difficulty is incorporating canon source. I had Tucker and Reed all set to be together when "Desert Crossing" aired, and the slashy subtext between Archer and Tucker in this episode absolutely had to be dealt with. I had to break up a committed pair and get Archer and Tucker together, and I had to make it all believable and fit it into canon. I had trouble seeing Archer and Tucker together sexually—they've always struck me as just friends—and there was a long delay while I got my head around it and wrote in an Archer/Tucker pairing. But on the whole, it's gotten easier to write, and my stories, at about 6,000 words each, already long for fanfic, are getting longer.

Although my motivation for writing the story was, as always, to explain the slashy subtext I saw on screen, another motivation is to please the fan community. They read my stuff, they write me nice notes with feedback, and they like the sex, although fanfic readers much prefer sex inside an emotional context. I responded to feedback by having the boys actually declare their love for each other in words, something I am reluctant to do because I have a hard time seeing the characters, as portrayed in canon, doing this. However, I have also discovered that the fanfic audience needs to have things spelled out overtly; simply implying emotion, or using physical gesture to stand in for a declaration, is not enough, and my betas invariably call me on it when I try to do this, forcing me to spell it out. But I must say that it's very fulfilling to write for an appreciative audience. I post my stories online because I want the feedback. I have also discovered, to my dismay, that when I write fiction in an unpopular pairing, it doesn't get read. Tucker/Reed stories generated enthusiastic responses, but Archer/Mayweather (admittedly an odd pairing) got much less.

The question, of course, arises: why do I, a member of the slash community, write slash? Much criticism on slash has focused on appropriation and power. Henry Jenkins, in "*Star Trek* Rerun, Reread, Rewritten," uses de Certeau's notion of poaching, arguing that slashers are "'poachers' of textual meanings," that "fandom is a way of appropriating media texts and rereading them in a fashion that serves different interests." Patricia Frazer Lamb and Diana L. Veith, in "Romantic Myth, Transcendence, and *Star Trek* Zines," argue that slash posits a loving relationship between two equals, and by removing "gender as a governing and determining force in the love relationship," unequal power between men and women is negated. Penley argues that "the slash phenomenon [was] one of the most radical and intriguing female appropriations of a popular culture product that I had ever seen," noting that it illustrates how "women, and people, resist, negotiate, and adapt to their own desires this overwhelming media environment that we all inhabit." Lawrence Grossberg, in "Is There a Fan in the House?," comments that in consumer culture, "the transition from consumer to fan is accomplished," and it is here "that we seek actively to construct our own identities, partly because there seems to be no other space available . . . . The consumer industries increasingly appeal to the possibilities of investing in popular images, pleasures, fantasies, and desires." The fan is active, the consumer passive. And because of this activity, Grossberg argues, the fan is affectively empowered. He concludes that "Fans' investment in certain practices and texts provides them with strategies which enable them to gain a certain amount of control over their affective life, which further enables them to invest in new forms of meaning, pleasure and identity" in order to cope with the world. And John Fiske, in "The Cultural Economy of Fandom," notes that slash (although he doesn't use that term) writers "fill the gaps in the original text" and write "elaborated and public versions of the interior, semiotic productions of more normal viewers, many of whom might imagine for themselves similar 'extra-textual' relationships among the crew of the *SS Enterprise*." Fiske suggests, in short, that slashers imagine themselves to have relationships, likely sexual ones, with the characters, and that these relationships are simply articulations that many viewers ("more normal viewers"? what the heck does that mean? have I been insulted?) hold.

Thus, according to these notions (some of which, I hasten to add, are true for fanfic in general, not slash in particular, although because I'm a slash writer, I view it with slash goggles on), I write slash because I want to place the characters in romantic positions of equal power; because I want to engage actively, rather than passively, with media, in this case *Enterprise*; because I have an agenda, such as rewriting the canon source with a preferred reading; because I have desires that I want to articulate; because the stories I see on the screen contain gaps that I feel motivated to fill; and because I myself want to engage in sexual relationships with the crew, and thus writing slash is just an expression of this sexual fantasy. But when, á la Jenkins, I confront myself as a member of the slash community, it comes down to pleasure—the pleasure of the text, if you will, both canon source and slashy rewriting. Because of slash, engaging with the canon source has become a true joy. When I watched "Minefield," an early Season 2 episode, I rewound and rewatched the incredibly awkward breakfast scene between Lieutenant Malcolm Reed and Captain Jonathan Archer—three times. I knew then that this scene alone would spawn dozens of slash stories, and I was right. (I wrote one of them.) This kind of active watching is tremendously satisfying. It's a lot of fun to study facial expressions, gestures, the actors' use of props, their physical proximity. It's even more fun to read into them: in this example, I like Archer's pouring Reed some orange juice, and I like Reed's hands as he carefully sets his PADD down as Archer attempts to force him to engage in chitchat about sports, Reed's discomfort plainly evident. And yes, I feel motivated to rewrite this text, to explore the relationships between the men, to fill in the gaps in the characters' private lives—*Enterprise* is, after all, about a bunch of people who work together, and I'm interested in what they do off duty. But I'm not filling in gaps because I'm unhappy with the story; I'm filling in the gaps because I want there to be *more* to the story. Rich canon source means there's a lot to play with. Although I lost interest in *Enterprise* before its cancellation, in part because it created a canonical heterosexual relationship between the Vulcan first officer, T'Pol, and Tucker, thus taking Tucker, a major slash player, out of the action, I began writing in other fandoms, including *Firefly* (another canceled show), *NCIS*, and *Stargate SG-1*, and *Stargate Atlantis*. In other fandoms, I find my writerly motivations to be much the same.

But the pleasure is more than my delight in watching the canon source and spotting slashy subtext. There's the pleasure of watching a television program with a cast of incredibly attractive, buff men. There's the real pleasure of creating the slash text itself. There's the literal physical pleasure of arousal as one writes or reads. Then there's the giddy pleasure of getting e-mails from people saying they really liked your work—e-mails that make me laugh out loud in delight.

So why do I write slash? I write it because I feel compelled to. In the fan community, this is known as getting bitten by a plot bunny. I write it because it's hot and sexy and fun. I enjoy the steamy sex. I write it because I want to read the kind of stuff I write, but few people write it: stories that are as true as possible to the characters as they are presented on the screen, but with that slashy twist (and, I hope, hot sex). I like to read texts that are in character, canonical, fraught, and full of angst that resolves into joy. Finding texts that fit my idea of "canonical" is more of a chore than it should be. I prefer to set the stories within or on the peripheries of canon episodes, rather than making up my own action-adventure stories. It's my niche as a writer. No doubt it's my literary criticism background: I am critiquing texts, only slash is far more fun than deconstruction, even if they're basically doing the same thing. Henry Jenkins, in an interview, notes that queer theorists such as Alex Doty or Eve Sedgwick are slashers: "They are writing academic slash in the ways in which they are reading the text and constructing these relationships that other readers are reluctant to see." And it's a good fit for me as a writer: I like having the boundaries of the situations and the characters set for me.

But the primary reason I write slash? That one's easy.

It just makes me so damn happy.

Notebook

1. Perhaps more than some of the other subcultures in this book, the slash fiction writers that Kylie Lee describes are actually "underground"—their participation in the subculture is often a secret, even to those closest to them, and they feel the need to maintain secret identities in order to participate. Such subculture members are hard to research and study, for obvious reasons, and so we're lucky to have a piece by an insider. But what are the disadvantages of writing about a subculture from within? What problems, if any, do you see arising from Lee's closeness to her subject in this piece? How will you counter such problems if you write about a subculture to which you belong?

2. Try your own hand at fanfic: Have you ever wished a TV series or book or movie had gone on longer than it did? Have there been minor characters that you would like to know more about? How would you continue, or alter, the plot?

3. Kylie Lee mentions media critic Henry Jenkins. Check out his book *Textual Poachers: Television Fans & Participatory Culture* (Routledge, 1992) for a new way at looking at the "passive" act of watching TV.

4. This chapter has three pieces that are written in the first person—Mimi Nguyen's film review, Heidi Schubert's convention report, and Kylie Lee's fanfic memoir. How does that style affect how you read these pieces? What do you think would be gained, and lost, if they were written as third-person accounts?

CHAPTER 3

Myths and Truths

OVERVIEW

Much of what you know—or think you know—about subcultures is probably based not on research or direct observations, but on rumors or representations in TV shows or movies. This kind of knowledge often falls under the category of stereotypes. But as you're well aware, stereotypes are often too general, judgmental, and erroneous to be useful information. When doing cultural analysis, however, we shouldn't pretend that the stereotypes don't exist. It's more helpful to be aware of the stereotypes, and to understand that stereotypes, although mostly fiction, often arise out of some kind of fact, and that the way subcultures are stereotyped can often have very real impact on the way the culture is treated and feels about itself.

When doing your own research, you may have the urge to do what some of the authors do here, and try to prove that what everyone assumes is true about a subculture is actually in some ways false. Or you may discover that the stereotypes have some validity—or that the subculture is in so much flux that it's impossible to say what is and is not true about it. Such issues could become the substance of a great argumentative essay.

From Geeks to Freaks: Goth and the Middle Class

AMY WILKINS

One could argue that few youth subcultures are as misunderstood as the Goth subculture, which, because of its interest in the macabre, is often associated with criminal intent or violence, even though, as Amy Wilkins observes here, its members are often highly productive, brainy, even cheerful members of society. Wilkins is an assistant professor of sociology at the University of Colorado–Boulder. Her work focuses on youth culture, identity, and social inequality. She is currently working on a book that explores three young adult cultural projects: Goth, "Puerto Rican Wannabes," and evangelical Christians.

✦

"Like if I were to see a pool of blood by candlelight, most people would probably be horrified, but I'd see the different ways light reflected in it."—Siobhan

In the mainstream mind, Goths are perhaps best associated with Columbine, in which the Goth scene was held accountable for spurring the two socially isolated, black trench coat-clad boys to enact the tragic school massacre. In the wake of Columbine, the Goth subculture has been treated with a good deal of fear. Goth is often perceived to be a dangerous, even satanic subculture, an image that is fed by comments like Siobhan's, as well as the dark clothes and the dark attitudes flaunted by most Goths. Like most scapegoating, however, this stereotype is misleading. Not only does it hyperbolize and misinterpret many elements of the Goth scene, but it also ignores the ways in which many Goths are preparing themselves to take on white, middle class adult identities despite their freakiness.

I write about Goths from the position of an ethnographer. For a period of over eighteen months, I conducted participant-observation in a northeastern, non-urban Goth scene located in a university community known for its liberal attitudes. In addition to conducting formal interviews with seventeen self-identified Goths (ten women and seven men), I hung out with Goths at their dance club, at private parties, and individually. For six months, I also participated on their weblist. Although I am not and have never been Goth, I became close friends with one of the central members of this Goth community, and so have had the additional benefit of being able to discuss my ideas about the Goths extensively with an insider.

In contrast to the stereotype of anti-social pathology, the Goths in this study are integrated into mainstream institutions, mostly attending college or employed. Their claims of diversity notwithstanding, they are primarily white, middle class, liberal, unmarried, and childless. They come together regularly through an internet listserv and Tuesday nights at the local Goth club night. Their scene, they inform me, is atypical for Goths scenes, in that there is more tolerance of people moving in and out of the scene. Because of this tolerance, these Goths describe their local scene as less "hardcore" than other Goth scenes.

Goths, as I will discuss, *are* freaky. Goths revel in this freakiness, taking on the label with pride. Using style, emotions, and sexuality, they draw deliberate, bold boundaries between themselves and mainstream "sheep" or "norms" (for "normals"). But although Goths shock the sensibilities of the mainstream, their strategy does not undermine their long-term status as members of the white middle class. Instead, their freakiness allows them to carve out a middle terrain that provides some of the benefits associated with being shocking, rebellious, and hip, but without sacrificing the security of their white middle class origins.

Goth, I was told repeatedly, is an "aesthetic." "It's seeing a set of things as beautiful, things that are darker and frightening to most people," as Honeyblossom told me. The Goth "aesthetic" is dark, "eerie," isolationist. Goths claim a shared aversion to the sun and a fascination with the macabre: cemeteries, nighttime, vampires. Like members of other subcultures, they use their self-presentations to advertise their rejection of conventional style, emotions, and sexual norms.

Most Goths were high school geeks. Anne's description of her social position in high school is characteristic, if mild: "I was never one of the populars to begin with." Zoe embellishes this point, suggesting that the experience of being a social outcast in high school is both widespread and traumatic; "I've talked to a lot of people— their whole junior high, high school was horrible. They had no friends until college, the haven." Indeed, almost everyone I spoke with began their tale with an account of social discomfort in high school—of being too smart or too shy, of being picked last for sports teams, of not playing soccer in a town where "if you didn't play soccer, you weren't anyone," of wearing the wrong kind of clothes. Some were picked on, others were simply invisible. Regardless of the specific experience of high school geekiness, finding the Goth scene changed everything—not because the ideas were new, but because, as Crow says, finding the Goth scene "gave a name to something I was already experiencing."

Becoming Goth not only provides socially isolated young people with a community, but it also transforms their social locations. Goths are "freaks." The transition from geek to freak moves Goths out of the shadows they occupied as geeks. Their outlandishness forces acknowledgment of their existence and gives them social power. While geeks are just losers, freaks must stand for something, even if we can't figure out what it is. Freaks are shocking. With pride and amusement, Goths tell stories about people recoiling when they see them, pulling their children away, crossing to the other side of the street. They recount reactions to their self-presentation: of having their photos snapped—"You know, when they pretend to be taking pictures of their kids and just *accidentally* move the camera up and to the left to capture us in film"—of being left to sit by themselves on the Greyhound, of "being able to clear a path to a crowded public bathroom sink just by standing there . . . (and) being able to successfully intimidate people I otherwise could not" (unnamed woman, listserv posting).

As these comments show, Goth freakiness is powerfully embodied through style. The Goth style juxtaposes Medieval romanticism with bondage wear, puffy velvet with skin-tight PVC. Dramatic make-up on whitened faces, jet black or brightly hued hair, and copious tattoos and body piercings accessorize dark, sumptuous outfits. Goths may sport dog collars and spikes, or fishnets and corsets—all in somber colors: black or blood red. The dark exterior symbolizes interior difference, as Dallas explains: "In poetry class, I write darker poetry and stuff. [The Goth clothing] explains it for people who don't know me." The dark clothes, then, bespeak dark emotions.

But while Goths revel in stories of the power of public freakiness, they are also able to downplay, or even take off, their freakiness when it is socially necessary. Dallas, for example, dresses in non-Goth style when she visits her grandparents, while both Beth and Zoe explain their decisions to de-Goth their appearances for work. Zoe says, "But when I got a job as a supervisor, I was dying my hair back to brown. I was afraid I wouldn't be taken seriously with green hair." These changes indicate the possibility of moving in and out of embodied freakiness even while maintaining a primary Goth identity.

The impermanence of style also enables a transition out of the Goth subculture. The freaky style can be shed and left behind, with few ongoing reminders that it was ever affected. While impermanence is a general characteristic of style, its benefit is particularly salient for young adults located relatively securely within the white middle class. For these Goths, stylistic rebellion is an expected part of the life course. Even parental alarm is an anticipated part of the middle class adolescent (and young adult) script, while other parents may even support experimentation out of a middle class belief in the importance of "finding oneself." For example, Dallas' mother supported her daughter's development of a Goth identity by willingly funding a new wardrobe.

Moreover, Beth points out: "Parents usually don't like [the Goth style]; they associate it with devil worship, think it's scary. They're conservative—want their kids to dress a certain way. [Parents] associate [the Goth style] with not being successful or doing well in school, but when people do well in school, parents are more accepting."

Beth's observation indicates that, in the presence of other class signifiers (like school attendance and success), some middle class parents are able to accept their kids' stylistic rebellion. Thus, while the shock value of Goth style clearly marks Goth disaffection with the mainstream, and provides Goths with social power in public spaces, it also builds in the possibility of remaining socially integrated in key middle class institutions, including work, school, and their families of origin.

Despite this integration, the construction of a visibly freaky self validates Goth claims to nonconformity and symbolizes their disdain for "mainstream" opinion. It thus angers and frightens (older) adults and sidesteps non-Goth peer approval (by denigrating non-freaky styles). This purposeful and collective nonconformity is itself status producing, as subcultures traditionally disparage the "mainstream" as unhip, as Sarah Thornton argues in her book *Club Cultures: Music, Media and Subcultural Capital* (Wesleyan University Press, 1996). The deliberate embracing of an alternative presentation of self changes the terms of the competition, so that hipness accrues to the presentation of self most at odds with "mainstream" styles. By turning freakiness into a point of pride, Goths establish internal criteria for approval—increasing their chances of success by ranking themselves according to a hierarchy on which they are already near the top.

Freakiness has other benefits as well. The scene is a space in which feelings of alienation are recognized and shared. Greg comments, "A lot of us had to deal with a lot of shit in life: outcasts, freaks in high school, whatever. Either deal with it or deny it.

Death doesn't bother me in a sense. If somebody's dead, they're dead. You move on. People [in the scene] had lots of negativity and trouble." Both Beth and Crow describe the Goth scene as a "sanctuary"—a space in which their stigmatized attitudes and behaviors are embraced. "You are yourself and can do whatever you want and it's not going to be criticized," Crow explains. These descriptions suggest the psychological benefits of having a shared space.

For many Goths, the validation of their psychic crises is indeed an affirming experience. Matt explains that when he found the Goth scene, he was "going through a break up" and that the "loud, thrashing" music by Goth bands "appealed" to him. He says, "I think [the scene] appeals to people who have gone through hard times." Rory similarly comments, "There's something refreshing about finding people to talk to who, when you say you want to die, won't tell you to get meds, lock you up, etc."

It is this fascination with darkness and death that frequently frightens outsiders, who perceive Goths as perhaps pathologically anti-social. But Goths themselves patrol the limits of their own darkness, censoring uses of the taboo that would result in socially harmful outcomes. Zoe remarks, for example, "For a bunch of people who glorify being alone, [Goths are] awfully social. . . . Goths brag about being depressed and suicidal but [they're] not really." And Lili explains that "in the Goth subculture, people can play at different things, and go over the top, and it's okay—to be overly angst, overly hurt. Drama can be a way of interacting and can be entertaining as long as people know it's there." Comments like these blunt the dangerous edges of Goth darkness, turning it instead into a psychological tool. Although it seems ironic, Goths use their negative emotions to create social connections; this community, in turn, helps them moderate their own destructive impulses.

Moreover, Goth freakiness does not require the wholesale abandonment of geeky traits. Instead, the geeky traits that are most clearly associated with socio-economic success are integrated into Goth culture. Goths are overwhelmingly technologically adept, articulate, and literate in both current events and "classic" cultural texts. The outward appearance of marginality does not preclude Goth participation in mainstream middle class institutions.

For the young people in this study, becoming Goth solves some of the problems they face as socially isolated young people. Although it often provokes open derision, the freaky Goth identity nevertheless provides community, an identity, emotional support, and a frightening and/or shocking self-presentation that commands social distance. And it does all this without creating significant long-term status costs: Goths are able to achieve these benefits without sacrificing their commitments to education, careers, and their families. For these young people, then, Goth is a subcultural strategy of limited liability.

Notebook

1. What stereotypes do you hold about Goths? Do you know any Goths? In what ways do they fit the stereotypes? In what ways do they dispel them? Could you conduct an interview or some research that would help you understand them better?

2. Wilkins argues that Goths find a certain amount of power in their status as "freaks." Based on what you've read here, do you agree? How do other subcultures you've read about, studied, or known seem to find power in their position as outsiders? What kind of power is it? What sorts of power or access do they have to give up to use this power?

3. If you're brave, you could try dressing up like a Goth, or punk, or skateboarder for a day (with the help of a subculture member to make sure you look authentic!) to see the world through the eyes of that subculture. Go to a fast food restaurant, an upscale store, a bank, or places you usually go dressed as yourself and notice any differences in the ways you're treated. This experiment is a lesser version of the one famously documented in John Howard Griffin's book *Black Like Me*, in which Griffin, a white man, pretended to be black in the 1950s South.

4. On a sheet of paper, create a "T" chart. Label the left side "Myths" and the right side "Truths." Starting with myths, write down all the Myths you've known or learned about the specific subculture you're studying. When you've completed that list, do some research and then fill in the Truths. Get into a group and discuss your findings.

How the Internet Is Changing Straightedge
J. PATRICK WILLIAMS

J. Patrick Williams uses the straightedge subculture—itself a subcategory of the punk subculture—to look at the ways in which contemporary subcultures are shaped by the way they exist as virtual communities online. If we can't even see the other members of our subculture face-to-face, how, we might ask, are we really members of the same community at all? J. Patrick Williams is an assistant professor at Arkansas State University. During the mid- to late-1980s, Williams self-identified as punk and straightedge in a local scene in the southeast United States. Since the late 1980s, he has played drums in several metal bands, and has been an active participant in the death metal scene since the early 1990s. He earned his doctorate in Sociology and Cultural Studies from the University of Tennessee in 2003.

———————— ✦ ————————

What does it mean to be "real?" The phrase "keeping it real," for example, has come to mean something specific in hip-hop subculture, and has spread throughout American pop culture vernacular. How do we know when someone is being genuine, versus faking it? There are many situations in which we find ourselves feeling or believing that people we know are not being honest with us, nor with themselves, about who they "really" are.

People in subcultures—whom we can call "subculturalists"— have always been concerned with maintaining a boundary between the real and the fake. Who is authentic, and who is a poseur? In 1983, D.R.I. (a.k.a., Dirty Rotten Imbeciles) wrote a song about "closet punks"—kids who sometimes dress up to look like punks but are considered inauthentic because they don't embrace the appearance all the time. Later in the 1980s and throughout the 1990s, hardcore straightedge bands such Bold and Earth Crisis wrote songs about kids who were not keeping it real. These kids are typically labeled as "sell outs." There's a popular straightedge saying, "If you're not [straightedge] now, you never were!"

But how can subculturalists tell who is and who is not an authentic member? Is it "faking it" when kids do not dress according to subcultural norms? When kids engage in activities that other subcultural members disapprove of? When kids keep the wrong kinds of friends? When their interests change and they drop out of the scene? When they do not like certain kinds of music or certain bands that are considered integral to the subculture? These kinds of questions are integral to my research on contemporary subcultures.

There are many examples of music-based subcultures in contemporary society, each with their own distinctive sounds, styles, values and argot (e.g., punk, hardcore, hip-hop, rave, goth, or straightedge). Each of these subcultures—and many others—are typically understood as music-based phenomena. Yet, however important music might be, there are changes occurring in contemporary society which require that we question the degree of music's importance for subcultures. In particular, information and communication technologies like the internet are changing the ways in which many subcultural youth participate in what have traditionally been considered music subcultures. In this essay I explore these changes in terms of one particular subculture called straightedge. A remarkable shift appears to be occurring within straightedge, in which the centrality of music is being challenged. I suggest that the internet now competes with music as a key resource for identity and participation. To do this, I analyze the symbolic interaction among participants in a straightedge internet forum and focus on the meanings that forum members attach to music and the internet, respectively. The shift grows as more internet users learn about straightedge online and begin self-identifying as straightedge without participating in punk or hardcore music scenes. By exposing the debate among participants over what constitutes authentic straightedge identity and what counts as a straightedge "scene," I highlight the role the internet plays in facilitating subcultural growth and change.

THE AMERICAN STRAIGHTEDGE MUSIC SCENE

The straightedge subculture arose around the 1981 song "Straight Edge" by the Washington D.C. punk band Minor Threat. In that song, lyricist Ian MacKaye emphasized how he differed from other youth in his disdain for drug use and promiscuity. Taken as a whole, Minor Threat's lyrics address in various ways central concerns of the band—the apathy of youth and the positive contribution of punk subculture. Hardcore straightedge was partly a reaction to the disaffection and subsequent self-destructive tendencies of many punks, and partly a collective search for meaning in a world characterized by the dissolution of authentic selfhood. The band's ideology of resistance to mainstream culture's emphasis on passive consumerism was not exceptional among punk bands, but the term "straight edge" seemed to strike a chord with punk youth around the US. Within a year or two of the song's release, kids around the country had begun claiming to be straightedge.

Straightedge subcultural norms regarding drug use and promiscuity have been articulated in a variety of ways through music lyrics. More important for our discussion here, however, is that subcultural norms have been spread in recent years via non-music media such as the internet. In tandem with this subcultural diffusion, individuals have discovered straightedge in a dislocated form, fractured from its musical roots. Of the individuals who encounter straightedge online and subsequently claim to be straightedge, many join face-to-face straightedge scenes, though many others do not. When the straightedgers I studied wrote, they made distinctions between two types of straightedger, which I will name music-straightedger and net-straightedger. Members of these two groups argued with each other about what constitutes being a "real" straightedger.

AUTHENTICITY AND "THE SCENE"

For subculturalists, it is important to be seen as an authentic participant. Subculturalists regularly claim to be "real" while charging others with simply doing subcultural things, such as dressing or speaking a certain way, in order to appear cool or fit in. Those unable to convince others of their authenticity are often labeled as poseurs, pretenders, wannabes, or week-enders.

Authenticity is a complex concept with multiple expressive forms. In this essay, I highlight two dimensions as discussed originally by Kembrew McLeod—the *social-psychological* dimension, which refers to staying true to one's beliefs versus following mass trends; and the *social locational* dimension, which refers to being an insider versus an outsider.

In the *social psychological* dimension, subcultural participants may, for example, tell stories about themselves that highlight their commitment to a subcultural lifestyle. Such narratives often articulate subcultural identity as something innate or self-owned and thus beyond another's control. In such cases, a subcultural identity serves to strengthen an individual's claim of "keeping it real" by legitimating her own behaviors and identity as authentic.

Then there is the *social locational* dimension of authenticity. Consuming specific subcultural products (e.g., music) or actively participating in a local scene, community, or network of friends can be just as important as believing yourself to be a "real" subculturalist. Those who are not part of these groups are labeled as "outsiders." By monitoring where and how individuals participate, subcultural members engage in a game of exclusion whereby only those participants who meet certain criteria are considered "insiders."

Most importantly, participants may not realize that they are using different measures of authenticity in their everyday lives. Rather, the answers subculturalists give to the kinds of questions I asked at the beginning of this essay depend on which dimension of authenticity they rely upon, often unconsciously. Like subculturalists themselves, many researchers assume that subcultural members all measure authenticity the same way. Unfortunately, this means that researchers do not adequately consider how individuals define their own authenticity as subcultural members. Many researchers privilege the voices of some participants over others. We should never assume that subculturalists all share a homogeneous perspective of their subculture because various members often have different views of what is appropriate versus inappropriate, right versus wrong.

Finally, how subcultural members measure authenticity can be linked to the symbolic value they attach to a subcultural scene. A scene is not objectively real; that is, it is impossible to see a scene or determine its boundaries precisely. However, the collective meaning of scene must appear to be objective before it can be experienced. Thus, even though I will argue below that internet forums may constitute a new type of subcultural scene, the idea of an internet scene is not yet salient to most subculturalists. The dominant view that all scenes are face-to-face scenes helps legitimize the assumption that all members give equal value to the social location dimension of authenticity. In order to demonstrate that this is not always the case, I will highlight how definitions of the scene are tied up in how straightedgers identify themselves and others as (in)authentic.

METHODS

My data come from an internet forum and from interviews with participants from that forum. The forum is located on a public website that is dedicated to the straightedge subculture. The website has more than 1,300 registered users from around the world, including Australia, Canada, Germany, Italy, New Zealand, the UK, and the US. I collected the data over a two year period, between autumn 2001 and autumn 2003.

My work was ethnographic, meaning that I participated in forum discussions even as I observed others' participation. I considered myself a regular member of the forum and behaved accordingly. When I had questions that I wanted answered, I took one of two steps. First, I posted questions on the forum, typically as a new thread. (Threads are chronologically arranged topical conversations that participants can see from the forum's main page.) After posting questions, I monitored responses and regularly asked follow-up questions. Second, I did nine qualitative interviews to gain clarification on the meaning of subcultural activities. The interviews lasted between 90 and 180 minutes and were done online using instant messaging or chat software. I asked open-ended questions, which allowed the interview to progress naturally. Some of the individuals I interviewed considered themselves straightedge music fans, while others did not. Some had participated in the forum more than a year, while others were relative newcomers. This variety enabled me to develop a better understanding of how different participants felt about issues of authenticity, the straightedge music scene, and the internet.

The messages young people posted in the forum were the sociological object of study, rather than the individuals themselves. Therefore I never tried to discover the "real life" identities of any of the participants. I have given pseudonyms to all the participants mentioned in the paper to protect their online identities as well.

CLAIMING AUTHENTIC STRAIGHTEDGE IDENTITY

Posted by: MeanBug

> I've been officially straightedge for about 1.5 years now. I believe this is a lifelong promise. However, some guy said I wasn't straightedge because I don't listen to any straightedge hardcore type bands or go to straightedge shows. I tried to explain I live in Idaho (self-explanatory there) but he said hanging out with other straightedge people was a must. Now, I'm the only one I know. Do I have a problem?[*]

In this post from the straightedge forum, a participant, Mean-Bug, expressed concern about her/his authenticity as an "official" straightedger. Questions like this, and the answers given by other participants, represent a debate going on in the forum between

---

[*]Forum participants regularly use the acronym sXe as shorthand for "straightedge." It is comprised of the S and E from straightedge surrounding an X, which is a straightedge symbol.

music-straightedgers and net-straightedgers. Individuals supported either the notion that only people who follow straightedge norms and participate in a hardcore music scene could be straightedge or the idea that anyone who follows straightedge norms could be straightedge. There was one particular thread in the forums that clearly contextualized the debate about the meaning of the scene and how members measured authenticity. The first post came from Old-SkoolSk8r, who asked, "Does punk rock, hardcore or whatever it is called nowadays still have a role in the straight edge movement? [. . .] I think the music and the 'punk rock' culture is what makes straight edge unique so the two cannot and should not be separated." Music-straightedgers tended to support OldSkoolSk8r's claim that straightedge was a part of the punk and hardcore music subcultures. Net-straightedgers typically disagreed, while other participants stated that the issue was more complicated than a simple "agree" or "disagree" answer. One straightedge music fan argued that "straight edge can't be independent of the music. It's a subculture centered around a style of music. You take away the music, you take away the subculture, and all you have left is a bunch of drug free kids." Another post represented the opposite view: "I don't believe so at all. Music may have 'spawned' straight edge, but I believe straight edge is fully independent from any musical 'scene'. Besides, I don't listen to punk rock." In both posts, we can see how participants make claims for what counts as "real" straightedge culture.

The main sticking point was whether or not straightedgers must belong to a local music scene in order to be credited as authentic. One hardcore participant, XantagX, authoritatively stated that "without the scene, without the music, there is straight but no edge." In response, a net-straightedger asked, "Where do you get the idea that if you don't listen to a certain style of music you're not edge? Or if you don't "go to shows" or are "in the scene" you're not edge? [. . .] Straight edge is a commitment till death of being drug free. [It] is a bond."

Implicit in their dialogue is the larger debate about authenticity, which is alternately conceived either in social locational terms (by being a member of a local music scene), or in social psychological terms (by making a "commitment till death" to follow straightedge rules against drug use and promiscuity). XantagX and OldSkoolSk8r both pointed to hardcore music as a subcultural boundary, first by suggesting that straightedge bands are all hardcore and second by suggesting cultural differences between straightedgers and people who are just "straight." One music-straightedger even asked rhetorically whether his abstinent grandmother should be considered straightedge since she did not engage in drug use or promiscuous sex. Another music-straightedger supported this allegedly absurd assumption by asking others to imagine a "granny mosh pit." Through such laughable imagery, music-straightedgers sought to show that "real" straightedgers differed qualitatively from members of mainstream culture, even from those who shared similar beliefs about clean living. Grandmothers, and implicitly anyone else who did not participate in the straightedge music scene, were not credited as authentic straightedgers.

Net-straightedgers, on the other hand, made claims to authentic straightedge identity by focusing on lifestyle choices. They often expressed straightedge as a commitment to subcultural norms. One forum member argued that a commitment to clean living (a "commitment till death") was the true source of straightedge identity, not musical preference. Others supported such claims by arguing that interaction on straightedge internet sites significantly diffused the straightedge subculture beyond the boundaries of local straightedge music scenes. In the post below, Nebula describes a variety of methods through which individuals could be introduced to the subculture and implicitly defends the authenticity of such people as straightedge.

Posted by: Nebula

Let's go like this: XantagX heard "Straight Edge" by Minor Threat. He heard about straightedge from bands & his friends. [. . .] A girl who listens to Korn [a non-straightedge, non-hardcore band] would like to be part of a philosophy that embraces anti-drugs. She hears about it from the internet. [. . .] A boy who listens to Metallica & Megadeath gets made fun of because he doesn't do pot. He finds someone with X's on their hands who tells him about straightedge. He decides to put X's on his hand & to hang out with the other kid as to make a statement about not doing drugs.

Here we see three hypothetical cases in which a person was exposed to and expressed support for a drug free lifestyle. In each case, the source of information about straightedge was different. This post served as a challenge to other participants to prove why or how one person is more or less authentic than anyone else. In other posts, Nebula expressed his conviction that an individual could be straightedge without participating in a face-to-face straightedge music scene. Indeed, he criticized hardcore straightedgers as simply following music trends and not recognizing the "true" meaning of straightedge, namely a drug free lifestyle.

Authentic straightedge identity seemed to be constructed around the idea of commitment, yet the value of commitment was measured using competing assumptions about authenticity. Straightedge music scene members argued for authenticity based on an in-depth knowledge of, and participation in, the straightedge music scene, while net-straightedgers emphasized that those who expressed and maintain a "true till death" ethos were also authentic.

WRITING THE SCENE

Music-straightedgers wrote about the scene as a necessary element in constructing a straightedge identity. According to one hardcore interviewee, the scene was defined by whom one associates with. "Well I hang out with a lot of kids that share my anti-drug beliefs within the hardcore community. [. . .] it's generally the same kids hanging out together almost every weekend and exchanging ideas. It is a scene, because it's at least somewhat based on the fact that we have mutual interests and goals." Other definitions of scene placed explicit emphasis on music. One poster wrote that "going to shows would be the base [of being in the scene] I guess, but not just that. I think it's a lot in helping out to fuel that scene in anyway you can whether it be posting flyers, helping set up gear at a show, working the door, doing favors for bands etc." Those individuals who engaged in these and similar activities gained respect from others in the subculture and the ability to influence others in the scene.

For these forum participants, the scene had to do with their relationship to the production, distribution, and consumption of hardcore/straightedge music. Authenticity involved listening to straightedge music and actively helping to keep the music scene alive. One music-straightedger explicitly stated that the scene was "more than just kids sitting around not doing drugs." Only those who actively participated in local subcultural events such as concerts represented the scene, and thus only they were "keeping it real." During an interview, another hardcore forum participant described the embeddedness of straightedge within the larger punk/hardcore subcultures and claimed that it was senseless to think of straightedge any other way. To him, "a lot of those kids [who claim to be straightedge but do not participate in local music scenes] I think are becoming 'straight but not edge.'" They were "straight" because they did not use drugs, yet they lacked the rebellious "edge" that he claimed characterizes members in the music scene. He created a distinction between those whom he considered authentic participants of the straightedge subculture and those who were not. He did not challenge the beliefs of non-hardcore forum participants, nor did he grant them any authenticity. Many participants agreed that straightedge was about a scene, but were not certain whether the scene was only about music. One participant, XdoitdoitX, noted in a post that the internet offered a source of information to individuals outside of punk/hardcore music scenes, some of whom subsequently found the subculture appealing and began to self-identify as members. This happened "because of the education through the internet and other media." Other participants, who at one point supported the music-straightedge position, come to accept at some level the idea that the definition of scene was negotiable. They came to acknowledge that internet participation was worth something, though music preference remained a key definitional component. That is, internet participation and commitment to subcultural norms was not enough. Without investing time, money or energy into a local straightedge music scene, or at least supporting the scene by purchasing straightedge CDs, net-straightedgers lost credibility in the eyes of straightedge music scene members. They remained "straight but not edge."

THE INTERNET AS A STRAIGHTEDGE SCENE

I have suggested that music-straightedgers ground their authenticity claims in a commitment to the face-to-face music scene. This is what I have referred to as the social locational dimension of authenticity. Where one participates from—from in front of a stage watching straightedge bands play, or from one's bedroom sitting in from of the computer—has everything to do with whether one is accepted by others as straightedge. Meanwhile, net-straightedgers grounded their claims in commitment to subcultural norms. For them, it does not matter whether one is a straightedge music fan, nor does it matter whether one lives in large city with an active scene or in a small rural community where nobody has ever heard of straightedge. As long as one self-identifies as straightedge and follows straightedge norms, she is straightedge. This is what I have called the social psychological dimension of authenticity: being true to oneself rather than to a group. Yet, it would be foolish to argue that there is a one-to-one correlation between a straightedge type (e.g., music-straightedge) and a dimension of authenticity (e.g., the social locational dimension).

The data support the notion that both dimensions of authenticity are important to both straightedge types. Music-straightedgers believed that scene participation was important *in addition to* following straightedge norms. Likewise, net-straightedgers believed that there was more to the subculture than simply following rules. In fact, that is why they were participating online in the first place—to find people with similar interests and experiences so that they could collectively express their identification with straightedge subculture. Net-straightedgers typically relied on the internet as their primary, if not sole, source of straightedge information and activity. Most knew no other straightedgers in the face-to-face world. For many of them, the internet was a social space that enabled them to create and express a subcultural identity that could not find support in the face-to-face world. Others chose not to participate in face-to-face straightedge scenes because they did not enjoy the music. Still others reject participating in a local straightedge music scenes because of the people who populated them. As one participant wrote: "I hate scene drama. I hate that there is a hierarchy within the scene, almost like a caste system. I hate everything having to do with them. The world is falling apart and somewhere there is a kid worried because the scene looks bad." From this perspective, we come to see a line between the scene and its proto-typical constituent, the "scenester." The scene was a neutral medium for subcultural participation, while the scenester represented the shallowness of many music-scene members.

Criticism of scenesters is used by net-straightedgers as a wedge to open up the subculture to re-evaluation, with emphasis on their belief that straightedge was changing, and that this change was necessary for the subculture's survival. Among some of the net-straightedgers I interviewed, there was a belief that straightedge was a positive youth subculture which was limited by its association with music scenes. Net-straightedgers made observations about subcultural configurations that worked to exclude people who did not belong to face-to-face music scenes and explained why and how straightedge was changing to incorporate a larger pool of participants. For them, the internet served as a more inclusive subcultural space.

One participant described the straightedge scene in this way: "It's just about creating a posi[tive] space that's drug free and supporting it. That's all, I guess it's about making a difference. Small as it may be, it's something, you know?" Importantly, this definition came from a music-straightedger who stated explicitly elsewhere in the forum that non-hardcore participants were not "really" straightedge. Yet this definition describes exactly what all straightedgers on the internet forum were doing—creating a positive social space to support individual's decision to live a straightedge lifestyle.

THE INTERNET AND SUBCULTURAL LIFE

The diffusion of subcultures through the internet is indicative of the extent to which information and communication technologies inundate our everyday lives. Sherry Turkle, a well-known internet researcher, argues that as people spend more and more time in virtual places, there is a push to break down the boundaries between "real life" and "life on the screen." Breaking down such boundaries will give people more and better opportunities for action, communication and political power. Certainly, we can see such desire in the discourse of net-straightedgers as they work to deconstruct the barriers not only between the online and face-to-face worlds, but between mainstream and sub-cultures. The quality and quantity of debates concerning the differences between music-straightedgers and net-straightedgers represents just how much computer-mediated communication affects subcultures.

The growth of the internet and its continuing penetration into our everyday lives confounds the idea that a face-to-face scene is necessary for subcultures because it allows more individuals who are disconnected from face-to-face hardcore music scenes to nevertheless interact within the subculture. The case under investigation suggests that straightedge is undergoing a noticeable shift in who has access to subcultures and how those people affiliate with them. These shifts are noticeable from a perspective that accepts the fluid and contingent characteristics of identity and culture.

Notebook

1. Straightedge is a subculture within a subculture—it's a branch of punk. (There's a "roots and origins" topic idea for you!) In the next chapter there's an essay about another punk subculture, emo. What other mini-subcultures exist within music subculture, or other subcultures? Consider a project about death or speed metal, queercore punk, or another such sub-subculture.

2. Think about the two dimensions of subcultural participation that Kembrew McLeod developed and J. Patrick Williams explores here. How can you apply this theory to the other subcultures in this book? To the subculture you're studying?

3. In this essay, Williams criticizes "researchers [who] assume that subcultural members all measure authenticity the same way." What do you think about

a scholar who critiques other scholars in his or her own scholarship? Have you come across scholarship elsewhere in this book, or in your research into your own topic, that you feel is flawed in some way?

4. Did you know about straightedge before you read this article? What did you know? How did your sense of the culture change after reading this? To find out more, check out Yahoo's "Society and Culture" directory, which has a straightedge category with many links to online straightedge sources.

My Night as a Wiccan: Dusting Away the Stereotypes

SARAH NORTON

What better night than Halloween to explore the subculture of "witches" in the guise of the pagan religion of Wicca? In a paper she wrote for a composition class on subcultures—the one that inspired this book—Sarah Norton does just that. Norton graduated from Bentley College in 2003 in Marketing. Originally from Orrington, Maine, her plans for the immediate future include pursuing life and a career owning her own business, either in marketing consulting or event planning.

─────────── ✦ ───────────

When considering topics for my final paper on subcultures, I was unsure of what to pick. I started to ask myself questions about subcultures. Which one seems the most intimidating? Which one do the most "freaks" join? Which subculture are the most people afraid of? Why are they afraid? And what makes people exclude, judge and label this different group of people?

I ended up choosing to study Wiccans because of a personal experience I had with stereotyping a few summers ago. I was having lunch with a co-worker; we were talking about her twenty-year-old daughter, Kim. My co-worker told me that Kim had experienced a rough childhood, but that things were starting to turn around for her. Kim was in college, she had a summer job, and was dating a new man, who was twice Kim's age. Some of Kim's friends disapproved of the relationship, but her mother thought the new man had been good for Kim.

One of the things that had changed about Kim since she'd been with the new man was that she'd stopped practicing Wicca, the religion associated with witchcraft. When Kim's mother told me this, I stopped eating and immediately asked if I'd heard her correctly. Like many people, I was confused about the role witches play in society, and many of my attitudes came from television and movies: that they are evil, that they have green skin, ride a broomstick and seek revenge through spells and potions.

In choosing to study Wicca for this paper, I had a mission, first to figure out who these people are, and second, to open not only my own mind but others' as well, especially the minds of some of my stubborn friends who believe their religion offers the only way. I began to research Wicca's origins, and found that although it has roots in earlier forms of witchcraft, today's Wicca was started in the 1960s by a man named Gerald Gardner, who based it on old traditions but modified it to address modern themes and issues. A part of Neo-Paganism, Wicca is an earth-based religion which focuses on the life force of the planet and the skies, and it usually follows the earth's seasonal changes.

I also found out that Wiccans—and many other Pagans—can worship solo or in a group, but that most start solo and eventually join a group, or coven. Like in any group, relationships are shaped and formed in the coven, and roles are established and families created. While some outsiders think that the coven is a "hideout" from the real world, it is actually the focal point of a Wiccan's life, where they live, work, play and learn from the other members.

I started to understand through my research is that being a Wiccan is not about weirdos joining together to dress in black; that they are not vampires; they do not worship the devil. They have just found a new way to practice old religions, and the religion is a chosen path and a lifestyle of positive thought and a loving, accepting, inviting atmosphere. But that didn't stop me from getting nervous when I went to experience it firsthand.

It started like any other day in college; class, work, endless group meetings, a week's worth of homework to do in a night, but this one night in late October I took a break from my studies and grabbed a classmate, Jeff, to go on an adventure: to participate in a Samhain ritual so I could write a paper for the English class we shared.

In the Wiccan tradition, Samhain, which is the origin of the mainstream holiday Halloween, is a time to celebrate the cycle of death and rebirth; it is the beginning of the witch's year. According to Wiccan beliefs, it is the only time of the year when there is an overlap in the underworld and our world, opening up a window for communication with the dead. During this time they honor the memory of those that have passed on, and look forward to the future.

After getting lost on the confusing one-way streets of Boston, we finally arrived at the small chapel on the MIT campus. A long line waited outside of the building; we parked the car and when we returned the line had disappeared. We looked at each other and laughed nervously. The large wooden doors of the chapel opened with ease, and we entered a dim narrow hallway lit only by a few candles. The hallway was full of people who were chanting praise to their female deity.

My heart pounded as I looked around and realized that suddenly society's roles had reversed: we were now the ones who were being looked at as "different." My friend and I exchanged looks again, realizing this was the last chance we had to leave if we felt uncomfortable. But although we felt uncomfortable, there was no reason to: no one had offended us, pushed us to do anything, or made us feel vulnerable in any way. We walked on.

I searched the room to analyze the types of people who had come together to celebrate Samhain. There were people there from all walks of life—many races, ages, and both men and women both represented and led the group at different times. I had come expecting the expected: long black robes, black boots, black make-up, chains and piercings. But I was completely wrong. For the most part, those who put on the ritual were dressed festively in reds, greens and blues. The Wiccans who surrounded us were dressed in street clothes.

Even so, Jeff and I thought it was obvious to others who was there for the first time. We tried to stay under the radar as much as possible, being as quiet and as meek as we could be. We walked forward, following the crowd of people. Sandalwood and pine filled the air, and softly, next to my ear, I could hear Jeff joining in on the chant, humming the words he didn't know. I followed his lead and joined in when I could. The chant stopped and another set of wooden doors opened. At the entrance a man in a green robe, with a large staff in one hand, greeted us warmly as the other hand motioned for us to step inside. Unsure, we stepped ahead. The large circular room was completely empty and only housed a small set of candles that barely lit the room. We followed the walls in and found a place on the floor to stand. Even though we were silent I could tell what Jeff was thinking: this was our last chance to disappear unnoticed if we wanted to.

There were three or four people who started the ceremony. The first was a woman dressed in a long robe, just like the man who had greeted us. She asked everyone to find their spots on the wall and to take two steps forward, and with that a circle was cast. The circle is a tradition in Wiccan culture, demonstrating there is no front and back, that everyone is equal. Another chant had begun—"we are a circle within a circle, with no beginnings and never ending." Again we followed the lead and joined in. We took two more steps forward and a woman dusted the outside of the circle, first with water, then salt, and finally with a broom, to represent aspects of nature and to cleanse it of any evil spirits.

The next step in the Samhain ritual was to show the importance of nature by lighting a candle in honor of the four elements; the Earth, water, fire, and wind. Each candle was the placed to the North, South, East or West of the circle. All the elements pertained to the growth and the need for each element in that year's harvest.

One by one we were led to the center of the room where we built a "boat" to the underworld. We were approached by the head priestess and asked what we feared most; I told her death. She then replied with a reason not to be afraid and lead me to the "boat" where I knelt on my knees. Unsteadily I placed my hand on the stranger's shoulder in front of me and repeated the words over and over, "Hecate, Ceridwen, Dark Mother take us in. Hecate, Ceridwen, let us be reborn." It first started slow and low, but by the time everyone was involved, the chant had grown louder and stronger as the boat that now resembled a large V-shaped ship in the middle of the room was built.

The next step was to be led to the underworld. Trying not to look anxious I looked around for Jeff, but I couldn't find him. I was nervous. I had no idea where we were being led or what was going to happen next, but again, it turned out to be nothing to worry about. We walked down a set of stairs and crossed through a black veil, where a pomegranate seed was handed to us. Our first stop was a small dark room filled with candles and memorabilia of loved ones who were no longer with us. Some participants cried, others reached out to those in pain to comfort and consol them. I just observed and tried to make sense of the whole thing. It was very powerful and inspiring to watch as total strangers comforted each other in their time of hurt and pain. Finally Jeff entered the room, and I sighed with relief.

Following a dark twisting hallway, we were led to a set of stairs that brought us back to the same circular room we had left earlier. Each step in the ritual was narrated as to what was going to happen and why it was happening. We were told that the resurgence back into the original room was meant to signify life and rebirth.

The last ritual in the Samhain ceremony was a spiral dance. The circle was broken and we formed a single file line. We split the line in two and began to pass by each other, holding hands and making sure to look everyone we passed in the eye. We continued to do this until our lines made a huge spiral that raveled and unraveled again.

At the end of the dance we reformed into a circle and reflected upon what we had just experienced. Apple slices were given out to represent the fruit of life; we also had apple cider and shortbread. After refreshments we sang goodbye to the elements, the ocean, the breezes and the mountains. The priestess opened the circle and we sang "Merry we have met, merry we have been, merry shall we part, and merry meet again, blessed be."

After the priest and priestess said their closing words, they asked the group to introduce themselves. One by one, people stated their names, schools, and how long they had been practicing. For many it was their first time experiencing a coven. The floor was then opened for thoughts and comments. Lots of people were comfortable expressing how they felt. Before the priest opened to the doors to let us out, he went around to each individual and hugged us and thanked us for coming, and invited us to stay afterward to make new friends.

All of the anxiety that I had before I attended this ceremony turned out to be a waste of time. The ceremony was not strange or scary in any way; it actually made a lot of sense and the people were very inviting. Although I am not a practicing Wiccan, I can appreciate what they worship and I can look at them with new eyes.

Notebook

1. Do you think religious groups count as subcultures? Why or why not?
2. Conduct an interview with a few people that examines their views on Wicca and its followers. Write an essay that discusses the findings and compares them to your own attitude toward Wicca before and after reading this essay.
3. Some states have legislated rights for Wicca so that it can enjoy the benefits of other religious groups. Research recent legislation about Wicca in your state.
4. For more information on Wicca, check out these two books: *Belief Beyond Boundaries: Wicca, Celtic Spirituality and the New Age*, by Joanne Pearson (Ashgate, 2002), and *Magic and Witchcraft: From Shamanism to the Technopageans*, by Nevill Drury (Thames & Hudson, 2003). Or check the shelves at your local public library or New Age bookstore—they are sure to have a number of titles.
5. With the class, play "Subculture Ritual Charades." As a group, come up with a ritual particular to a specific subculture and act it out for the class without any sound, so that they can guess the ritual and subculture to which it belongs.

She Rips When She Skates: Female Skateboarders as Active Subcultural Participants

NATALIE PORTER

What happens when women become members of a subculture almost exclusively dominated by men? In what ways do they gain satisfaction and power if the very subculture itself resists their participation? Natalie Porter asks these questions in an essay based on her thesis paper, "Female Skateboarders and Their Negotiation of Space and Identity." Porter graduated in 2003 from Concordia University in Montreal, Canada with an MA in Media Studies. She has been skateboarding since 1995 and is currently working on a book called A Visual History of Women in Skateboarding.

———————— ✦ ————————

The scholarly definition of a "subculture" has evolved over the past century, but is generally recognized for the way in which a group of individuals with common interests come together and direct a challenge towards dominant structures and mainstream ways of thinking. Whether or not this challenge is effective or beneficial to society is another topic for debate, but for the purposes of this paper I have focused upon skateboarders who form a subculture and contest the boundaries surrounding the use of "public" space. Skateboarders often ignore restrictions such as city by-laws imposed upon them to limit and condemn their movements. But, for female skateboarders, the situation is more complex because they must also overcome socially-constructed barriers to even participate.

To pursue and excel at skateboarding women must disregard traditional expectations for girls to remain passive, compliant and subordinate, expectations often perpetuated in the media, especially women's magazines. They must also negotiate attitudes from within the subculture that attempt to ignore or dismiss their involvement. According to Iain Borden in his book *Skateboarding, Space and the City: Architecture and the Body* (Oxford, 2001), "skateboard companies and magazines have increasingly used misogynist treatment of women as a way of selling skateboards," and meanwhile, "female skaters are not explicitly discouraged, their relative absence is only occasionally noted and implicitly condoned."

And yet, despite this lack of support, female skateboarders have persevered by creating their own visibility and networks of support through websites, videos, zines, and organizing "all-girls" competitions, which has established a unique, international community. In this essay, I will trace a history of women in skateboarding, describe their activities as cultural producers, highlighting my own group of skateboarding peers in Montréal, Canada.

THE HISTORY OF WOMEN IN SKATEBOARDING

Skateboarding has gone through several trends and cycles of popularity, and these movements have had significant affect on female skateboarders. Skateboards emerged in the 1950s as a child's toy, two sets of roller skates applied to a board, and the first commercial skateboards called the Roller Derby Skateboard hit the marketplace in 1959.

In 1963, the first skateboard contest was held in Hermosa, California, and skateboarding was established as a popular youth activity. In the 1960s and early 1970s women excelled at the freestyle and slalom disciplines, which consisted of performing flat-ground tricks like spinning 360 degrees, and weaving through obstacles down a hill. Borden states, "Female skaters have always existed even while broader conventions discourage them from skateboarding. As one female skater put it, 'we are few and far between, but we are out here,'" and he speculates that possibly 25 percent of skaters in Southern California in the 1970s were female. Female legends from this early era include Pat McGee, who appeared on the cover of *Life* magazine in May 14, 1965 doing a hand-stand on her skateboard, and competitive skateboarders such as Ellen O'Neal, Robin Logan, Ellen Berryman, Kim Cespedes, Laura Thornhill, and Peggy Oki.

Oki was the only female member of the notorious Zephyr Skate Team from an area in Los Angeles nicknamed "Dogtown," featured in the documentary film, *Dogtown and Z-Boys* (Dir. Stacy Peralta, 2001). Oki, a hardcore surfer, joined the Zephyr Team at age 18 and fit in well with the rebellious group. At the Del Mar National competition in 1975, Oki's performance was particularly controversial because the tricks she performed were the same ones performed by the male skateboarders, even though she was good enough to win the prize in the freestyle competition.

As a result of the female competitors protesting Oki's unconventional style, her name was not included on the winner's list, and after several frustrating experiences at contests, she made the decision to focus on her education, while other Z-Boys went on to acquire fame and sponsorships. Oki continues to skate and surf today, as well as pursue an activist/environmental lifestyle that is reflected in her artwork.

With their roots in surfing, the Z-Boys transferred their skills from the waves to skateboarding in empty pools often on private property, which they would access by trespassing. A skateboard session at a pool was an intense affair since it was known that the police would be quickly contacted if they were discovered. During these sessions there was a feeling of tension and energy because skateboarders were very territorial, and information regarding the pool's location was often secretive. As skateboarders sought out the risky terrain of the pool, male skateboarders took on a more macho attitude that reflected their social-outcast status, and rejected female participation. According to Borden, "the pools in particular thus became places of initiation, dangerous (through accident or social confrontation) places where young men might prove themselves to their peers . . . The focus here was on danger, pain and bodily injury, but also on the competitively collective nature of the group, created from a set of extreme individual attitudes and actions."

Female skateboarders were rarely included in these sessions, because it was assumed that they could not handle the aggressive scene, skate the steep transition, or defend themselves when pursued by the police. And perhaps women were just not interested in being intimidated by male skateboarders within this confined space.

Cement skateboard parks were then designed and built for public use and allowed more skateboarders to gain confidence riding this terrain. Vicki Vickers was not to be fazed by the new vertical concrete skateboarding or the macho attitude that ensued during the late 1970s. As Michael Brooke writes in *The Concrete Wave: The History of Skateboarding*, "In an interview with *SkateBoarder* [December 1979], Vicki lamented the poor coverage of female skaters and the lack of respect that pro women skaters were receiving. 'I'll be damned if we're not out there breakin' our necks just like the guys . . . we're getting burned. How many issues has it been since you've seen a girl's face? About five.'" This sort of statement could easily be directed towards popular skateboard magazines today, but what has changed is that female skateboarders are no longer waiting for male-owned and operated productions to accommodate them. This attitude has emerged due to the persistence of several talented female skateboarders.

After a short-lived boom in popularity, skateboarding went into decline as parks closed due to concerns over insurance and injuries, and only a few individuals continued to skate into the early 1980s. A skateboarder named Carabeth Burnside maintained her passion for vertical ramps and pool-riding during this period. Burnside began skateboarding in the mid-1970s as a child. When skateboarding stopped being a popular youth activity Burnside took up soccer and karate, but returned to it while attending university, although women skateboarders had practically disappeared. Burnside soon found herself riding only with men and often felt uncomfortable. She pointed out that it was difficult for females to feel part of the skateboarding scene because, as she told Jennifer Egan for her *Conde Nast: Sports for Women article* "Girl Over Board," "Who wants to go skateboarding at 13 and get made fun of by guys?" Burnside briefly established her own board company and competed against the men in the vert competitions, but it was only in 1998, with the growing popularity of extreme sports, did she receive significant recognition from *Vans* skateboard shoe-company. *Vans* sponsored her, designed a popular "signature" Carabeth shoe, featured her in several advertisements, and promoted her reputation as a skateboard legend. Burnside continues to compete professionally in both skateboarding and snowboarding, and organized all-female skateboarding tours in the summers of 2002 and 2003, where the participants performed demonstrations at skateboard parks across the United States.

In the late 1980s, skateboarding made another development, where urban obstacles found in the streets like curbs, ledges, handrails and stairs began to be utilized. It is within the streets that the identity of skateboarding as a subculture was established and as a result, female skateboarders were further marginalized since, according to feminist subcultural theorist Angela McRobbie, "it has always been on the street that most subcultural activity takes place . . . it both proclaims the publicisation of the group and at the same time ensures its male dominance. For the street remains in some ways taboo for women." There are always exceptions to these rules, but it became increasingly difficult for female skateboarders to gain acceptance in this era. A hardcore punk attitude was prevalent among the skateboard community in the 1980s, with aggressive music accompanying their activities, board graphics that displayed sexualized images of women, and several professional male skateboarders who made statements that females should not skate at all.

FEMALE SKATERS AS CULTURAL PRODUCERS

It has been a frustrating process for young women to feel recognized and appreciated by the skateboard industry, especially among media representations of skateboarding from both the mainstream and inside of the subculture. Skaters are shown to be predominantly young men in their teens and early twenties, with broadly accommodating dispositions toward skaters of different classes and ethnicity. Gender relations are, however, more problematic, with female skaters usually discouraged by the forces of convention, including within skateboarding those of sexual objectification.

As Becky Beal and Lisa Weidman write in their article "Authenticity in the Skateboarding World," "This sexual objectification is often exhibited through skateboard advertisements, where companies attempt to appeal to the male majority and display masculine (hetero)sexuality and sexual prowess through the use of female models who . . . sometimes function as trophies or adornments for fully-clothed (and usually recognizable) male skateboarders. In other cases, the female models appear only with the products being advertised (or even without the products) and function as sexual enticements to the young male readers."

These stereotypes reflect a common tactic used by the male-dominated sportsworld to ridicule women athletes and discredit them by implying that they are lesbians, as Susan Birrell and Nancy Theberge posit in their article "Ideological Control of Women in Sport." This practice has been questioned and challenged, but women athletes still feel pressure to conform to a certain heterosexualized image, especially if they want to be sponsored. Mainstream media representations of skateboarding often reflect this practice of exclusion and dismissal, and when they do include female skateboarders, such as in the recent Warner Bros. film *Grind* (dir. Casey LaScala, 2003) with the "sexy skater chick" character named Jamie, there is an attempt to capitalize off the recent "cool" skater-girl image.

Fortunately, some young women are able to ignore the media's practices. Skateboarders like Elissa Steamer have begun to challenge assumptions that there are only male skateboarders. Steamer is of particular importance to this movement because the skateboard media industry had no choice but to recognize her skills. The skateboarding world was completely disrupted when she became sponsored by *Toy Machine* skateboard-company, and produced ground-breaking feature parts in their videos, *Welcome to Hell* (Toy Machine, 1996), and in *Jump Off a Building* (Toy Machine, 1998).

To some critics, Steamer was regarded as a "token girl skater" with unusual and exceptional talent, and many felt threatened by her, regarding her style and appearance as masculine. Others, though, felt that regardless of this response, Steamer was a vision of the future for female skateboarders and a role-model. For many girls, Steamer was recognized as living proof that they had a right to occupy space at skateboard parks and in the city streets, and enjoy skateboarding. Steamer's talent has also provided her with a professional "signature" skateboard model by *Bootleg* board-company, a shoe sponsorship with *Etnies*, a character playing-figure in the video-game *Tony Hawk: Pro Skater*, and meanwhile, she continues to be seen in skateboarding advertisements and videos.

Due to Steamer's visibility, female skateboarders began to elevate their performance standards and gain confidence in their identity, even though they are still in a minority. While it has become obvious that women athletes are capable of performing aggressive or rough activities, some male skateboarders still assume that there are fewer girls skateboarding because, "girls don't want to have scars on their shins," as Beal writes in her article "The Subculture of Skateboarding: Beyond Social Resistance," or because they "don't look good with bruises," rather than questioning social expectations of feminine passivity or the lack of encouragement from the skateboard media industry. During an interview, Mathilde, who is 22 years old and has been skateboarding for 6 years, was reflecting upon the argument made by some male skateboarders who say that girls only skateboard to find a boyfriend. She exclaimed that, "I wouldn't break my ass everyday just to go out with guy skateboarders . . . I wouldn't get bruises and stuff!" Her friend Amy, who is 21 years old and has been skateboarding for 3 years, responded by saying, "When you spend the whole summer trying to learn something and then you do it and you did it, and you were like, 'That was so much better than anything ever' it doesn't matter that the last thirty times I tried to do it I broke my legs and smashed myself up. I think it feels good to get beat up by a skateboard sometimes."

Just like male skateboarders, female skateboarders often celebrate and document their bruises and injuries as proof of their active participation, as well as a rejection of feminine standards that expect women to appear flawless and perfect. Amy explained that she was aware of being different from most people she sees on the streets:

"I feel different when I'm walking past people with my skateboard or I'm skating. They sort of look and realize that I'm not a boy even though I look like a boy. I don't have a problem with it. I feel unique. There's not a lot a people who wear what they want to . . . I didn't want to have to wear a uniform and be somebody I'm not, or buy clothes that I am not comfortable in . . . You can still be feminine — I'm kind of a crusty feminine."

Amy feels proud of her skateboarder identity because it distinguishes her as an individual who was pursuing her passion and not compromising her own sense of femininity.

For a female skateboarder to feel confident in her identity it is often necessary that she find like-minded women to share stories and encourage each other, and it was in the mid-to-late 1990s that women came together with more focus than previous attempts. An important development was the New York City-based, *Rookie* skateboards, the first female-owned skateboard-company which gathered a strong team of primarily female skateboarders in 1996 and began featuring them in their advertisements.

This was the beginning of a slow infiltration of images of female skateboarders into the skateboard media industry. The message was that female skateboarders were "out there," and there would always be a buzz of excitement among my friends when a new Rookie photo was printed of sponsored riders Jesse Van Roechoudt, Jamie Reyes, Lauren Mollica and Lisa Whitaker. The owners, Catherine Lyons and Elska Sandor, were irritated when they were initially labeled and dismissed as a "girls' company," but when this wore off *Rookie* emerged as a respected skateboard company with a unique mentality, that has even appealed to some male skateboarders, rather than as a specialty company just for girls. *Rookie* also came to represent a status symbol among female skateboarders, who would wear their clothing and ride their boards to suggest that they were "in the know" regarding the significance of this company.

Female skateboarders were and continue to be considered a novelty because they are often isolated geographically or dispersed in a major city. But, in an attempt to interact with each other, an alternative community through zines, websites and internet forums was developed. The *Villa Villa Cola* zine was started in 1997 by skateboarding sisters Tiffany and Nicole Morgan from San Diego, and ran for three years before the members chose to pursue other projects. It featured photographs, artwork, travel diaries, reviews, and an advice column for readers. The zine had an international following, and expanded into a website, clothing-line and an independent video called *Striking Fear into Teenage Girls Hearts*, featuring their group of friends, Faye Jamie, Van Nguyen, Lori D., Jamie Sinift, and

Lisa Whitaker. The production inspired many others to do the same: *Bruisers* made by Heidi in New Orleans, *Check it Out Girls* by Liza and Ana Paula in Brazil, a zine out of California called *SwashBuckler*, and *50-50: Skateboarding and Gender* made by Zanna in Portland.

Young women gain a sense of community through zines and more confidence to skateboard in public spaces, even when they might not be in physical contact with other female skateboarders. The virtual territory that girl skaters are creating include "Betty-boards," "Girls Skate Better," "Gurlz on Boardz," "Skate of Mind," "The Side Project," and "Frontside Betty." In "Frontside Betty" Denise Williams wrote,

> Once upon a time, I was a lonely girl skater in a big city. I went to the indoor park a few days a week, but there were never any other girls there and the guys seemed to want little to do with the girl in the corner teaching herself kickturns. As much as I loved skating, it was necessary to give myself a serious pep talk to get motivated to go back to the park each day.
>
> On the wall beside my desk there was a picture of Jessie Van that I'd torn out of a magazine, one of the few pictures of a female skater that I'd seen in print. Each time I needed motivation, I looked at that picture and it reminded me how much I enjoyed skateboarding, how much I had a right to be a skateboarder, and how it wasn't worth it to let loneliness and lame people get in the way of that. I went back to the park.
>
> So began Frontside Betty, a site for girl skateboarders and anyone who loves them. We're frustrated by the small amount of skate resources online (and off) that include girls in the skateboarding world. The ratio of male to female skaters is ridiculously lopsided, and the representation of girl skaters in the skateboarding media is even more so. Frontside aims to be a resource of images, reviews, information, and stories for the world of girls' skating. Because not only do we deserve it, but sometimes we need it.

"Frontside Betty" has a detailed links section of other related sites of interest to female skateboarders, a chat forum to connect the users, and the site itself is always expanding, accepting written and visual contributions from female skateboarders.

The rest of the skateboard community is finally taking notice, and the responses are generally positive. In a review of the "Frontside Betty" site in *Transworld Skateboarding* magazine, it began, "A whole Web site devoted to females on skateboards? Yep. It's pretty damn cool, too . . . Overall, there's excellent pictures and coverage, a good links section, and a Web forum to keep everyone in touch." This brief mention of the website in the most popular skateboard magazine is worth noting, but amongst the hundreds of pages of advertisements and articles featuring male professional skateboarders, I was fortunate to happen upon it. And yet women like Williams have not been deterred by the rare inclusion of female-oriented skateboard activities and as of the winter 2003 she began producing the first-ever, free skateboard magazine called *Push*, devoted solely to female skateboarders. These zines, websites and now the *Push* skateboard magazine have established an alternative skateboard media industry, in contrast to those magazines sold in skateboard shops or at the corner store, which tend to have a rigid format that rarely gives female skateboarders any recognition.

The subculture of skateboarding is unique in the way that its members have consistently documented their performance, style, and evolution through photography and film. With the increasing accessibility of video equipment, skateboarders have used this technology to exhibit the dynamic energy of skateboarding, with hundreds of video titles by both large-scale and small, local productions being made each year worldwide. Representation of female skateboarders in videos occur primarily when sponsored women are given a part in a company video, which was the case with Elissa Steamer. Besides these rare cameos, there have been several documentaries on female skateboarders, including *Live and Let Ride* (1999), an independent film by Tara Cooper, and the most recent being *AKA: Girl Skater* (Dir. Mike Hill, 2002). The film documents a team of professional female skateboarders who are sponsored by Gallaz, a skateboard shoe company designed for women, and their adventures while on a trip to Australia, where they compete in the 2002 "Globe World Cup of Skateboarding" girls' street event.

Like *Dogtown and Z-Boys*, the *AKA: Girl Skater* documentary reflects an influential period and group within the subculture's history. Even though it has not attracted mainstream attention to the same degree, the girls' contribution is now being recognized among the skateboarding community. *AKA: Girl Skater* was reviewed in the popular skateboard magazine *Slap*, which acknowledged how skateboarding tends to act like a fraternity, but that it is important to support female skateboarders.

The popular skateboard media industry is slowly realizing that female participants are genuine members of the subculture, and do not necessarily have to become "one of the guys" to be accepted.

It was often the case for the lone female skateboarder who wanted the support of male skateboarders to prove that she was not a "groupie" by adopting a masculine standard of dress and attitude. Fortunately, with the growing network of female skateboarders, the attitude is gradually shifting towards an acceptance of a variety of styles. For example, at the 5th Annual Transworld Skateboarding Awards ceremony, May 2003, the Female Vert Skater of the Year, Jen O'Brien, was photographed beside the Female Street Skater, Amy Caron and the contrast was quite apparent. O'Brien looked feminine, as though she was ready to go to the prom, while Caron was wearing a mesh baseball cap and "Anti-Social" t-shirt. And yet, both skateboarders and their styles are legitimate and respected.

THE STORY OF THE FEMALE SKATEBOARDERS OF MONTREAL

This is an exciting time for female skateboarders. The scene continues to gain momentum, which is apparent within my own community of female skateboarders in Montréal, Canada. While the women in *AKA: Girl Skater* are validated due to their high level of skill, I want to also offer an insider perspective from everyday participants through observations of and interviews with my peers over a two-year period. It is important to recognize a variety of female voices, because by offering their own version of subcultural reality, female skateboarders undercut various methods to ignore women and their experiences, and proclaim their right to occupy and enjoy public spaces for their own personal benefit.

In Montréal, there is a core group of fourteen women who skateboard and socialize together consistently. I interviewed nine of the women between the ages of 21 and 33, primarily in their early twenties, and also a woman who was 18 and had made the decision to take up skateboarding instead of observing her boyfriend skateboard from the sidelines.

I generally tried to let the discussion flow towards their interests, inspirations and concerns, but would initiate the conversation by inquiring about how they first began skateboarding. Brigitte, who is 29 years old and has been skateboarding for 7 years, explained that she saw a skateboard in a store window when she was twelve and thought it looked like fun, but her father thought it was too dangerous.

"So," she said. "I negotiated with him for six months, he made me sign a contract, and the contract stated that I would wear my helmet and my wrist guards every time . . . I began cruising to school. But guess what I did? I brought my backpack and once I was down my street and around the corner, I took off my helmet and pads!" Brigitte continued to skate with some boys in her neighborhood until she turned sixteen and took a break for several years to work and, "There were issues with my father because he felt it was socially unacceptable to be a skateboarder. He said that 'Oh, you have to grow up.'" It was only after she took up snowboarding and became more independent that Brigitte decided to begin skateboarding again.

Louise, who is 22 years old and has been skateboarding for 10 years, was very self-motivated when it came to learning how to skateboard and eventually she competed at an international level. She told me that, "Nobody was encouraging, some guys tried to not let me skateboard. I just became addicted to it . . . my guy friends would skateboard a lot, and I would always want to try their skateboards. But, they kept on telling me, 'Skateboarding is not for girls!' So, I just said, 'Fuck it!' and one day I went out and bought myself a skateboard. I started learning ollies in my street all by myself, and then, when it would rain I would just go in my garage and ollie on flatground."

Louise was not deterred by the young men who attempted to intimidate her and preserve the skatepark as a male domain. She remarked that, "I think skateboarding made me meet so many different people, now I'm able to deal with any situation."

Louise's story is in contrast to Mathilde's experience, which was very positive because she learned to skate in her rural town with her brother and his friends, and was welcomed into the skateboard community of Montréal without hesitation. Julie, who is 23 years old and has been skateboarding for 7 years, also had a brother to skate with, but she preferred to skateboard alone until she began to go to the skatepark regularly, where she became accepted as part of the local scene. Amy was actually introduced to skateboarding by a female friend who gave her a skateboard. "My friend was like, 'Hey, you should come skate at the park.' I was really scared, but finally one day I went, it was fun and I didn't stop going back."

Going to a skateboard park can often be a very intimidating experience and one's first time takes some courage, especially as a lone female. Sometimes the group of guys can be encouraging, while at other times they can be distant and rude. Gaby, who is 24 years old and has been skateboarding for 4 years, recalled going to the indoor skatepark in Montréal called the "Tazmahal," where she felt intimidated.

It was like everyone turned and looked at me, all the guys, and they're all watching me while I do something because you're a girl and they want to see if you can really skate. . . . Nobody really approached me, the guys who would approach me, it would just seem like they would hit on me . . . . It was weird because I just wanted to go there and skateboard . . . it was so intimidating, my knees were shaking so hard I couldn't do anything. . . . It felt like nobody really wanted to let me into the "inner circle" and I skated there for the entire winter.

Meanwhile, Aida, who is 23 years old and has been skateboarding for 5 years, was oblivious to these attitudes and stated that she never had problems except that, there was "one person that told me one day, 'Get out of my way!' But I said, 'Fuck, the Tazmahal is not yours!'" Aida acknowledged that perhaps people stared at her, "But, I wasn't even looking over, I was just like, 'I want to skateboard, I need a break.'" Gaby expressed admiration for Aida because, "She goes all the time regardless of who is there, if it's men or women. She wouldn't even dream of letting anyone make her feel intimidated about it." It is often up to the individual and whether or not they will let external attitudes hinder their participation.

Most of the women I interviewed also recognized the positive influence of certain male skateboarders. Marie France referred fondly to various individuals, such as the guys who worked at the skateshop called "Spin" because they gave her free skateboard equipment and made her feel welcome by acknowledging her at skatespots and offering advice. Aida also referred to "Spin," where she works, and how much she appreciated the encouragement of her male co-workers.

Gaby noticed how it often seemed that it was the guys who were the most secure and confident in their ability that did not dismiss or judge her. She described meeting a new friend named Joe, who is a well-known skateboarder in Montréal.

I was talking to him and he was saying, "Yeah, I saw you on the mini ramp, that's really cool!" And I was like, "Yeah, I felt kinda bad because all these guys were skating and I just feel like I'm taking up their time and stuff." And Joe was like, "Who cares man? You're a body, I'm a body, you're entitled to your space!" And he's a really good skateboarder, you know what I mean? He's also somebody who could like, go around pretending like he rules, he owns the place and everything, and meanwhile, he's telling me, who can't even ollie, that I'm entitled to the same amount of space and the same amount of time as he is. And it's true!

The comment that Joe made was particularly perceptive and exceptional, but it reveals that there are some young men who do take into consideration issues of space and equality, which are put into practice when young women position themselves in such situations that demand a re-evaluation of constructed norms.

While many female skateboarders appreciate the encouragement from male skateboarders, especially when they are beginning and perhaps have no female peers, others are fortunate to find women who share their passion and create a network of support. In many of the interviews, the girls described when they encountered another female skateboarder and how friendships were developed. Marie France recalled meeting a very talented skateboarder named Alison who was visiting the city for the summer: "She was really good . . . and that's what really told me, 'Okay, you can skate, no matter if you're a girl'. . . . She has a nice style, she has a good attitude, she's funny, and she did this video part and I thought that was pretty cool . . . she 'heel-flipped' six stairs, and 'switch ollies' up the block!"

As the group came together during the summer of 2002, Julie remarked that, "I love it, now that all the girls have met and we are a team. It's so good, man. We're always together. I know that I can call you and know that you are going to come or if you can't come I got a list of ten persons to call, you know, other girls." Julie then recalled meeting her friend Anne-Sophie at a local competition and how they began skating the mini ramp together. They both shared an interest in competitions and traveled together to the 2002 "All Girls Skate Jam" in New York City placing 2nd and 3rd in the amateur street division. This competition series was established in 1997 by Patty Segovia, a skateboarder and photographer who responded to the fact that her female friends were not getting recognition from the skateboard media industry or opportunities to compete like they deserved, and organized the competition series, primarily in the U.S. The "All Girls Skate Jam" encourages female skateboarders of all abilities to participate within both the vert and street disciplines. The event has also inspired similar events in other countries, such as the "Girls Skate Out" in Britain, the "Gallaz Jam" series in Australia and France, and "Ride Like a Girl" competition in Canada.

Several of the girls in Montréal enjoy competitions, but Mathilde noted that, "nobody between us is in competition with each other, you know what I mean, we're all different, we all have a different style, a different type of trick and we all do our own thing. And, we still do it together." Among this group, there is diverse range of skills, ages, and backgrounds: lower to middle upper class, broken homes, strict religious upbringings, and intimate families. However, it must be acknowledged that just because there is a common interest in skateboarding among a group of females does not guarantee that everyone will be close friends, and I have observed personality conflicts that threatened to break up this newly formed group. Fortunately, there seems to be an understanding that tensions are to be forgotten when skateboarding becomes the priority and an experience is shared.

Erika was the most articulate skateboarder that I interviewed regarding feminist issues and values, which she had the confidence to act out within the skateboard "session" environment. Erika's specialty is skating the mini-ramp and bowl, and she described a session she had in California with a group of male friends. The session was suddenly interrupted by two cameramen, who barged onto the ramp and proceeded to set-up a scene where a young woman model wearing a bikini, barefoot, holding a skateboarding, was pretending to "drop-in" to the ramp. Erika was insulted and explained, "I'm not a person that's just like, 'whatever' . . . therefore, the only thing to do was to 'drop in' in front of her because I was so mad . . . I said, 'I think we're skating here! I think we were just fucking skating! We were having a session!' And I dropped in, and I 'kickturn' right next to her foot, like I scared her . . . And I kept skating."

Erika was concerned that her group of male peers would ostracize her as a result of this daring move, especially since some of the guys thought the model was cute and were concerned that she could have been hurt, but some of the guys applauded her actions. Erika was adamant that people should be more questioning of the world, and has decided to create a zine called "Armpit," to be a vehicle for presenting her ideas. The first edition was released in July 2003.

Female skateboarders are clearly inhabiting and sharing the same spaces as their male peers, but on different terms. I know that when I take over a skatespot downtown with my friends, or cruise past streams of traffic in a jam, forcing the drivers to acknowledge my existence, I feel powerful. These actions may not be overtly challenging society, but they are statements of resistance, which feminist scholar Lauraine Leblanc regards as key to girls' subcultural participation. In her book *Pretty in Punk: Girls' Gender Resistance in a Boys' Subculture* (Rutgers University Press, 1999), Leblanc write, "This resistance against gender roles must be considered when we examine girls' deviance. While it may be true that males use subcultures to explore masculinity, it is also the case that some females use subcultures to repudiate or reconstruct femininity."

One way to showcase this reconstruction is through the medium of film. One of my interviewees, Mathilde, had not planned on making an all-girls skateboard video, but what resulted after accumulating more and more footage of her friends was a fifteen minute video called "Boy," the first of its kind in Canada. Mathilde explained that she started filming because she observed her male friends working on a video, and imagined herself in the same position.

The process of filming was a rewarding experience for Mathilde and the others in our group who were filmed, and when the video was completed in March 2003 we organized a video premiere at a local bar downtown, where a crowd of approximately two hundred skateboarders, friends and family, came to support the production. The response and the demand for copies of the video have been encouraging, with female and male skateboarders from Australia, Britain, U.S.A., and across Canada, requesting copies. The video was of interest to Lisa Whitaker, a filmer/skateboarder in California who was enthusiastic to meet women like Mathilde who shared similar interests, and is now selling the video through her website, "The Side Project." The video has also sparked local interest, and the editors of the skateboard magazine *Exposé* reviewed the film, and asked the girls to contribute two pages of female-oriented skateboard stories and interviews each issue.

Through cultural production and the use of media technology, female skateboarders challenge past subcultural research and position themselves as independent members of the subculture, rather than simply accessories to male activities. As Erika explains, "through skateboarding, I feel like I have my own life. That's where I feel so much different from girls my own age . . . I am very confident that I am doing the right thing. That's crazy, it goes against everything especially when living in a big city. For guys it's easy. But when I'm in the metro . . . and people stare at me, like I'm weird, there's definitely envy because you're doing something that you like. You're true to yourself and it's the most precious thing in life. Skateboarding saved my life."

For girls like Erika, skateboarding is not just an image but rather a chosen lifestyle based on their own standard of authenticity, and a rejection of mainstream visions of success. If individuals are recognized for being part of a subculture based on their refusal to accept dominant attitudes, it is apparent that female skateboarders are doing exactly this. They have overcome acceptable notions of passive femininity, as well as, exclusionary practices from within the subculture, to establish a community of their own.

Endnote: The title of this essay refers to a song called "Possessed to Skate" by the Suicidal Tendencies, which was a popular skate anthem in the 1980s. When learning to skate, I would hum the chorus, "He rips/ when he skates/ cause he never hesitates . . ." to motivate myself, but would change the gender in the lyrics.

Notebook

1. What stereotypes do you hold about women your age? About men? Have those stereotypes changed over the course of your life? How and why? How do you think the dominant culture's stereotypes about men and women have changed?

2. Compare the female skateboarders in Natalie Porter's essay to the male skaters described in "The Lords of Dogtown" in the first chapter. How would you characterize the difference? What different things do the girls get out of the subculture than the boys get? What different things do they bring to it? How do the rhetorical styles of the essays differ, and how do you see that difference as related to the different subject matters?

3. Are there other subcultures like skateboarding where most of the participants are one gender or the other? Could you write an essay about the men who participate in a female-centered subculture?

4. What do you think about Porter's choice to include lots of quotes from the female skateboarders? What do you think the advantages and disadvantages could be of letting subculture members speak in their own words in a scholarly essay such as this one, or the one you're writing?

A Different View of Hackers
ZHI ZHU

Sometimes a subculture that is perceived as negative by the mainstream culture is actually contributing a service to society, as Zhi Zhu argues here about computer hackers. Zhu majored in business at Bentley College and plans to pursue a career in finance. His inspiration for this paper came from his lifelong interest in computers and electronics. In his spare time, Zhi works with inner-city youth from the city of Boston where he now resides.

◆

There was a time when the Internet was only a niche, a novelty, something intriguing but cool, a toy for tech wizards and cyber geeks. Fast-forward ten years: never has one technology so rapidly and completely transformed everything. It is no longer a novelty, but an essential tool for commerce, communication, and information. Those who are not connected are now supposedly on the wrong side of the "digital divide" and endangered by their lack of access.

However, as the importance of information technology has increased, there has been a growing concern about the security, vulnerability, and privacy of these networks. Is it safe to send my credit card number to E*Trade? Is WebMD selling my health information to pharmaceutical companies? Will this supposedly confidential information be used against me? The relatively anonymous and decentralized nature of the Internet has only exacerbated these problems.

With this recent boom in information technology, a fear surrounding malicious teenage hackers has re-emerged in the minds of the public. Computer hackers have become the subject of widespread scrutiny in the media, which has resulted in intense monitoring by the government. Stories about hackers bringing e-commerce sites such as Amazon.com and Ebay to their knees have become commonplace in mainstream publications. Due to unfavorable coverage of these isolated incidents, the American public has held many misconceptions of the average hacker. However, the teen hacking subculture contributes to the development of the Internet rather than serving as a detriment to its progress. I hope that my research will serve to dismiss these popular misconceptions about the hacker subculture, and provide background for a greater understanding of the role hackers play in cyberspace and society at large.

The term hackers first came into usage in the late 1960s and early 1970s in the Artificial Intelligence lab at the Massachusetts Institute of Technology. As the 2001 TV documentary *Hackers: Computer Outlaws* on The Learning Channel pointed out, the term was an honorable title for the teenage lab workers back then, and it originated when MIT students created hacks—programming shortcuts—so they could execute programs on a mainframe with greater speed. In the early days, hacking mostly involved the telephone system. These types of hackers were better known as "phone phreaks." "Phone phreaks" were curious teens who cracked the phone systems in order to make free long distance calls by using a device called a Blue Box. Essentially, what the Blue Box did was make distinctive sounds into the receiver of the telephone, tricking the phone company's computer into thinking that the noise was made by its own equipment. This practice went on for a couple of years until the officials at the phone company caught up with the hackers' practice. It was because of this incident that the media began to pay attention to the world of hacking and the public began to acknowledge the existence of hackers.

According to The Learning Channel documentary, the subculture of hacking exploded with the introduction of the Altair personal computer. For the first time, computer enthusiasts were able to have a machine of their own. These enthusiasts realized they could do fascinating things on these tiny, self-built home machines. With a few adjustments and a couple lines of code, amateur computer programmers were able to create games and play music on these little gadgets. By having a machine of their own, both programmers and enthusiasts could learn the inner workings of the computer and improve their skills in computing.

Later, the introduction of the Internet allowed hackers to take their computing skills onto the net. Soon, computer buffs discovered the usefulness this new technology had for them. Electronic Bulletin Boards, where users dial in via a modem, began popping up.

These bulletin boards allowed users all over the world to share information and knowledge with each other. At the same time, many individuals discovered that they could use the Internet to penetrate other peoples' machines. Their intention was not to cause harm to the systems that they hacked into, but was out of mere curiosity for how things work. These hackers would break into computer systems of corporations and analyze the hardware and software that control those systems. Many times, they would dissect the codes on many of the company's software to understand the logic behind it. Because computer technology was relatively new at the time, there were not many laws or consequences surrounding the hacking of other people's systems.

It was during this time that many of today's famous hackers, such as Kevin Mitnick, Mark Abene a.k.a. "Phiber Optik," and Robert Morris, became known to the world, according to the book *Cybercrime: Law Enforcement, Security and Surveillance in the Information Age* (Routledge, 2000). Things began to turn from fun to ugly for the hackers in 1983 when the movie *War Games* shone a light into the hidden faces of hacking, and warned audiences nationwide that hackers could get into any computer system. Not long after the movie's release, Congress passed the Federal Computer Fraud and Abuse Act of 1986 to combat the problem of hacking. The freedom hackers possessed is now gone.

In the early days of computer hacking, the availability of computers was scarce, and teens penetrated systems to get a better understanding of how computers worked. Doing so allowed them to discover flaws in software code or hardware design in the system they hacked, which in turn allowed system engineers to correct them and improve the quality of their product. This tradition continues today: many security experts spend most of their time hacking into other people's computer to find vulnerability in them. The results are usually reported back to the designer or corporation allowing them to correct it. Because of their hard work and code of morality of hackers, many system security issues have been discovered, and are prevented from landing in the wrong hands.

Hackers have been in existence since the creation of personal computers, but what exactly makes them tick? Marc Rogers, a behavioral science researcher at the University of Manitoba in Winnipeg, Canada, has identified some basic trends of computer hackers. In his article *Psychology of Hackers: Steps toward a New Taxonomy*, Rogers has broken down the evolution of the term hacker to the following four generations. According to Rogers, the first generation of hackers was a group of talented individuals—students, programmers, and computer scientists. These people were interested in pursuing academic and professional challenges in the field of computers. Their hacking process involved dissecting lines of code or sets of instructions in order to gain a better understanding of the program. They did not have a malicious intent, thought they may have had a lack of concern for privacy and proprietary information because they believed the Internet was designed to be an open system. They were often considered pioneers in their field.

The second generation of hackers evolved from the technically elite. Rogers points out that these hackers "were more the technological radicals who were forward thinking and recognized the potential of a second computer niche from mainframe to personal computer." Because of the often "radical aspect" of these individuals, minor criminal activity was common. In fact, Rogers points toward examples of two founders of a now prominent computer company that once had been active in tampering with the telephone system and sold Blue Boxes.

The third generation of hackers involved young people who embraced their computers. They recognized the potential entertainment value of the PC and began to find ways to obtain free software, games, and other programs. Because many of the games and programs are protected by code from being copied illegally, individuals tried to find ways of breaking the copyright codes in order to obtain copies.

The current, fourth generation of hackers has embraced criminal activity as if it is some sort of game or sport. The motivation of some hackers appears not to be curiosity, or a hunger for knowledge, although this is often presented as a rationale by arrested hackers. Their actual motivation seems to be greed, power, revenge, or some other malicious intent. Roger, however, is quick to point out that the term hacker has been misused to represent a very diverse group of people. "Hackers are not a homogenous group," he writes. In fact, many of the studies that have been done had hardly represented the entire hacker community because they involve only a certain number of individuals.

The hacker lifestyle is in many ways the lifestyle of typical American teenagers. Despite what the media might portray, these teens are not isolated individuals, spending most of their days hacking away on a computer. "Many of the hackers hang out at the mall, play sports in their high school, and socialize with their friends," my hacker friend, who goes by the code-name Morpheus, said during my interview with him. "They are no different than the John Doe that is living up the street from you. Hackers do not wear 'geeky' glasses or dress in an uptight shirt and pants as the stereotypes illustrate. Many of the teens in this subculture have body piercings (i.e. nipple ring, tongue ring) and tend to go with the punk look. In fact, many of them see themselves as party animals rather than boring computer geeks."

Hackers in America today have their own conferences, clothing styles, and lingo as well. They hold meetings in chat rooms once a week to trade information with one another on things from hacking software to cracking the code to a specific site. Hackers also have a tradition of holding a yearly security convention in Las Vegas called DefCon. It is during this convention that hackers from all over the country meet and discuss the projects they have been working on or secrets they have uncovered. The main objective to this convention is to socialize, drink, and debug. These hackers believe knowledge is free and open to anyone that wants to learn. Hackers share their findings, accomplishments, and failures much like scientists at scientific conventions. This is also an opportunity for hackers of all ages and experiences to show off the latest hacking tool they created or programs they designed. The convention becomes a place where new hackers can learn about happenings in the underground world, and maybe even meet the person on the other end of the chat room that they have been talking to throughout the year.

Hackers are a very intellectual group of people. Their lingo is so vast and important that hackers have *The New Hacker's*

Dictionary—also known online as *The Jargon File*—published by the MIT press to keep track of the language. In this publication, one can find every term that has been or is being used in the world of hacking. The objective in creating this document was to create a reference where people from a different technical background could decipher what another hacker might have said—very much like a regular dictionary.

Like many cultures that do not use money or wealth to sustain ranking in the group, hackers use reputation to gain status. You gain reputation and "points" among the group only when other hackers of greater technical knowledge consider your actions clever or interesting. Hence, one does not become a hacker until other hackers consistently call you one. The subculture of hackers is considered a gift culture. As Eric Raymond points out on his website *How to Become a Hacker*, a hacker does not gain status "by dominating other people, being beautiful, or having things that other people want, but rather by giving things away (i.e. your time, your creativity, and results of your skills)."

According to Raymond's website, there are five things one can do to be respected by hackers. The first is to write open-source software, programs that other hackers think are fun or useful, and give the program sources to the whole hacker culture to use. The role of open-source programmers in the culture is so important that they are viewed as the gods and goddesses of the culture. Open-source software is valued as the foundation of the subculture, because hackers realize the need to share knowledge without paying a price, and have held firmly onto that idea. Another way to gain status in the culture is by testing and debugging open-source software. In fact, almost half the time it takes a person to develop a new program is spent on debugging. Other ways to being a good hacker include publishing work and volunteering. Like a scientist, keeping good data and publishing your work is significant to the hacker subculture. The attitude of a hacker is also very important. According to Morpheus, "hackers like to solve problems and build things. They believe in freedom and helping others. Hackers view the fascinating world of computing as programs that are waiting to be solved. They get thrills from solving problems, sharpening their skills, and exercising their intelligence. This is the hacker's attitude towards life."

In order to arrive at some type of understanding about the motivation of individuals engaged in hacking, attempts have been made to categorize the term hackers by both criminologists and psychologists alike. One of the first attempts to define the hacker community was by Bill Landreth in his 1985 book *Out of the Inner Circle: A Hacker's Guide to Computer Security*. He proposed a five category classification system based on the activities the hackers were involved with: novice, student, tourist, crasher, and thief. The novice is the least experienced. Their activities are viewed as plain mischief rather than harm. The student is just what the name stands for, a student. Instead of homework, they occupy their time exploring other people's computer system. They are usually bright and find school boring and unchallenging. The tourist hacks out of a sense of adventure with the reward being the thrill of having been there and done that. The crasher is a destructive hacker who intentionally damaged other's information and systems; they are believed by Landreth to be the most unpleasant. The last is the thief, the most rare and dangerous of all hackers according to Landreth. Thieves are professionals that profit from their activities. They are the ones that are involved in espionages for governments or corporations.

Marc Rogers himself, in his revised publication *A New Hacker Taxonomy*, has broken down the term hacker into seven distinct sub-categories: newbies, cyber-punks, internals, coders, old guard hackers, professional criminals, and cyber-terrorists. From my research of popular media, survey-reports, academic journals, and personal observations, I have found most of his categorizations to be similar to the way hackers view themselves. The cyber-punks are the group that generate the most media attention and create hysteria in the minds of the general public. This group is also the one who most frequently is caught by the authorities because they often like to brag about their achievements and exploits on the web. Through the answers to many of the question I posted online and in chat rooms, I have found that the cyber-punk group of hacker is generally between the age of 12 and 30 years old. They are predominately white and male, and on average have a grade 12 education. Though the cyber-punks are by far the largest category of the term hacker, they are nevertheless not the most technological group. They possess more knowledge than the novice, but still have a limited capacity of the types of systems they could break into.

Another group that I have had minor interactions with during my research is the programmers and virus writers. This group of hackers is made up of professionals who know the ins and outs of a computer system like the back of their hands. Based on my observation in chat rooms and dialogue with various hackers, I have learned that the coders consider themselves to be an elite group. They do not brag about their findings as the cyber-punks would; therefore, they are a group that has not caught much attention with the media or the public. They are very sophisticated and some of the virus they write could bring total chaos to the world of computers. However, they do not have any malicious intent and their viruses are meant only as an experiment on their own computer systems as opposed to getting out into the real world and infecting other systems.

The last category of hacker, and one that I have found to be the most dangerous, are the career criminals or "black hats" as referred to by the media. These hackers do not get involved with the "foolishness" of teenage hackers, but target government agencies and big corporations instead. Their intent, unlike those of the cyber-punks who hack out of mere curiosity, is motivated by their desire for profit, vengeance, theft, or espionage. They are usually hired by government agencies and corporations to perform espionage on other countries or rival corporations. Their skills are unlike any others in that they are very sophisticated around the systems they hack, and they cover their tracks very well. In fact, many times a system administrator would not even know that they have been hacked unless notified by the hacker. Because of their level of sophistication and skills in leaving no evidence behind, they are rarely apprehended by law-enforcement.

The importance and benefits hackers have contributed to the United States and the world became more apparent after the attack on the World Trade Center on September 11, 2001. Prior to the incident, hackers had been active in helping the U.S. government in evaluating and exploiting its computer's security vulnerabilities. In fact, according to an article in the 1998 issue of *Business Weekly* by Ira Sager, then Attorney General Janet Reno had quietly committed $1 million dollars for the hire up to sixteen hackers after intruders vandalized the Justice Department's website. After the attack of the 11th, hackers have been actively assisting the government in their quest to hunt down Osama Bin Laden. These hackers are also working hard to protect the U.S. government's information from being leaked out to terrorists groups that are trying to break into government computers. According to a November 13, 2001 *Boston Globe* article by Nicholas Thompson, a group of Pakistani hackers calling themselves "Al Qaeda Coalition Online" has already been successful in breaking into American government and military web sites, and plastering it with pro-Taliban rhetoric and the slogan "Osama Bin Laden is a holy fighter." On the other side of the fight, however, is a group that call themselves the Young Intelligent Hackers Against Terrorism (YIHAT) led by ex-hacker and millionaire Kim Schmitz.

Although there have not been many reports about the group YIHAT in the media, Thompson writes that YIHAT claimed to have broken into the Al Shamal Islamic Bank in Sudan in its effort to track down Bin Laden's assets. "We have forwarded information from accounts held by Bin Laden associates to the FBI," said a source with the group, a report that the FBI has not confirmed.

Besides providing support to the government, hackers have been a great asset to corporate America. This is true in the case of a personal video recording company called TiVo Inc., which has welcomed the help of hackers in providing support for its TV recording system, as David Iler points out in his Multichannel News report "TiVo, Hackers Enjoy Special Relationship." Essentially, a TiVo system is similar to VCR that allows consumer to record their favorite TV show. Instead of using VHS tapes to record, the TiVo system records the information digitally on a computer hard-drive built into the system. Because of the limited hard-drive space that these systems have, hackers conceived ways to allow owners of the systems to upgrade the storage-challenged TiVo to a bigger hard-drive at a lower cost. As an alternative to paying high-price proprietary hard-drives that the system was design for, hackers manipulated few lines of coding, thereby allowing the TiVO's hard drive to be upgraded by using hardware from other vendors. These types of activities are legal because they do not infringe any copyright laws, but are merely a modification of the system permitting it to accept after-market parts. This is the same as when you decide to use an after-market part in your car rather than an original-manufacture part that the car was design for. One might think that the manufacturer of TiVo would be weary of hackers tampering with the proprietary system. However, according to Iler's article, TiVo's Richard Buliwinkle said, "Our position is that if what you do to your box involves no harm, no foul—and it makes you a happier TiVo customer—then we're all for it." Buliwinkle has credited hackers for their work in sharing potential problems and security issues with the company. In fact, because TiVo is tolerant of the hacker community with their system, "they'll protect us," Buliwinkle predicted.

Hackers are a group that is often misunderstood. Many people feel that hackers are teens with bad intentions and should be severely punished. The media portrays hackers as geniuses who can penetrate systems at will. While there are hackers who are geniuses, the majority of hackers do not fit into this category, nor do they break into systems for malicious destruction. In fact, hackers condemn those who use their hacker skills to profit from causing harm to individuals or organizations—hackers refer to these criminals as "crackers." Crackers are the *deviant* form of hackers. They hold an opposite ideology to hackers and pay no attention to the code of morality that the hacker community emphasizes.

This code of morality includes the belief that the information they obtained on the vulnerability of other people's systems should be distributed and shared among individuals of the community, but is never to be used illegally to attack that system. This idea stems from hackers' belief that knowledge should be freely available to all—hence the concept behind Linux, a freely distributed operating system. This is one of the way hackers have contributed to our growing society. By opening up their source-code, people are able to contribute their knowledge, making the software better. In addition, many people—including myself—enjoy the idea of not having to pay corporations like Microsoft huge sums of money for their software, eventually giving them a monopoly in the software market.

In recent years however, there have been numerous laws designed to restrict the activities of the hacker community. One of these laws, the Digital Millennium Copyright Act (DMCA) passed in 1998, was intended to prevent copyright infringements that many people feel is an uncontrollable problem in a world with hackers. The new law was design to address the growing concern for protecting the rights of software authors. However, many critics have argued that the law has gone too far. They feel the act will impose a ban on certain kinds of technical innovations and result in stiff penalties for violating that ban. In one recent highly publicized case, a Russian computer programmer name Dmitry Sklyarov was arrested by federal law enforcements outside of the DefCon conference in Las Vegas. As reporter Shannon Lafferty writes in her article for the law magazine *The Reporter*, Sklyarov was the first charged under the new DMCA law for writing a program for his Russian employer Elcom-Soft, which allows e-Book owners to translate from Adobe's secure e-Book format into the more common Portable Document Format (PDF). The software only works on legitimately purchased e-Books. It has been used by blind people to read otherwise-inaccessible PDF user manuals, and by people who wish to move an e-Book from one computer to another (like moving a CD from a home stereo to the car stereo). Sklyarov was charged with distributing a product designed to circumvent copyright protection measures because the program unlocks the e-Book allowing it to be use with systems that might not be compatible with Adobe's software.

The hacker community is outraged at this new law, because not only was Dmitry arrested outside of the DefCon conference—a symbol for the hacker community—but also because they feel the law will bar them from exposing weaknesses and security flaws in computer systems. In order for security researchers to discover flaws on an encrypted system, they have to develop tools that are able to crack the encryption. This, however, is not permissible under the new law because it means creating a system that circumvents copyright technology. The main goal of hackers has always been to discover flaws that exist on computer systems and share them with the author and the public for swift correction. By limiting their ability to do so, the new law has eradicated the pride hackers have in doing their job.

We live in a world that relies heavily on computer technology to alleviate many of the challenges in our daily life. Computers allow us to work more effectively, bank more efficiently, shop more conveniently, and meet people more easily. However, worries about information security and privacy looms in our mind each time the word "hacker" is mentioned. Laws have been passed to calm the fear inside of people, but what the legislature had not thought about is the vast number of computer vulnerabilities and security holes that are open to computer criminals for exploitation. In fact, according to the Honeynet Project—a project whose main goal is to detect the number of hacker intrusions by using a simple computer network that are similar to ones in most homes and small businesses—their systems were probed, scanned, and exploited a total of 524 times in a thirty day period. Because the project was design to simulate a small, unpublicized business network, the author of the project warned that corporations with greater publicity and value are probably probed by as many as ten times the frequency as the smaller networks. By taking away the hackers' ability to discover these flaws, Congress has consequentially jeopardized individuals and companies more than it has helped. As a culture that has benefited so much from the contribution of hackers, we should not be wary of them, but rather appreciate the hard work and achievements they have contributed to the technological world instead.

Notebook

1. Zhi Zhu's essay tries to argue against a commonly held perception or idea. After reading it, do you consider hacking a subculture or a criminal enterprise? What about the essay convinced you, one way or another? How do you think the essay could have been more convincing? How would you imagine structuring your own argumentative essay?

2. This article was written several years ago, ancient history in the digital age. How do you think the hacking culture has changed? How has the media portrayal of it changed? Are hackers still presented as the enemy?

3. Conduct some more research into the hacking underworld—you might choose to start with the books *Hackers: Heroes of the Computer Revolution* by Steven Levy (Penguin Putnam, 2001), or *Hackers: Crime in the Digital Sublime* by Paul A. Taylor (Routledge, 1999)—and hold a class debate on whether or not hacking is a constructive culture.

4. Now that you are more than halfway through the book (if you started at the beginning), what are some of the subcultures that you see missing from this book? Are there any new subcultures or outgrowths of older subcultures on the horizon? What about African-American college step teams, or cowgirls—would either of those be considered subcultures?

CHAPTER 4

Merchandise, Commercialism, and Co-opting the Scene

OVERVIEW

As evidenced by many of the people interviewed for the essays in this book, authenticity—being "real" instead of a "poseur" or a "wannabe"—is a central issue both for young adults in general and for subculture members in particular. In order for a subculture to retain its credibility (or "cred") as an edgy, alternative, underground, or otherwise nonmainstream entity, its members must find ways to prove their refusal to be like everyone else. Often this gets expressed by what the subculture members wear and buy, or how they spend their money and time. We can see this in the way punks style their hair, or in the hard-edged, dark music beloved by Goths.

So what happens when supposedly nonmainstream markers— green hair dye or Marilyn Manson videoes, for example—become popular "above ground," and can be found and bought at your local drug store or mall? The relationship between the identity of a subculture and the merchandising of that identity to the mass culture is often referred to as "co-opting," a derogatory way of talking about incorporation that implies a kind of thievery. In our fast-paced consumer culture, we are always on the hunt for the next new thing, and sometimes that new thing comes from a subculture that has been holding on to it, trying to keep it meaningful and secret, for years. When the mass culture picks up on a previously subcultural trend, what kind of reverberations does this have within the subculture itself? Have you ever been in the situation where something you owned and treasured because you thought it made you unique turned out to be a trend? How is identity shaped by what we consume?

Towards a Critical Understanding of "Asian Cute Culture"

ADRIENNE LAI

Can shopping for cute Hello Kitty stickers be a political act? Here, Adrienne Lai, a visual artist, writer, freelance curator, and educator, explores how purchasing cute Asian products helps her define a subversive identity for herself. Lai received her MFA with a Graduate Emphasis in Asian American Studies from the University of California, Irvine, in 2001. In 2004, she guest-curated "I Am the Remix" at the Western Front Artist-Run Centre, an exhibition with an accompanying roundtable discussion investigating the use of DJ culture by contemporary artists. She is currently an instructor in Critical and Cultural Studies at the Emily Carr Institute in Vancouver, BC, Canada.

❖

A few years ago, I purchased a black muscle T-shirt with the head of Hello Kitty emblazoned on the front in silver studs. When I wore it, a friend commented that he'd seen the shirt in a store window and knew that I'd be drawn to it: "It's Hello Kitty, but it's *tough*." I am interested in how the assumptions and stereotypes about what young Asian women and feminists are supposed to look like can be disrupted through these contradictory visual messages. What does it mean for an adorable cartoon cat to be depicted in a vernacular normally found on punk rock leather jackets? And what does it mean if this cute/tough character adorns the chest of a feminist university instructor, or a young Asian American woman? What if they are one and the same? More than anything, this use of cute culture is a tongue-in-cheek defiance of overly prescriptive and proscriptive ideals of race and gender.

My adult-years participation in Asian cute culture is influenced by a number of strategies and motivations: it is a mixture of Asian girl pride, nostalgia for youth and childhood, ironic and defiant engagement with the stereotypes the dominant culture imposes on me, and pure aesthetic pleasure. Furthermore, Asian cute culture provides a means for me to adopt cultural forms that are coded as Asian, but which are also based in the current language of a North American media and consumer-based life. Like many individuals of Asian heritage who were raised in North

America, I have little familiarity with traditional forms of Asian culture (language, music, literature, dance, etc.), some of which seem somewhat antiquated and distant from my everyday life. To adopt one of those forms in the name of exploring my "Asian" identity seems a bit arbitrary and nostalgic, an attempt to reclaim an authentic culture to which I am no longer connected. Asian popular culture may provide a possible avenue for the exploration of contemporary cultural forms, one that may seem more relevant and/or attractive to the experiences of North American youth in an era of global exchange and media saturation. Through the consumption of kung-fu films, Japanimation, or Sanrio products, young Asian Americans such as myself can express an affiliation to an Asian identity, one that is based in less fixed or conventional notions of culture and "Asianness."

When I set out to purchase the products of Asian cute culture, it usually involves a shopping expedition to one of the Asian malls located in one of the suburbs of my hometown. Friends who are Asian American males, Asian American females, or Caucasian females usually accompany me on these shopping trips. These trips are undertaken with the intention of consuming Asian popular culture—to browse through the fashions imported from Japan and Hong Kong, to stock up on Asian sweets (usually baked goods or candy), and to check out the latest cute characters and products at the fancy goods store. I have noticed some subtle differences in these excursions, however, depending on whether I am with individuals from an Asian or non-Asian background. In the former instance, there is an element of self-conscious performance: that in visiting these sites and consuming these products, we are sharing the experience of communing with the Asian parts of our identities. In contrast, with my non-Asian friends, I tend to assume the role of the insider/guide, the source for explanation of items whose meanings and uses are strange or unclear. This occurs in spite of the fact that I do not have any particular linguistic skills or cultural experiences that may provide a basis for such expertise. In both cases, however, there is a definite sense of cultural tourism: although the spaces and products of the Asian malls are familiar to me, they still feel foreign, originating in a world separate from my own. The allegiances and affinities I hold towards them are deliberately adopted, rather than naturally present.

As a cultural phenomenon, "cuteness" remains largely unexamined by feminist, postcolonial, and cultural theorists. Perhaps this lack of regard (or even trivialization) stems from cuteness's inherent diminutive and unassuming characteristics. However, as a young woman, and an Asian American in particular, I can testify to the central position that cuteness holds in my life and identity, and the role that cute culture has played in their formation. In this essay I will provide a starting point for further examination of the impact and cultural significance of cute culture. Focusing specifically on Asian cute culture (and the Sanrio corporation as the quintessential purveyor thereof), I will trace its effects on women in Japan and North America while making linkages to ongoing changes in feminist thought. Ideally, this project would include an ethnographic survey of young women's attitudes and responses to cute culture. In lieu of this, I will insert my own personal narrative into the discussion, as I am an active participant in and consumer of cute culture. In doing so, I hope to provide a critical and multifaceted (though incomplete) examination of the power relationships and political repercussions of cute culture, taking into account the complex processes involved in the formation of individual and collective identities.

To begin, an analysis of "cuteness" is necessary. Although the definition of cuteness is a value judgment based on personal taste, it seems that there is some general consensus around some of its predominant characteristics. In the few scholarly articles on cuteness I have read, cuteness has been overwhelmingly associated with children and infants, and more specifically, with girls. Furthermore, cute people or things are described as possessing an inherent charm based on vulnerability and inability to care for themselves. This correlation between cuteness and powerlessness is explored in "Commodifying Affection: Authority and Gender in the Everyday Objects of Japan," an essay by Brian McVeigh published in 1996 in *The Journal of Material Culture*. McVeigh positions the characteristics of cuteness relationally to their opposites in two lists:

Powerlessness: controllable/controlled	**Power:** controlling/controller
females	strength
femininity	males
weakness	masculinity
cheerful	gloomy
bright colors	dark colors
infants, children	adults
youth	maturity
light hearted	serious
outgoing	taciturn
small	large

Here, McVeigh enumerates the characteristics of cuteness as defined by lack in relation to the characteristics possessed by the patriarchal ruling class of society. This dualistic model will resurface in my later analyses of cuteness and power.

The embracing of cuteness as a positive and desirable quality is exemplified in a phenomenon that I will term "Asian cute culture." Asian cute culture originated as a youth subculture in Japan in the early 1970s. What started as a handwriting and fashion fad amongst teenage girls became quickly appropriated by the economic boom in Japan. The Sanrio Company began printing its own cute versions of American-style cartoon characters on writing paper and stationary. Soon it expanded its line to stickers, diaries, toiletries, candy, etc.—the assortment of merchandise housed under the category of "fancy goods." The cute characters created by Sanrio are generally small, anthropomorphized animals, which are given names, personalities, and histories. The pre-eminent figure of Sanrio and Asian cute culture in general is Hello Kitty, a white cartoon cat with a large head, no mouth, and a red bow tied around one ear. The popularity of Hello Kitty and her Sanrio compatriots spread from Japan to North America in the late 1970s and continues to grow, spawning imitators from fledgling fancy goods companies such as Korea's Morning Glory. The global success of Sanrio (and Asian cute culture by association) is exemplified by its 1996 $1.2 billion in worldwide sales and recent rioting at McDonalds restaurants in Hong Kong over a Hello Kitty stuffed toy promotion.

Although one would assume Asian cute culture to be marketed primarily towards young girls and preadolescents, it is also significantly consumed by adolescent girls and adult women. This is indicated by the range of Sanrio products specifically not geared towards children, including cellular phone cases, sequined purses, day planners, rice steamers, maxi pads, condoms, and vibrators. Asian cute culture is a subculture that celebrates girlhood but which does not require physical girlhood of its members. My own participation in Asian cute culture probably began around the age of six and spans over twenty years (with some gaps of non-involvement) to the present day; where, as an adult woman, I continue to purchase significant amounts of "fancy goods": mostly stationery, stickers, house wares, and miscellaneous tchotchkes. Asian cute culture, although mainly associated with young Asian girls, is not limited to this group: I know many non-Asian women and some Asian and non-Asian men who revel in the joys of consuming cute products. Finally, as demonstrated by the above descriptions, it is a culture that is characterized by its essential commercial nature. In the essay "Cuties in Japan," Sharon Kinsella, a scholar of Japanese popular and material culture, observes: "cute . . . seem[s] to be accessible *exclusively* through consumption." It is important to note that this characteristic is not exclusive to Asian cute culture: in most youth subcultures, consuming commodities (music, clothing, etc.) is a central activity.

As a consumer practice and symbol of weakness, naiveté, and conventional ideas of femininity, cute culture is predictably not embraced by traditional feminist and anti-racist theorists. The process of infantilization inherent in the adoption of cuteness is generally perceived as counterproductive to an agenda that seeks to combat the oppression and paternalism present in the dominant culture's sexist and racist ideologies. The popularity of cute culture amongst Asian women would seem to be doubly problematic, as Asian women are bound by the dual oppression of their race and gender. In a notable 1972 essay titled "Racist Love," Asian American writers Frank Chin and Jeffrey Paul Chan describe the patronizing attitude the dominant culture has historically held towards Asians:

> The Chinese . . . are meek, timid, passive, docile, industrious . . . It's well known that the cloying overwhelming love of a protective, coddling mother produces an emotionally stunted, dependent child. This is the . . . bigoted love that has imprisoned the Chinese-American sensibility . . .

In this context, cute culture can be regarded as an oppressive force that prescribes stereotypical gender and racial roles. Brian McVeigh's essay particularly emphasizes this view. Although he briefly acknowledges that those who exercise power sometimes use cuteness as a means of masking the dominance of their positions, overall he regards cute culture as "objectified sentiment, commenting on and supporting a normative discourse about gender definitions." Similarly, in "Cuties in Japan," Sharon Kinsella notes: "In cute culture, young people became popular according to their apparent weakness, dependence and inability, rather than because of their strengths and capabilities." If cute culture is indeed an endorsement of conservative values, then by adopting said culture young women (myself included) internalize traditional gender and racial roles. In other words, empathy with the cute object (and the recognition of self therein) leads to the interiorization of normative ideals. This normalization process then necessitates the continued consumption and display of cute signifiers in order to affirm the subject's "cute" identity.

The disavowal of girlishness present in traditional Asian American feminist writings tends to support this critical view of cute culture. In a seminal text of Asian American feminism, *The Woman Warrior: Memoirs of a Girlhood Among Ghosts*, author Maxine Hong Kingston creates a girl protagonist who exhibits few of the usual traits of girlhood. This girl is preternaturally wise with a keen critical eye turned towards both Chinese and American cultures. She possesses a level of self-reflexivity lacking in most adults: instead of concerning herself with dolls or make-up, she muses about issues of voice and agency in Chinese girls. She develops a hatred for one of the other Chinese girls, a particularly quiet one with a "China doll hair cut." Hong Kingston describes an incident in which this protagonist tries to bully the quiet China dollish (in other words, cute) girl into speaking:

I looked into her face so I could hate it close up. She wore black bangs, and her cheeks were pink and white. She was baby-soft. I thought that I could put my thumb on her nose and push it bonelessly in, indent her face. I could poke dimples into her cheeks. I could work her face around like dough. She stood still, and I did not want to look at her face anymore; I hated fragility.

In this passage, Hong Kingston's narrator confronts the stereotype of the cute, quiet Asian girl and lashes out at it with enmity and violence. She voices her desire to grow tough skin and strong yellow teeth, and to wear only black in order to distance herself from the cute stereotype she despises. The *Woman Warrior* is a literary work that clearly attempts to disassociate Asian women from the infantilized images the dominant culture has imposed on them.

While traditional feminism's critical rejection of cuteness, femininity, and all things associated with conventional gender roles make sense in a historical context; there are problems with the unilateral adoption of this position. It reacts against a stereotyped, polarized, and oversimplified conception of gender by taking up an oppositional, and equally polarized, stance. This stance continues to operate within the same prejudiced binary model that posits femininity and its accompanying attributes (i.e. passivity, weakness, emotionalism) as the lacking opposite of masculinity. To uncritically accept this model is to abandon the intricacies and variations of experience and subjectivity for a reactionary and simplistic assessment. Can we really accept the idea that if something is small, cheerful, or young it cannot be serious or strong? Does participation in cuteness or cute culture necessitate an automatic relinquishing of power? More recently, some feminists have attempted to reclaim the contested ground prohibited by older generations. The notion of "postfeminism" can be regarded as a current stage in the ongoing transformation(s) of the feminist movement. It is precisely because of the advances made by the hard-line (and at times moralistic) stance of earlier generations that postfeminism is able to begin to address the pluralist and contradictory nature of women's experiences. This includes the theorizing of "trivial" areas like popular culture, the reconsideration of "oppressive" mechanisms such as pornography and heterosexual male desire, and the reassessment of the "powerless" concepts of femininity and girlhood. The emphasis has shifted from the criticism of dominant culture as an all-encompassing structure of oppression to an investigation on how ordinary people can appropriate the products of dominant culture in order to produce their own meanings. Postfeminist cultural theorists such as Angela McRobbie have taken up the study of girl cultures in order to investigate the various ways girls and women produce meaning with the representations available to them. As Ann Brooks observes in her 1997 overview of issues in contemporary feminism(s), *Postfeminisms: Feminism, Cultural Theory and Cultural Forms*, McRobbie recognizes that "femininity is no longer the 'other' of feminism and that femininity is constructed as the product of less stable, emergent subject positions which tally with the more fluid subjectivities of postmodernism." Following this recognition, we are able to rethink girlhood in such a manner that "girl power" is now regarded as an affirmative mantra, not an oxymoron.

Taking into consideration the potential of alternative analyses, cute culture can be re-examined in order to discover how young women use it as a tool for self-representation and even empowerment. The meanings conveyed by cute culture will of course vary in accordance with its users. Although I cannot speak on behalf of all participants in cute culture, I am interested in suggesting some possible ways that young women can consciously and unconsciously use this consumer practice in order to undermine dominant discourses. What meanings do young women invest in the objects of cute culture? What meanings are embedded in the objects of cute culture? Can the normalizing features of cute culture be transcended? How can cute culture be utilized as a subversive tool?

A significant feature of cute culture is that it is a subculture that originated amongst young women in Japan. As Sharon

Kinsella notes (and Angela McRobbie echoes this sentiment about the male-centred tendencies of subcultures in her book *Feminism and Youth Culture*):

> Nearly all originally western youth cultures in the post-war period—such as mods, rockers, new romantics, techno, punk and hip hop—have been dominated by young men with young women playing a more passive, side-kick role. . . . Consequently, the creation of cute youth culture around young women has attracted a lot of notice.

Cute culture is one of a number of recent female-centred subcultures—such as the riot grrls, the "women in rock"/Lilith Fair phenomenon, and the Spice Girls—most of which have been well documented in the media. However, as with the first few waves of feminism, these feminist youth cultures are characterized by a predominantly white membership. Despite the many criticisms that can be levelled against cute culture—the consumerism, the infantile aspects—I cannot think of another subculture that features such prominent participation by Asian girls and women. This dominance can also be found on the production side: Mary Roach's 1999 *Wired* article on the business of Japan's cute culture estimates that 90% of the Japanese "cute" industry's character designers are women. Even if cute culture holds no other positive aspects, it provides a spot in the marketplace where the concerns, interests and desires of Asian women hold center court.

Another crucial distinction between cute culture and other female-oriented subcultures is that the latter still partially hold on to a traditional conception of feminism as they highlight the advancement of women into male-dominated spheres (a prime example of this is Lilith Fair's celebration of the presence of women in the testosterone-driven arena of rock and roll). Aside from its admittedly problematic involvement with capitalism, cute culture shows no interest in the male adult world. Its alliance with things child-like and girlish signals a rebellion against, and refusal to participate in, adulthood and society. Similar to Generation X/Slacker culture of the 1990s, which favoured an extended period of adolescence, cute culture celebrates a pre-socialized world that explicitly refuses to engage in the trappings of mainstream adult society. Kinsella describes this operation of cute culture in Japanese society:

> Women debased as infantile and irresponsible began to fetishize and flaunt their *shojo* [adolescent girl] personality still more,

almost as a means of ridiculing male condemnation and making clear their stubborn refusal to stop playing, go home, and accept less from life.

This analysis emphasizes cute culture's possibilities as a form of resistance. While cute culture has had a different reception and function in the less gender-repressive society of North America, its "girls-only" sentiment remains. Although males can (and do) become members of this cute club, they can only achieve this through participation in the girly domains of animal mascots, stickers, notepaper, and stuffed toys.

One strategy by which the users of cute culture can subvert dominant culture is via the process of mimicry, a notion I appropriate from noted postcolonial theorist Homi Bhabha. In Bhabha's 1994 book *The Location of Culture*, he describes a process of mimicry where the colonized (oppressed) subject takes on the appearance of the colonizer (oppressor), affirming his or her difference from the oppressor by attempting to deny it—a kind of "protesting too much." In other words, mimicry is a kind of strategic inadequacy: because the colonized can never fully take on the identity prescribed by the colonizer, it points to the failure of the total colonizing project. Homi Bhabha notes the necessity of this failure in the use of mimicry by the oppressed subject: "[T]he discourse of mimicry is constructed around an ambivalence; in order to be effective, mimicry must continually produce its slippage, its excess, its difference." By surrounding themselves with the pastel-colored, cartoon animal-festooned objects of cute culture, adult women take on normative, ultra-young and ultra-feminine appearances. However, because they cannot fully *become* little girls, they become *imitations* of little girls. Through the lived experiences of these imitations, there are almost always incongruities that surface: the pink purse in the shape of a kitten that holds a day planner, cell phone and car keys; the girl in the bunny rabbit t-shirt at the bar drinking gin and tonic; the university seminar that is interrupted by graduate students comparing Sanrio stickers, pencils, and note paper. By running around in the (not-quite right) personae of little girls, these adult women simultaneously reinforce and disrupt the patriarchal logic that seeks to treat adult women like little girls.

The element of parody figures importantly in the use of mimicked cuteness as a tool for subverting the normative power discourses around cute culture. This aspect of cute culture is most prominent in its North American incarnation. As *The Encyclopedia of Japanese Pop Culture* indicates, "There was a heavy dose of irony in the American take on Hello Kitty totally absent among Japanese Sanrio fans." Many (although not all) of the adult women who revel in girl culture are keenly aware of the incongruous picture they paint. A drastic example of this would be the assumption of baby-doll clothing by the female grunge/punk bands of the early 1990s: women like Hole's Courtney Love dressed in lacy dresses and pink barrettes while screaming out obscenities and defiance.

It is through this ironic adoption of sweetness and light that they cast a sarcastic sneer in the direction of dominant culture. This has been one of the motivating factors in my own personal involvement with cute culture. Through my alignment with an exaggerated, highly stylized, artificial, and inconsistent version of Asian femaleness, as in the story about the black studded Hello Kitty t-shirt, I seek to poke fun at the notion that such an "authentic" version exists.

However, I also recognize that these uses of cute culture are not radical forms of disputing dominant social norms; rather, they are everyday forms of resistance. They do not fundamentally change the systems of oppression. Instead, they allow young people to take the objects presented to them by consumer culture and reinvest them with new meanings. Angela McRobbie described this process as it has functioned amongst working-class girls' subcultures in England in *Feminism and Youth Culture*:

> Here they can at least exert some power in their choice of commodities. These commodities often come to be a hallmark of the subcultural group in question but not exactly in their original forms. The group subverts the original meaning by bestowing additional implied connotations to the object thereby extending the range of its signifying power. These new meanings undermine and can even negate the previous or established meanings so that the objects come to represent an oppositional ideology linked to the subculture or youth grouping in question.

McRobbie puts forth several ideas of interest. One is the linking of consumerism and the power of choice as voice. The second is that consumer objects can be used by youth cultures to articulate their specific concerns and identities. The third is that the meanings of these consumer objects can be subverted and even changed to the extent that their original meanings are lost. In essence, the adoption and reworking of normalized consumer identities can be a means of changing the system from within—of using the master's tools against him. By reclaiming cuteness, young women can appear to remain within the dominant discourse while simultaneously subtly changing the meanings of cute within that discourse, thereby, in small ways, transforming it.

In closing, I wish to posit a caveat in my endorsement of cute culture as a subversive practice. This use of cute culture is but one strategy of resistance, and it can (and probably should) be used in conjunction with other—perhaps more traditional—ways of defying oppression. Cute culture, fundamentally, is a consumer practice and a style; it is dangerous to conflate it with or substitute it for aggressive, active political lobbying for change. I do not wish to suggest that purchasing and displaying a Hello Kitty item is a revolutionary act; I merely wish to suggest that it isn't necessarily complicit with oppression. Cute culture continues to be problematic in its corporate, commodified essence. Despite all the new meanings I may be investing in these objects, despite the subversive uses I intend, despite the ways I feel empowered by my participation in this culture, I know that some businessperson is profiting from my purchases—not to mention the fact that these products are often made in Asian countries associated with sweatshop labour, which exploits young female labour. This is one aspect of cute culture that, like most other consumer-based and/or appropriated youth cultures, may prove impossible to subvert.

With this investigation into the uses and significations of cute culture, I wish to highlight the notions of criticality and self-reflexivity in the consideration of girl and/or youth subcultures. While it is true that cute culture is at times nothing more than an expression of personal style, it is important to note that in the adoption of *any* fashion we become coded in a particular way. However, it is far too simplistic to dismiss the social and stylistic activities of young women as trivial or completely formed by the inculcating twin forces of social normalization and consumerism. Furthermore, as a young woman who engages in the complex performance of identity and representation, I want to be lucidly aware of both my resistance to and complicity with the discourses of dominant culture. Hello Kitty and the rest of the Sanrio characters are the mascots of a subculture that is coded as specifically Asian, young, and female—a combination that conjures up particular associations, histories, and stereotypes within North American culture. It is up to me, and anyone else who wishes to engage in cute culture, to consider which parts of these mythologies should be celebrated, and which parts need to be thwarted.

Notebook

1. Are you part of any consumer-based subcultures? In other words, are you part of a group because you buy something?

2. In her essay, Lai claims that while "cuteness" can be an empowering trait and is a female-centered culture, "cute culture can [also] be regarded as an oppressive force that prescribes stereotypical gender and racial roles." Can you think of any other examples of subcultures in which the rituals, values, or objects of the culture actually work to disempower the members?

3. This essay begins with a personal anecdote, but then goes on to be a much less chatty, more theoretical kind of piece. What are the effects of such a rhetorical move on you, the reader? Would you try something like this in your own essay? Why or why not?

4. Think about the things you buy. How are the consumer choices you make based on ideology? For example, do you shop at an independent record store rather than a chain store? Discuss your consumer choices—and their political implications—with the class. You could experiment by changing those choices for one week and seeing how becoming a different kind of consumer effects the rest of your life.

5. Sanrio products like Hello Kitty have become mascots for certain alternative cultures, as Lai describes here. Does the subculture you're studying have a mascot? If so, find an artifact that depicts this mascot (such as a sticker or a t-shirt), and bring it into class to explain its relationship to your subculture. If your subculture doesn't have a mascot, could you create one you think would be appropriate? What kind of design or emblem would appeal to the members of that subculture, and why?

6. In thinking about "Asian cute culture," can you come up with other subcultures based around buying certain products? For example, do people who buy and ride Vespa motor scooters make a subculture? Why or why not? What about teenagers who ride and race Big Wheels tricycles, or tricked-out bikes? What about collectors of vintage trading cards?

So Emo It Hurts

EMILY LAMISON

As a communication major at Chatham College in Pittsburgh, Emily Lamison conducted research on the appropriation of subcultures in mass culture, which culminated in her undergraduate thesis entitled "Different Like Everyone Else: The Merging of Underground and

Mass Culture in Modern Society," from which this essay about emo music—a subgenre of punk rock characterized by its emotional lyrics—is excerpted. Emily currently divides her time between work as a freelance writer and as a communications specialist for a non-profit that provides adoption and foster care services. Her writing has appeared in the Pittsburgh weekly alternative papers, as well as the nationally distributed music zine, Kitty Magik. *In the fall of 2006, she began graduate work in leadership and organizational transformation at Chatham College.*

—————————— ✦ ——————————

Since late 1990s, the word "emo" has been casually tossed around the music press. However, many people—including musicians and music fans—are unfamiliar with the exact criteria of the genre. The current incarnation of emo is fluid and ever changing, like the pop cultural landscape in which it has recently found a niche. Its meaning and origins vary in the popular lore, but some commonly held perceptions follow.

Emo is best defined as a post-punk genre that first appeared in the 1980s. It is commonly—but not exclusively—viewed as an extension of the hardcore and straight edge punk scenes that emerged in and around Washington, D.C. in that era. The straight edge movement enforced a drug- and alcohol-free lifestyle, and also encouraged a strict vegetarian—often vegan—diet and abstinence from sex. The application of straight edge values to music is most evident in the group Fugazi, who is often cited as a primary influence of contemporary emo bands.

The term "emo" derives from the intense emotional content of the music. The emotion in question is often glorified teen angst, mirroring the social relationship traumas of its primarily adolescent and young adult fan base. Some proponents of the genre maintain a jagged, hard, post-punk sound, while others—like Bright Eyes and Dashboard Confessional—opt for stripped-down, acoustic subtlety. Confessional, diary-style lyrics characterize the genre.

The popularity of the emo style is a distinctly modern phenomenon, as dependent on technology and the dissemination of information as it is on the quality of the music itself. In American society, which is increasingly defined by developing technologies and diminishing attention spans, the mass media plays a greater role than ever in determining the direction of culture. At the turn of the century, we reached an apex of technological advancement, with myriad communication tools at our disposal. But before the Internet, before I-Pods and MP3s, there was MTV.

Since the advent of MTV in 1981, Americans have grown accustomed to split-second montages of flashy imagery and sound bytes. Ironically, the first video ever aired on MTV was the Buggles' "Video Killed the Radio Star." Though the network executives couldn't have then realized the full scope of their future impact, that premiere video choice foreshadowed a huge shift in popular culture and the media.

Before music television, performers remained virtually unseen outside of live performance: musical talent ranked above fashion; the aesthetics of sound took precedence over visual appearance. In the last two decades, however, style and fads have ruled over substance. Ours is now a society of instant gratification and perpetual change. Pop culture trends are chewed up and spit out at lightning speed, constantly making way for the latest craze. These trends, though seemingly affected by the whims of the general public, are pre-determined by a select few who rarely participate in the culture they produce. As Thomas Frank points out in his essay, "Alternative to What?":

> Under no condition is "popular culture" something that we make ourselves, in the garage with electric guitars and second-hand amplifiers, on the office photocopier when nobody's looking. It is, strictly and exclusively, the stuff provided for us in a thousand corporate boardrooms and demographic studies.

Underground culture—also deemed "subculture" or "counterculture"—has followed a path parallel to that of popular culture in the last twenty-odd years, becoming co-opted and commodified for mass consumption. Therefore, it is no coincidence that the disposable cultural trends of recent years can be directly correlated to the rise of MTV and similar media outlets, such as *Spin* magazine, a popular music publication with roots in alternative and underground music scenes. According to John Seabrook, a regular contributor to *The New Yorker* and author of *Nobrow: The culture of marketing—the marketing of culture*:

> This was the thing that MTV had changed most about the world: it broke down the old barrier between . . . mainstream and underground, mass and cult, it and you. Before MTV, art made for the mass audience and the art made for a cult audience had been mostly detached and distinct from each other.

Seabrook elaborates, "Thanks to MTV, the avant-garde could become the mainstream so quickly that it made meaningless the old antithesis—either avant-garde or mainstream—on which so much critical theory . . . rested." America's current social climate allows for such blurring to continue because ever-evolving technologies allow for faster and broader communication, while tastemakers rarely make the distinction between folk, mass and elite culture. Terms like "underground" and "mainstream" no longer distinguish cultural categories. For many—particularly young people—commodities define identity. In his essay, "The Advertised Life," Tom Vanderbilt addresses this issue when he states, "The consumption of goods is now so closely linked to identity that a new form of social analysis has emerged in which classes are defined not by property or profession or even income but by what products they purchase."

The phenomenon of identity-based marketing raises several questions: If the identity markers of emo and other once-underground music genres are readily accessible to any suburban pre-teen with an elastic allowance, do they retain their original symbolism within the subcultural community? Does this shift in meaning force members of the subculture to seek alternate means of expression to continue subverting the status quo? Without clearly defined distinctions, how, then, do members of subcultures distinguish authentic supporters from identity-hungry consumers? In such a fluid environment, it is difficult to arrive at concrete answers to these questions. However, we may consider cultural theory, the artistic output of subcultures and the effects of mainstream marketing on their production to help make sense of this postmodern occurrence.

Since subcultures first emerged as a means of expression and resistance, members—particularly of underground music subcultures, like punk—used clothing and alternative media outlets as external markers of their marginalization. Their do-it-yourself—or DIY—spirit and social statements of have recently been diluted for mass appeal by national department stores; niche shops like Hot Topic and Gadzooks; teen-targeted catalogues and boutiques like Delia*s; and the hipster-chic retailer for the college set, Urban Outfitters. Most commonly, the commodification, or appropriation, of subculture in fashion becomes evident through T-shirt slogans and graphics. However, other articles of clothing also reflect influence from the counter-culture. For example, particular designs and patterns may indicate a specific time period or cultural movement. An anarchy symbol splashed across a T-shirt often indicates an association with early punk rock, while Doc Martens boots and flannel shirts have become synonymous with the early 1990s grunge scene. These styles hold symbolic power but maintain very little authenticity once removed from their original contexts. As Frankfurt School theorist Walter Benjamin states in his essay, "The Work of Art in the Age of Mechanical Reproduction," "Formerly unique objects, located in a particular space, lost their singularity as they became accessible to many people in diverse places. Lost too was the 'aura' that was attached to a work of Art which was now open to many different readings and interpretations."

Though Benjamin's essay focuses on visual art, its concepts can easily be applied to music subcultures. The fashion, iconography and communication tools of subcultures are co-opted by the mainstream, offering access across borders. Though the demystification of the artistic process democratizes the art in question, it also creates new opportunities for distortion and misinterpretation.

For example, the communication methods of subcultures are often appropriated by mass culture. The zine culture that flourished in riot grrl communities a decade ago influenced countless contemporary publications, in their edgier writing styles and "cut-and-paste" layouts. Similarly, online journals called weblogs, or "blogs," originated within the emo scene and have since become the mainstream self-publishing mode of choice. The sensitive nature of the emo genre attracts a demographic predisposed towards diary writing; as a youth subculture, emo has always embraced modern technology. Those two elements combined to create a pop culture phenomenon. In each example, the underground attributes of subcultural communication tools have been simultaneously exoticized and watered down for mass consumption.

In his book, *An Introduction to Theories of Popular Culture*, Dominic Strinati quotes the writings of Karl Marx in *The German Ideology*: "The ideas of the ruling class are, in every age, the ruling ideas: i.e., the class, which is the dominant *material* force in society, is at the same time the dominant *intellectual* force." The ruling class—in this case, purveyors of mass culture—both mass-produces commodities for consumption and sets the parameters of intellectual discourse. Marx continues, "The class which has the means of material production at its disposal, has control at the same time over the means of mental production, so that in consequence the ideas of those who lack the means of mental production are, in general, subject to it."

Mass culture holds power over the means of production and, therefore, becomes the source for ideas, cultural movements and trends. Subcultures lack such immediately accessible means of production; in order for the ideologies, aesthetics and media of the counter-culture to reach a mass audience, they are appropriated and transformed, filtered through the lens of mass culture. But subcultures and counter-culture movements typically arise in opposition to mainstream society and resist assimilation into the dominant culture; herein lies the ongoing tension between the underground and the mainstream. Examples of this struggle are scattered across music history; however, subcultural dissent reached its apex with the punk movement and its offshoots. In the mid-seventies, the British punk movement arose against a back-drop of economic depression. The genre conveyed an intensely anti-Establishment message and style. To this day, the mass cul-ture appropriates symbols from the English punk movement and applies them to all punk genres: the Union Jack, anarchy symbols, leather and safety pins each carry punk connotations in mass con-sciousness. Similarly, the riot grrl movement of the early 1990s sprang from discontent. In the punk scenes of Olympia, Washing-ton and Washington, D.C., women became increasingly frustrated by their double-marginalized position: their "otherness" as punks, in relation to mainstream society, and their distinction as females in a predominantly male subculture. Ironically, the fiercely feminist riot grrls later became assimilated into an apolitical mass culture, when in the mid-1990s, "Girl power" messages peppered the mainstream landscape, and riot grrl rhetoric was reduced to simplistic catch phrases spouted by the likes of the Spice Girls.

Occasionally, though, it is possible for counter-culture and mass culture to establish a symbiotic relationship. In these instances, the underground takes advantage of the means of production accessible via mass culture outlets in order to suit its own purposes. As previ-ously mentioned, this has become especially evident within the last decade because of constantly growing access to new technologies and the blurring of boundaries between sub- and popular cultural trends.

It may come as no surprise that, as part of a genre that has come into its own completely in an era of such technological advances, some purveyors of emo culture make little attempt to resist appropriation. The style has already provided soundtracks to the lives of several casts of MTV's *Real World* and, more recently, popular teen dramas, but its origins lie outside of the mainstream domain. Given the genre's politically-charged, punk-influenced history, its current, cartoonish incarnation understandably rubs some loyal followers the wrong way. Interestingly, though, the musicians themselves—the producers of emo culture—often embrace notoriety, utilizing the resources offered to them through mainstream success.

The style gained marginal popularity in the mainstream realm within in the last several years. The summer of 2002 marked the beginning of its mainstream transition. *Seventeen* magazine, along with other popular media outlets, had finally caught on to the genre. Always a pace or two behind the teen demographic it serves, *Seventeen* pounced on the opportunity to inform their readers of a burgeoning musical movement. A feature in their August 2002 issue reduced the emo phenomenon to a simplified, step-by-step guide called "am I emo?" What, in the 1980s, had been a significant socio-political development in underground music, had begun its descent into teenybopper fluff.

In the article, writer Mara Schwartz employs a paint-by-numbers approach to entering a once-underground scene. According to the piece, "emo" attributes include black hair dye; patterned socks; cuffed, dark denim jeans; vintage t-shirts; "geeky," horn-rimmed glasses; and shrunken sweaters. The accompanying visual representation of emo style features adolescents of both sexes decked out in emo garb—a perverse distortion of the style that appeared more Halloween costume than hipster uniform. To long-time emo listeners, this visual model appears to be a caricature of their lifestyle.

The clothing and accessories are diagrammed with descriptions of the emo connotations of each element. For example, under the headline, "Studded Belts & Bracelets," the girl's adornments are justified as such: "Show your punk roots with a biker belt. But don't dress too tough: After all, you're a sensitive soul. So wear lots of pretty bracelets to express your soft, girlie side."

Schwartz also ranks intelligence—whether genuine, or approximated with faux horn-rimmed specs—as an emo trait: A slick, stylish "emo" boy clutches a stack of books. The caption below reads: "A used copy of J.D. Salinger's *Franny and Zooey*, rock critic Greil Marcus' *Ranters & Crowd Pleasers*, and a notebook to express your innermost thoughts." This description falls under the headline "Deep Reads." The magazine does not explicitly recommend *reading* these books; readers are made implicitly aware that, when placed within the context of argyle socks and cuffed jeans, the recommended literature merely serves as another accessory.

The article continues by listing several attributes sensitive souls must adopt to distinguish themselves from "jocks" and "frat boys." Their message is this: athletic prowess and popularity go hand in hand. However, in the narrow classification system established by the magazine, these qualities also mutually exclude a proclivity for emotionally charged music. The description of a pair of sneakers reads: "Ratty old Converse or Vans. Avoid anything too obviously shiny or new—or risk looking like a jock."

The absurd irony is that, to fully embrace an emo lifestyle—one supposedly tied to emotion and authenticity—one must adopt a disguise. In a peculiar dichotomy that brings to mind its stock advice to wear make-up to create a natural look, *Seventeen* advises emo fans to make an effort to appear effortless; critical readers envision impressionable teens meticulously scuffing their shoes to the melancholy strains of Bright Eyes. In the same picture, a key chain dangles from this young man's waist. Its description is equally disturbing: "Wear it janitor-style. If you add the wallet, you might accidentally be mistaken for a nü-metal frat rocker." This serves to segregate teenagers who appreciate counter-culture products from those who are "normal." Rather than present subcultures as positive outlets for creativity, *Seventeen* magazine reduces them to mere cliques, creating an "us and them" dynamic. In its attempt to be progressive, the magazine promotes rigid categorizations.

This is not the first time this magazine—or countless others like it—has appropriated subcultural symbols without any consideration of context, lifestyle or history. At the time of our interview, Cindy Yogmas held the title of Assistant Arts & Entertainment Editor for the Pittsburgh-based alternative weekly paper, *Pulp*. Cindy—who experienced her pivotal teen years during the equally mass-marketed "grunge" phenomenon—recalls a similar trend nearly a decade ago:

> My friend and I would read *Sassy* and *Seventeen* when we were in middle school . . . I remember once when we were in eighth or ninth grade we were looking at magazines at her place and there was an article in there that really struck me. Instead of the usual bit on how to do your makeup or what kind of jeans are in style at the moment, this one told us what to listen to in order to be cool. It said, "Play Courtney Love," among other things, but what really bugged me was that there was no context behind it—there was no writing to back up what was so good about Courtney Love, or any other band for that matter. . . . It would have been one thing if they gave us a bio of the bands, or a review of their albums, or any type of story that backed up the idea that they were cool, and thus listening to them would make us cool. But they gave us no reasons, no context, just "play them."

As the recent resurgence of the punk trend proves, it has become increasingly difficult to assemble a credible underground image. With niche shops like Hot Topic cropping up in countless suburban malls, generalized symbols of punk and its offshoots create a false sense of authenticity. Customers blindly purchase assorted trinkets featuring anarchy symbols, safety pins and the Union Jack. The punks' emo counterparts voraciously gather black hair dye, fake glasses and "trucker hats"—exaggeratedly puffy baseball caps recently popularized by hotel heiress Paris Hilton, actor Ashton Kutcher, and their ilk. Knowledge of the symbols' history—or even the background of a musical genre—is irrelevant, as long as your jeans are cuffed just so. It's shallow consumption—with an edge.

Furthermore, in recent years, with the rising success of emo bands like Jimmy Eat World and Dashboard Confessional in the pop market, emo has traded underground credibility for fleeting popularity. Jimmy Eat World's self-titled sophomore release, originally entitled Bleed American, was a mere blip on the radar screen until the single, "The Middle" took off nearly a year after the CD's release. The popularity of that song and the follow-up single, "Sweetness," culminated in the release of a karaoke CD single featuring both songs. This demonstrates the marketability of the genre. Once, karaoke versions were only available for standards and Top 40 pop songs. Punk music, alternative rock and their various offshoots rarely cracked the Top 40, but in the summer of 2002, the relatively alternative genre of emo had somehow gained enough notoriety to join those ranks. In 2004, emo had gained such recognition that offshoots and sub-genres—including the "emo rap" style—had begun to surface.

Technological access and the whims of pop culture tastemakers conspired to boost the rise of the emo genre. Unlike past subcultures that resisted media attention and appropriation, some emo musicians and their fans enjoy riding the wave of popularity. With this shift into the mainstream, alongside other distinctively modern genres like nü-metal, pop punk and the garage rock revival deemed "retro alternative," emo did not merely blur the distinction between popular culture and counter-culture—it virtually erased it. Ten years ago, "alternative radio," though relatively accessible to the mainstream, did not earn nearly as much mainstream recognition as the current crop of alternative sub-genres. Emo is at the forefront of those styles, and with continued cooperation with the arbiters of taste, emo artists are crossing the boundary into territory previously reserved for mainstream pop stars.

It is not inherently "wrong" for a subculture to take advantage of mainstream success, but one must consider the separation between the original subculture and its pop culture counterpart. Typically, cultural critics will note a disconnect between a subculture and its mainstream version; often mass-produced representations of subculture lack the context and authenticity that made the original subculture so vital. Though the image and sounds may mimic those of the subculture's original, pure output, diluted, mass-produced knock-offs will never match the original in vitality and creativity.

Popular, accessible emo bands temper their melancholy message with radio-friendly pop hooks, abandoning the hardcore punk roots of the genre. Emo frontmen—like Dashboard Confessional's Chris Carabba, and, unwittingly, Bright Eyes' Conor Oberst—have become heartthrobs to female fans, gracing the pages of teenybopper rags alongside bubble-gum pop icons.

Ironically, it is "am I emo?" author Mara Schwartz who pinpoints the disenchantment of many emo fans in her *Seventeen* piece. The article inspired countless emo listeners to post to online message boards and write angry letters to the magazine, decrying the mainstream "posers" who would steal their subculture. Schwartz concludes: "The one thing these artists do have in common is that they're all independent-minded rock acts. Some, like Jimmy Eat World and Thursday have already been snatched up by major labels eager to make emo the next big thing. We kind of hope it's not."

Notebook

1. What music has meant the most to you in your life? Are you part of any music-based subcultures or fan groups? How are music-based subcultures different from other subcultures? Can a music-centered subculture exist without the music?

2. What do you think about "alternative" things being sold in the mass market—like Goth clothing at Hot Topic (a mall store), or Converse All-Star sneakers at Foot Locker, or tie-dye t-shirts at Target? Do you think this is okay? Why or why not?

3. Emily Lamison makes the point that many emo bands seem to have embraced the mass marketing of their genre. If emo bands happily join the mainstream in order to be financially successful, does this mean the subculture ceases to exist? Who "makes" a music-based subculture—the bands? The fans? The media that covers the phenomenon?

4. Emo is one of the newest subcultures written about for this book, and as such, it is one of the most subject to change—it hasn't even had time to fully solidify yet. What's the state of emo as you read this? Has it become something else, launched its own spin-offs? Is it over? How do you know, or how could you find out?

5. Andy Greenwald looks closer at the emo culture in his book *Nothing Feels Good: Punk Rock, Teenagers, and Emo*. Do your own research project on a music-based subculture: rap, punk, country, or metal. How has the subculture changed over the years? How has the commercialization of the subculture changed it, improved it, or killed it?

Economic Status and Raving

CHRISTINA ROBINSON

We often think about how people choose the subcultures they are in, but sometimes the circumstances of a subculture mean that it "chooses" its members. In this essay, Christina Robinson looks at how a certain amount of disposable income is required for, and therefore impacts, the rave subculture. Robinson was born in Maynard, Massachusetts, and completed her undergraduate studies at Bentley College, where she wrote the essay included here. The majority of her research for her essay was based on personal experiences during her first two years of college. Currently she is pursing a graduate degree in economics at North Carolina State University, and hopes to be a professor in the future.

———————— ✦ ————————

It has often been said the economy of the United States has had more influence on the global economy than any other. The US has the unique position of being the center of trade as well as a political powerhouse, so for most people the leap of faith that a booming economy could only lead to higher rates of employment, better pay rates, and an overall increase in worker satisfaction seems rational. And, while this is true, there are always two sides to the coin—as the economy booms, Americans often find they have larger disposable incomes; an increase in liquid cash inevitably increases the amount of purchasing that occurs. Many find that they are able to spend their cash without a second thought.

One could speculate that it is the increased disposable income, and the sense of power and self-importance that comes with such income, that causes parents to place extra pressure on their children. Parents who find that their life is suddenly an economic dream come true expect their children to follow suit: to be perfect in all areas of their life. My theory is that this increased pressure, coupled with the increase in available cash, is what drives many upper- and middle-class teenagers to become part of the drug-using, all-night-partying rave culture. Many of the ravers see raving as a means of escaping the pressure, and of separating themselves from the overbearing, repressive lifestyle many of them detest.

The original rave culture extended, grew, and morphed to create the rave culture of today. The culture was born on the Spanish island of Ibiza where clubs were wild, unmonitored, all night parties. According to Tara Pepper's 2001 article in *Newsweek*, "Partying for Profit," people at these parties would openly do drugs, engage in sexual acts, and dance to techno music well into the morning hours. This style of party quickly became commercialized and spread into other parts of Europe.

In Europe the rave culture prospered as people embraced the lifestyle that accompanied it: unconditional love, a place to dance and openly be whatever you want to be. Along with the rapid growth of the culture, however, came the awareness of the police, who broke up these parties and attempted to put an end to these all night free-for-alls. To an extent the officials were effective: the number of raves dramatically decreased. In the article "Degeneration X: The Artifacts and Lexicon of the Rave Subculture," Chrys Kahn-Egan claims that the decrease of European raves has led to the development and transplantation of the culture into several United States cities including New York and Detroit.

A typical U.S. raver is somewhere between fifteen and twenty-five, and is generally a member of upper- to middle-class society. When observing the demographics of a raver in conjunction with what the raving culture can provide, it is easy to understand the connection. For one thing, ravers tend to be at an experimental stage of their life, as well as being at an age where they may be experiencing rebellious urges against their parents. These urges are in large part related to the anger and pressure they feel stemming from their social position, their parents, their educators, and their government. Parents want their children to be more successful than they were and to live a better life. The main goal of any educator is to help a student achieve greatness, and now more than ever before there is an emphasis placed on the importance of a college education. While there isn't a direct pressure from the government, there is the constant fear that social security will run out, and that education and a good job will be necessary to retire comfortably when you have reached that point of life.

Most teenagers and young adults are living with the knowledge that they are paying taxes towards social security which will be of no benefit to them in their time of need. The pressures that are unique to today's middle-class are the same factors that entice people to join the rave subculture where they will be unconditionally accepted for who they are. These teenagers are often uncomfortable with the new expectations that are being bestowed upon them and seek a way to escape and deal with this change. Once the rave culture became firmly established, it began to develop its own rituals, rights of passage, and codes of membership, which are often centered around love and unconditional acceptance.

Most rave rituals are centered on the drugs—mainly ecstasy—and dancing. Experienced ravers often "baby sit" and "bless" first time or virgin ravers, who are about to have their first drug enhanced experience. A more experienced drug user will often "baby sit," or remain with, the virgin to ensure that if they become scared of what is happening to them, someone is there with them to help them regain control. Blessing a first timer is done as a symbol of comfort, and as a spiritual gesture to try and ensure the raver has a good experience. According to Kahn-Egan, one common blessing is "X out the bad trip. A perfect circle of endless light for a good trip. A kiss for good luck."

Rave dancing is done to techno music, which is electronically enhanced to have a very rapid beat; experienced ravers typically have dance moves that are done at a specific part of a song. The dancing often involves props, such as light sticks, which require skill to use properly, and to achieve the appropriate effect. As someone gains skill and experience their dance skills will improve and they will begin to blend with the more seasoned ravers.

There are two different rites of passage that ravers undergo; all ravers will undergo the first transition, while only some will experience the second. When somebody attends their first rave it is simply that, attending a dance party; however, with time these people may become initiated into becoming a full-fledged raver. While there are no specific rules, written or otherwise, to achieving raver status, most people describe a similar process. They went to a few raves with friends, fell in love with the atmosphere, and developed a longing to immerse themselves into the environment with increased frequency. At this point most people begin to view themselves as ravers, and often feel that the rave lifestyle is taking on a central focus in their day-to-day activities.

The second rite of passage is commonly experienced by those who join the culture at a young age—this is the transition from being a candy-raver to developing a more typical rave style. Candy ravers are those who often dress in a much younger manner, and wear many candy accessories, such as rings and necklaces. This transition consists of abandoning some of the candy necklaces and childish trip toys in favor of more adult toys, and wearing more traditional dress.

The codes of membership for a raver are simple—dress the part, behave the part, and truly love all aspects of raving. Dressing like a raver means wearing pants with oversized legs, a tee shirt, typically but not always childish—many rave tee shirts depict cartoon characters from the early eighties—and a backpack full of supplies needed, such as water, stuffed animals, and anything else one may need to get through the night. To behave as a raver one must truly appreciate the music, the others at the rave, and above all embrace the raver's code: PLUR. PLUR stands for peace, love, unity, and respect, and describes the ways ravers feel people should treat each other.

While in its basic profile raving appears as a subculture open to any who wish membership, there are certain costs which make it a fairly prohibitive culture to join. It is true no one would be turned away for the way they look, or the way they are dressed. The monetary costs of being a member, however, are large and require a certain amount of liquid income. Lower income teenagers are normally not capable of spending the amount of money that most people spend at an average rave. A typical rave has two costs: the cost of attending the rave (the cost of being allowed in the door), and the cost of any drugs or other items you would like to consume. Admittance to a typical rave is fairly modest, ranging from twenty to one hundred dollars for a ticket. The cost of drugs, however, is considerably higher. The most common drug consumed at these all night parties is ecstasy, a designer drug composed partially of a prescription drug from the nineteen eighties, metheylenedimethoxymethamphetamine (commonly called MDMA), and possibly mixed with crack, cocaine, speed, and traces of other illegal drugs. Ecstasy is normally sold in pill form and can cost anywhere from twenty to thirty dollars a pill on the street and up to fifty dollars per pill at an actual rave. With time, ecstasy users may begin to feel the drug has lost its magic, and doesn't provide the same sensation it once did. At this point users will most likely start taking more than one dosage at a given time. Thus, the average total cost of attending a rave ranges from anywhere between twenty to one hundred and fifty dollars.

Because of its age demographic, this is a subculture consisting mainly of students. Most students have only a part time job, which likely provides only a small amount of income, and raving is an activity that requires a considerable amount of financing, likely more than can be earned by working a part time job. Due to the prohibitive costs, many ravers are likely receiving external funding which they use for the activities. Since most college students report receiving a living allowance from their parents, it seems likely that those receiving a larger allowance are more willing to spend this money on parties and drugs than those who are trying to scrape by on their own incomes.

Along with the age-related financial constraints are the problems inherent to members of the middle class. Being a member of the middle-class goes far beyond financial standing, and extends into the social and psychological aspects of the human psyche. Many middle class children are brought up with the fear that one false move may cause their reality to unravel, the fear that they will not be able to satisfy their life's desires, and the fear that they will be forced to go without in their time of need. A great deal of middle class children grow up going to day care after school, while a great deal of upper income families can afford to have a parent or a nanny home to watch the children after school. Both upper and middle income teenagers grow up unsure of the role they do (or want to) play in society, and long for a place to belong.

Some of those youth find their place within the raving culture. Within this culture almost everything is accepted; who you are, where you are from, and what you look like has little to no bearing on acceptance into the raving culture. One of the most common reasons for attending a rave is the freedom to be a child; if you want to act like an infant you can: common elements of the rave scene include pacifiers, stuffed animals, and other childish paraphernalia. One could theorize that these are attempts by children who are growing up far too fast to remain young for as long as possible. It seems obvious that they would want to cling to things that remind them of their simpler, carefree childhood, not surprisingly such objects are a major attraction of the raving culture. This infantilism, coupled with the effects of ecstasy, creates an atmosphere that suits upper and middle income teenagers.

The pressures to get all As on a report card, to be the perfect son or daughter, or to fit into a societal mold seem to magically disappear once they enter the rave. Raving and other ravers provide a sense that drugs, and the underground raving scene are safe, acceptable, and commonplace.

The state of today's economy is assisting the rave culture in its rise. There are two types of existing goods: those that are demanded more when income and the economy are increasing, and those that are demanded more when the economy is faltering. The first category of goods are referred to as normal goods, and the latter are referred to as inferior goods. Simply being a normal

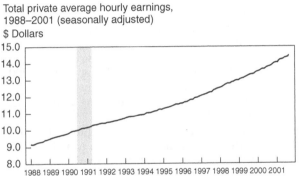

Total private average hourly earnings,
1988–2001 (seasonally adjusted)

Source: Bureau of Labor Statistics. Current Employment Statistics Survey.
Note: Shaded area denotes recession.

Unemployement rate, 1989–2001 (seasonally adjusted)

Source: Bureau of Labor Statistics. Current Population Survey.
Note: Shaded area represents recession. Break in series in January 1994 is due to
        the redesign of the survey.

good does not imply that something is a good product; it means that as the income rises, so too does the demand for the good. An inferior good is not something that is poorly made, or of little worth, but something for which the demand falls as income rises. Goods such as alcohol, tobacco, and education are considered normal, while things such as potatoes would be considered inferior; so when people have more money and want more of a good that is normal, but when their income increases and their demand declines that is considered inferior.

These graphs show that between 1994 and 2001 the economy was doing quite well; the unemployment rate fell from the high experienced in 1992, and the hourly earnings rates were increasing. The country was at a high. Between the years of 1998 and 1999, unemployment declined sharply and earnings were steadily rising; during the same time period the usage of illegal club drugs were also on the rise. As reported by the U.S. Senate Caucus on International Narcotics Control, lifetime use of this drug by high school students increased by 2.2 percent, going from 5.8 percent in 1998 to 8 percent in 1999. According to Doug McVey's 2001 report "Drug War Facts," the percentage of students reporting use of club drugs experienced a similar increase, going from 3.6 percent in 1998 to 5.6 percent in 1999.

It is statistics like these, and the demographics of the rave culture, that have put this subculture on the rise. A major subgroup of the raving culture consists of children of wealthy parents who are trying to escape from their monotonous life. Raving is an expensive activity, and requires disposable income, and what is more disposable than money that comes from your parents? Many ravers argue that they do not go to raves to use drugs, but rather that the usage of ecstasy and other such substances enhance the raving experience. These same people, however, also state that they would be unlikely to attend a rave if they didn't have enough money to go and be on their drug of choice. Statements like these make it possible to arrive at the conclusion that ecstasy use is a function of raves, and from there it is possible to assume that an increased use of ecstasy has been caused by an increase in raves. Similarly, as the amount of ecstasy use increases, so to does the occurrence of raves.

Drugs have always been a means of escaping problems. For a group of young people brought up by parents from the seventies who embraced drugs, turning to ecstasy and the raving culture should have been anticipated. The ecstasy enhanced/induced state of being relieves the pressures of living for a few magical hours. As the amount of drug usage increases, and the social position of the United States economy increases, members of the upper- and middle-class youth find themselves continually more drawn to the raving culture. I interviewed Walter, a young upper-class youth who would prefer to be referred to as Rave. Rave drives a brand new GMC Jimmy that his parents bought him for graduation from his military high school. He began raving because it seemed like a way of maintaining his own sanity, escaping the overbearing pressures to maintain an image that he despised. Rave didn't want to dress the way his parents wanted him to, and didn't want to work for his father at the family owned business either, so almost in a way of protest he began going to raves. At his low point, Rave was known to drop two to three bombs (ecstasy pills) in one day, whether at a rave or not. In a response to pressure to be the perfect child, and behave in a "respectable manner," he chose the almost perfect antithesis—a life of drug use and reckless partying.

Members of two different social classes can achieve an equal experience where they are on equal ground. Everyone at a rave is having a similar experience; they all have the same responsibilities and a shared reality. It isn't uncommon to speak to a raver that describes this experience as one in which it seems everyone has a responsibility to add something to the party. The economic differences between teenagers create a division, different growing experiences and an almost entirely separate culture. These differences, however, are put aside when at a rave creating an equality and respect that exemplify PLUR.

As my parents often tried to instill in me, I know that drug use in itself isn't good . . . but it isn't always bad either. In the sixties and seventies hippies smoked marijuana and used hallucinogens to enhance themselves, and created a culture based on love and peace. Today, in the early part of the twenty first century, the ravers are using ecstasy and other club drugs to enhance themselves, crossing many boundaries that the generation before them would never consider breaking. The recent increase and spreading of the rave culture is not only the rise of drug use, and illegal partying but also a rise in PLUR.

Does the rave culture exist because there is now more pressure to be successful, is it simply because people have more money and therefore are more likely to part with a dollar? The answer lies somewhere in between. Simply having more pressure and inadequate funds would not lend itself to the raving culture, and just having money is not a reason to rave, as few people would go to a rave simply because they could afford it. It is the combination of new, liquid money, an increase in pressure from parents, and the community that draws teenagers to this place where they can put that all aside for a while. As income increases, the demand and desire to attend a rave increases accordingly; when the income is low people still try to escape their problems, but are more apt to seek solace in some beers, and go to a local party.

Notebook

1. What have you bought in the last week? How do you feel that those items define who you are? Is there anything subversive about what you've bought? Since we live in a capitalist society that thrives on the consumption of goods and services, can we say that any subculture of consumption is really oppostional to the dominant ideology? What about the rave culture, which Christina Robinson describes as being dependent on a disposable income—can such a subculture be subversive, and if it's not, is it a subculture at all?

2. Robinson makes the case that one needs to be middle or upper class in order to fully participate in the rave culture. Given that most subcultures have merchandise and paraphernalia involved, does it follow that most members of subcultures are middle class? Are there working-class subcultures? (See the essays on heavy metal and the roots of skateboarding.) Do those subcultures fill a different set of needs for those of a different class? How do issues of class affect the subculture you're studying?

3. The author of this essay was an economics major, and this interest determined her approach to the subject. From what you can tell from their biographical notes, how have the other authors in this book used their own backgrounds and interests to determine the angle for their research or theories on subcultures? How will your own interests, skills, and knowledge help you write the paper you're going to write?

4. There are a number of good articles and books out there on the various aspects of the rave culture, which, because of its use of particular costumes, rituals, codes, and music, makes it a particularly fertile subculture for study. But it's also got a kind of glamour—having to do with "sex, drugs, and rock n' roll"—that appeals to the mainstream culture, and therefore it was often depicted on TV shows and in movies in the 90s. The movie *Groove*, directed by Greg Harrison, is a fictional account of rave culture. Check it out on DVD and compare its findings to those in more academic or journalistic sources.

Street Skateboarding and the Government Stamp of Approval
ROBERT RUNDQUIST

Skateboarding is a subculture that has made its way from its roots in working-class youth (see the essay "The Lords of Dogtown") to respectability and mainstream acceptance, as evidenced by the fact that it was featured on a U.S. postage stamp. Robert Rundquist considers that transformation and its effect on the skateboarders themselves. Born in Los Angles in 1974, Rundquist attended Los Angeles Valley Community College before transferring to the University of California, Berkeley, earning his B.A. with Highest Honors in English Literature. He returned to Los Angeles and received his M.A. in English at the University of Southern California. After working at various community college writing centers, Rundquist became the Instructional Specialist for the Chaffey College Writing Center in 2003.

---------------- ✦ ----------------

At the 1999 ESPN Summer X Games in San Francisco, California, the United States Postal Service unveiled the Xtreme Sports Stamp Collection, a four-piece set showcasing bmx, in-line skating, snowboarding, and skateboarding. Present on stage during the ceremony were ESPN anchor Chris Fowler, San Francisco Mayor Willie Brown, United States Postal Service Vice President John Ward, and a number of pioneering Xtreme Sports athletes. Fowler began the ceremony with the following words: "This is an exciting day for those of us at ESPN, especially those of us that have been involved with Xtreme Sports coverage, and a day that was impossible to imagine five years ago when the X Games started in Rhode Island. As of today, the USPS has given its stamp of approval to Xtreme Sports."

Since these activities have been historically viewed as "underground" and "deviant," many in the Xtreme Sports community viewed this national recognition as a welcomed form of social acceptance. Towards the end of the ceremony, Fowler interviewed skateboarding legend Tony Hawk. "What's your reaction? You've been doing this sport since you could walk basically, and you experienced the ups and downs, the rise in popularity, its status as a rebel sport. You've been heckled by cops over the years as well as

your fellow skateboarders. Now you're legit. You're on a stamp."
Hawk's response? "It's been a long time coming."
After decades of conflict between skateboarders and mainstream society—most specifically city governments and law enforcement—it has indeed taken a long time for skateboarding to
receive such cultural validation, in this case, an honor that carries
so much social currency that a person must usually be dead for at
least ten years before appearing on a stamp in order to ensure that
the individual's entire life and legacy meets the moral require-
ments for this iconographic representation of American culture.
So why have skateboarders been given such a venerated honor?
What explains such a radical turn of events? Although the fact that
skateboarding would be chosen for a stamp could reflect a growing acceptance of this Xtreme sport, the incorporation of skateboarding into the national iconography rather exemplifies the
dominant culture's attempt to dictate the nature of skateboarding,
in particular street skating, in order to confine the activity to a
government sanctioned frame of space and imagination.

Skateboarding indeed entered a new phase of unprecedented popularity at the end of the 20th century. According to
Skatepark.org's survey on participation statistics between 1997 and
2000, the Sporting Goods Manufacturing Association estimated
that more than 11.5 million people were skateboarding in the
United States in the year 2000. *Transworld Magazine* reported in
2001 that skateboarding clothing, especially shoes, became available in a wide variety of department stores and retail outlets, with
skateboarding merchandise annually contributing $1.4 billion to
the nation's economy. Video games offering young kids the virtual
ability to enjoy the incredible moves that only professional skaters
are capable of doing or even imagining found a place in homes
across the country. Cities began to build public skateboard parks
to serve the growing numbers and generations of skateboarders.
And competitive events like the X Games and Gravity Games
placed skateboarding (and other "Xtreme" activities) in the national spotlight of primetime television.

Packaging skateboarding as an "Xtreme Sport" and exposing
the general public to a competitive, structured side of skateboarding—via mainstream media, consumer products, and even
a government stamp—countered the long-held perception of
skateboarding, in particular street skating, as destructive and
criminal. Michael Brooke's *The Concrete Wave: The History of
Skateboarding* chronicles skateboarding's reception over the years
and relates skateboarding's "bad" reputation to the 1980s when

skateboarding took to the streets with a new style and attitude. *Thrasher* magazine encapsulated this era of skateboarding. Brooke quotes magazine founder Fausto Vitello summing up its hardcore philosophy this way: *"Thrasher* is not about hypocrisy or selling out to corporate America. We are about skate and destroy." The aggressive style of street skateboarding that hit the scene in the 80s did not reflect an inherently deviant nature in the skateboarder but rather demonstrated a change in the conditions surrounding the activity. In an interview with skateboarding legend Lance Mountain, he discussed how the birth of modern street skating corresponded with a bust in the industry that caused skateboarders to take their craft to the streets:

> During the times of the skatepark closures in the early 80s, when all the private cement parks closed down, skating moved directly to the street and parking lot adjacent to it. . . . That opened up the United States and the world to a new arena, which is the kid could just take whatever they had, a sidewalk, this parking block, anything, and adapt skateboarding to it and adapt tricks to it.

This loss of space intensified the rebellious attitude in the small contingency that remained loyal to skateboarding after the industry downturn, and that image has dominated the mainstream perception of skateboarding for most of the past two decades.

The in your face, "skate and destroy" mentality that emerged during the 80s undoubtedly widened the rift between skateboarders and the rest of society. Now in the plain view of the everyday public, the daring aerials and use of structures within the city landscape heightened concerns about liability risk and property damage—the two main arguments used against skateboarding throughout its history. Although property damage and liability risk are unintended results of street skating that cannot be ignored, skateboarders feel that these negative parts of skateboarding have been blown out of proportion. Skateboarding does often chip concrete surfaces and leave black streaks of dirty wax, but the amount of damage to the environment would seemingly pale in comparison to the negative environmental effects resulting from the use of automobiles and other daily activities that occur daily throughout the country. And while many skateboarders do get hurt while skateboarding, the statistics consistently reflect that skateboarding is one of the safer activity choices for today's youth. According to the United States Consumer Products Safety Commission, only

0.77% of skateboarders are seriously injured every year, when the percentages in traditional sports like baseball, basketball, and football are at least twice as high. The cultural focus on the negative aspects of skateboarding renders what attracts most young people to skateboarding as seemingly unimportant, but a better understanding of the passion young skateboarders have for this activity may open up an underlying, yet perhaps more significant, dimension to this issue that needs to be examined in order to appreciate today's antagonistic relationship between skateboarding and mainstream culture. For skateboarders, street skating is an unadulterated form of creative expression that empowers those who participate in it. Skateboarder Matt Rzeszutko describes the type of passion that is often overshadowed by mainstream complaints about skateboarding:

> I love skateboarding so much. I even tattooed a skateboard onto my arm. It sounds kind of crazy, but it's something I believe in. . . . Skateboarding to me is a reason to live my day. I . . . wake up in the morning and think, "skateboarding really gives my life meaning." I'll just go out and have fun. Skate with my friends. Skate by myself. . . . Like without skateboarding, I don't know where I'd be. I'd probably be some bum just sitting around with no reason to live, no happiness. Skateboarding's given me everything.

For most skateboarders, this type of passion and commitment is not out of the ordinary. And what draws most people to skateboarding is its unique form of personal expression.

The street skater's creative form of expression lies in the way that skateboarders view and interact with the world, and it is the nature of this expression that may contain the roots of "the skateboarding problem." Riding handrails, jumping gaps, and grinding combinations on ledges and objects that were never constructed with such purposes in mind are a creative form of expression that draws many young people to skateboarding. Professional skateboarder Andy MacDonald describes the skateboarder's interpretive process in the following way:

> Street skaters view the world with what I call "skate goggles." Like we'll look at a bridge and think, if the world was turned upside down one day, we would skate that. Normal people don't look at the world the way skateboarders do. Driving down the street, walking down the street, skateboarders are constantly searching for some new line, some new element in the urban

surroundings that the original architects never conceived of. And it's the skateboarders' interpretation of that that I think is really neat. 99.9% of the population view a handrail as something to stabilize you as you walk up or down, but the skateboarder sees it as hours and hours of fun, a challenge. Sliding down their boards. Who would have ever thought?

Brooke's title, *The Concrete Wave*, symbolically exemplifies the almost paradoxical nature of the street skater's way of viewing the world: treating what is concrete and fixed with the fluidity and instability of a wave.

In *The Practice of Everyday Life*, Michel de Certeau focuses on the generative actions of the pedestrian in the way that I wish to analyze the interpretive actions of the street skater. As de Certeau states of pedestrians, "trailblazers in the jungles of functionalist rationality . . . trace 'indeterminate trajectories' that are apparently meaningless, since they do not cohere with the constructed, written, and prefabricated space through which they move." As he later states, "Walking is to the urban system what the speech act is to language." De Certeau argues that although places are defined with proper meanings and uses, pedestrians—taking liberties with the textual landscape—modify spaces for their own purposes: taking short cuts, sitting on a ledge to tie one's shoes, etc. For de Certeau, consumption is always a process of production: "users make innumerable and infinitesimal transformations of and within the dominant cultural economy in order to adapt it to their own interest and their own rules."

Street skaters re-interpret the definitions of physical reality and utility institutionalized by previous generations in a much more radical manner than de Certeau's pedestrian. Donald Bell, in an issue of the skateboard magazine *Heckler*, articulates the cultural challenge present in the practices of the urban skateboarder:

> Street skaters use the surrounding concrete covered modern landscape as a canvas for personal artistic expression. The art of street skating lies in its ability to incorporate objects of architectural utility (curbs, benches, driveways, handrails) into a high speed dance that critiques the significance of the object and shows to those with open minds the beauty that can be found in the everyday. . . . Street skating's natural environment is the unnatural, the manmade concrete structures of our cities and suburbs, built with finite purpose and human utility in mind. I spent my youth destroying people's confidence in the absolute meaning of these

objects. . . . We are suburban subversion on four wheels. . . . It is the power of saying: This is not a curb. This is not a bench. This is not a dead-end suburb, or a thriving metropolis. This is my playground.

Bell's description of street skating borders on a social critique, and this spatial re-interpretation can be read in a way that carries significant cultural implications, for the street skater's practices undermine the symbolic stability of our cityscapes, the literal fabric and foundation of culture.

Cities are not "natural" places but constructions of human imagination with built-in values and beliefs. In the essay "The City," Robert Park states, "The city is . . . a state of mind, a body of customs and traditions, and of the organized attitudes and sentiments that inhere in these customs and are transmitted with this tradition. The city is not, in other words, merely a physical mechanism." Iain Borden, author of *Skateboarding: Space and the City*, relates this reality directly to the skateboarder:

> One of the interesting things about skateboarding is that skaters skate in relation to modern cities, which means that they're skating amongst modern buildings, modern cityscapes, modern landscapes. The point about this is that city's buildings, landscapes mean things to people. You'd be hard pressed to find a more important set of documents of civilization than buildings. . . . People expect cities to be full of certainty, predictability, zoning, and people behaving exactly as they should. Skateboarders don't do this. They think illogically. They ollie up into the air. They ride up onto pieces of street furniture. They go through bits of architecture that they shouldn't, and people don't like this. This is unpredictable, chaos, disorder.

Interpreting signals of the physical world in the "correct" manner is one of the fundamental ways that people with different subjective beliefs can still function and co-exist—literally stay out of each other's way. It is this order that skateboarders challenge with every grind, undermining the fixed notion of utility for cityscapes and the objects within those areas.

Although any intent involving a large-scale social critique may be beyond the scope of most skateboarders, the form of expression can be more directly tied to the specific conditions of this youth subculture. By operating in urban areas, the actions of this predominantly white, middle-class, male, youth subculture, may be construed as a form of rebellion against the white-collar work-place they are often being groomed for. The street skater's lifestyle, hanging out on the corner and constantly playing, supposedly fails to properly train an adolescent for his or her eventual development into a "productive" member of society. Skateboarding fails to instill a responsibility for utilizing one's time and body in a way that rigorously contributes back to the system (except for the small few that skateboard at the professional level). The wasting of energy and resources in a constant form of "unauthorized" play is a glaring violation of the work ethic that an adolescent should be learning during the transition to adulthood. The young skater's practices resist the "all work, no play" lives of their middle-class parents by violating the separation between those two activities and by doing it in the space of the aspect of modern life that the skateboarder seems to find empty and unsatisfying. For many young skateboarders, skateboarding offers a sense of empower-ment through this expression of rejection, and it is this message that seems to be even more socially problematic than property damage or liability risk.

The wide range of problems associated with street skating has resulted in the employment of a variety of strategies to eliminate skateboarding from the streets. Attempts to recuperate skate-boarding and its subculture have existed for decades. Laws banning skateboarding have existed since the 1960s, and "No Skateboarding!" signs dot cityscapes across the country. Street skaters are issued tickets and often have their boards confiscated by authorities. Many times, skateboarders even get arrested and go to jail for skateboarding. Graphic design artist and skateboarder Michael Leon tells a story that is quite common in the skate-boarding world: "Me and my friend use to skate this one painted curb in our small town. We would wax it and stuff. The owner of the strip mall was not too happy about it. . . . We ended up going to jail. We were in jail for two days for skating a curb."

Most of the punitive strategies have been unsuccessful since many skateboarders seem to thrive on their rebel status or do not believe that they are doing anything wrong, a stance reflected by the "Skateboarding is not a crime!" mantra. This reality has generated new strategies in recent years that focus attention on prevention rather than punishment. Devices called Skatestoppers® are now be-ing used all over the country in an attempt to make desirable terrain unskateable. By applying a piece of industrial-strength plastic or metal to a potential skating surface, Skatestoppers® make it more difficult for skateboarders to slide or grind on a ledge or rail.

Skatestoppers® have not been able to completely rid city streets of skateboarders, but the strategy reflects the continued commitment of local governments and businesses to address the skateboarding problem. At the forefront of these latest measures to remove skateboarding from the streets is the re-emergence of public skateboard parks. With facilities opening up nationwide, skateparks offer vertical ramps and concrete bowls, as well as rails, fun boxes, and other types of simulated urban conditions in "street courses." The public skatepark boom seen in the past few years was the direct result of the legal declaration of skateboarding as a "hazardous recreational activity." In California, Assembly Bill 1296 became effective on January 1, 1998, releasing cities from any liability for skateboarding injuries and allowing the construction of skateparks to proceed without the costly expense of liability insurance. This strategy is being adopted by a number of states around the country, creating an unprecedented commitment of public resources to skateboarding. Appearing next to baseball diamonds and basketball courts, the re-emergence of public skateparks demonstrates a social recognition on the same playing field as other traditional youth activities.

The designation of skateboarding as "recreational" also symbolically and practically marks skateboarding as an activity appropriate for areas of play and not city streets. By providing a space sanctioned for skateboarding, skateboard parks offer an alternative for skating the streets. Such a strategy has a historical analogue. At the beginning of the 20th century, when the widespread use of automobiles necessitated the regulation of children's play on the streets, city governments constructed alternative areas for play, what are now commonly known as playgrounds. In *City Play*, Amanda Dargan and Steven Zeitlin argue that "motorized vehicles redefined the use of streets and changed notions of public space. Adults used city ordinances to make street play illegal, and they used the playground movement and other reform efforts to coax children, especially poor immigrants, from the sidewalks." Providing a proper time and place for skateboarding, skateparks similarly function as a regulator of skateboarding, attempting to negate the problems caused by skateboarding on the streets.

The strong push to create a socially acceptable place for skateboarding is exemplified by the United States Postal Service skateboarding stamp. The stamp reflects the mainstream culture's desirable image of skateboarding, carefully constructed to represent skateboarders in their proper place and obeying the rules dictated by society. Wearing safety equipment now required by law in all skateparks and being in the middle of a maneuver most likely to be performed on a skatepark vert ramp, this image dictates the proper confines of skateboarding that the government wishes to create. The stamp and the process of stamping attempts to clarify, classify, and re-present skateboarding in order to solidify a positive and acceptable image of skateboarding in the cultural imagination. Such imagery solidification attempts to dictate and reinforce a culturally appropriate type of skateboarding, making all others inappropriate, illegal, and, down the road, possibly unimaginable.

As part of the long history of efforts to recuperate skateboarding, the stamp creates a new image of skateboarding for present and future generations, one that parallels the socially acceptable facet of skateboarding that has paved the way for the gradual entrance of skateboarding into mainstream society. So far, these efforts have not completely eradicated the "darker" side of skateboarding, and this reality lies in the fact that the creative expression of skateboarding constantly strives to push the limits of its own expression. The attempts at recuperation have failed and continue to fail because the mainstream solution operates within a paradigm that most skateboarders already reject. Street skating is antithetical to the single-minded viewpoint reflected in the strategies employed to negate the skateboarder's creative and transformative eye. And it is the street skater's bold-faced, unapologetic rejection of limits and semiotic closure that makes, and will probably continue to make, skateboarding a problem in the eyes of mainstream society.

On the streets, there are a variety of clues that the problems will continue. Skaters mock authority by changing "NO SKATE-BOARDING" signs to "kNOw SKATEBOARDING" or "Go Skateboarding." They run away from security guards who try to monitor them. Skateboarders break off Skatestoppers® or use them to make tricks even harder. Dissatisfied with the quality and rules of public skateparks, some groups of skaters have constructed their own underground skateparks in abandoned areas of cities. All in all, there is a part of the skateboarding community that rejects the ways that mainstream society attempts to control skateboarding. Joel Patterson, an editor for *Transworld* magazine, captured the feelings of dismay felt by many skateboarders who continue to ride the streets despite today's increased harassment and restrictions:

> Skateboarding runs in like this weird course. It's like sanding against the grain of wood. Is that bad? No. Is that good? No. It just is. It would be terrible to take it away. It's a really cool thing, especially when you participate in it. They're just kids, you know. We're just young people. Just people. No one's out there killing anybody. I don't know. I just don't see the purpose of why it has to go away, why street skating has to go away. But people want it to go away. They do . . . desperately.

My point is not to reinforce or propose an essentialist version of skateboarding. Many skateboarders love skateparks, and there is no hierarchy of value that should inherently privilege the streets over skateparks. But there are consequences when control shifts from the members of the subculture to an outside force, especially when that outside force intentionally places limits on behavior and practices. The current cultural agenda, symbolically punctuated in the Xtreme Sports stamp, attempts to represent only one type of skateboarding as legitimate, and although the prevailing of this government sanctioned construction of skateboarding may lead to a more positive relationship between the skateboarding subculture and mainstream society, there may be negative consequences as well. And these negative consequences must be questioned more thoroughly. What is the cost of social acceptance? What is the cost of receiving the government stamp of approval?

Notebook

1. In discussing street skaters, Rundquist makes the argument that "by operating in urban areas, the actions of this predominantly white, middle-class, male, youth subculture may be construed as a form of rebellion against the white-collar workplace they are often being groomed for," an argument nearly identical to Christina Robinson's analysis of ravers and Amy Wilkin's argument about Goths. Have you yourself ever felt the desire to rebel against "being groomed for the workforce"? How did this rebellion manifest itself? Why do you think some kids are happy to prepare for careers while others are attracted to raves, skateboarding, or Goth? Why would one middle-class white guy choose skateboarding and another Goth?

2. In his essay, Rundquist concludes, "there are consequences when control shifts from the members of the subculture to an outside force, especially when that outside force intentionally places limits on behavior and practices." What

outside forces have come to bear on the subculture you're studying? How have those outside forces changed the subculture?

3. Compare this essay to "She Rips When She Skates" and "Lords of Dogtown," the other two skateboarding essays in this book. How are they rhetorically similar? How are they different? How do their differing styles help support their different arguments?

4. Rundquist mentions the book *The Concrete Wave: The History of Skateboarding* by Michael Brooke. This could be a good place to start if you're interested in further researching the arc of this subculture from underground to acceptability.

CHAPTER 5

Dropping Out and Dropping Back In

OVERVIEW

So far, we've explored the way people enter and involve themselves in subcultures, and how rituals, beliefs, and a sense of community draw these people away from the mainstream culture. But we also know that being in a subculture usually means keeping one foot in the mainstream culture as well, and that most people who join subcultures also eventually leave them. In this chapter, we explore some of the reasons why people might leave a subculture, as well as the process they must undergo in order to depart.

The reasons and the processes vary. Some subculture members try to hang on to remnants of the culture as they grow older, while others fade out of the community and its activities as real-world, adult responsibilities—work, family, finances—take a greater hold. And while many people look back on their days in a subculture with fondness and nostalgia, others have more dramatic and tough transitions. New generations battle for the future of the subculture with the older members. The rituals or activities of the subculture prove too strenuous or dangerous to keep up. Or the members become disillusioned as they compare their idealistic hopes for the subculture with the flawed realities. What groups or activities have you joined and then left in your life? Looking back, what surprises you about yourself when you think about your participation in those activities? How did you make your break with that community?

As I write this, most of the subcultures explored in this book are still active: in 2006, there are still punks, straightedgers, ravers, hippies, and skateboarders in my city, Chicago. But by the time you read this, things may have changed. Some of these subcultures may no longer exist. Other, new ones may have popped up. This is part of the reason why it's important to document and study subcultures when and where you find them: blink twice and they might be gone.

The Graying of Aquarius

JERRY ADLER

"Not Fade Away" goes a song commonly associated with the hippie subculture. Like all subcultures, the hippie movement has waxed and waned over time, but it has shown a remarkable ability to keep going. Here, Jerry Adler visits some older hippies holding on to their identities as such. Adler is a senior editor and science writer at Newsweek *magazine. He received his B.A. in American History from Yale University in 1970.*

——————— ✦ ———————

The smell of incense still wafts down from Earth People's Park, outside Norton, Vt. From the mountains near Eugene, Ore., on a quiet night you can still hear the White Album being played. They cluster in remote communes from which they descend occasionally to sell some sandals or straighten out a problem with their welfare checks. Or they live in plant-laden Victorian houses in Cambridge or Boulder with $500 bikes in the halls and $200 cars in the driveway. They are hippies, survivors of that once vast band of romantics who imagined that the mighty river of American civilization could somehow be turned from its course by sex, drugs and rock and roll. They await the call that may never come, to dance again on that verdant field of memory, joining hands no longer young, real grannies behind those glasses.

It isn't easy being a hippie in 1987, having the only kid named Sequoia in a class full of girls named Farrah. The infrastructure of back-room LSD factories, head shops and crash pads has virtually disappeared. Neither sex nor drugs has turned out to be as innocent as they seemed 20 year ago, and as for rock and roll, its central place in the nation's intellectual life has been usurped by computer software. Long hair has lost its meaning as a symbol of cultural rebellion, just in time for the appearance of that bittersweet reminder of the passage of time, the balding hippie. That much of life is compromise has finally been borne home to this unforgiving generation. Harvey Wasserman, 41, a veteran of the civil-rights, antiwar and antinuclear movements who went from 1969 to 1975 without a haircut, still believes in "peace now." But instead of wearing it on a T shirt, he has it printed on his business card, as president of a family shoe company. Rodger T. Williams, 42, a San Francisco carpenter/artist who boasts the hippie equivalent of a Mayflower ancestor—he went to grade school with Ron McKernan of the Grateful Dead—must be one of the few American men who still wears beads. But he wears them inside his shirt.

They are still gentle. There is, on the whole, less bitterness in a whole forest's worth of hippies than in a single elevator of Yuppies on their way up. The grand political passions and anger of the '60s are mostly spent, although a Republican hippie remains a contradiction in terms—as does, for that matter, a Democratic hippie. Many will still rally for issues that grew out of the movement: apartheid, abortion rights, nuclear power. But an equally common attitude is expressed by Williams, who says: "The closest I get to politics is the Buddhist thing, personal transformation"—which, in fact, is the polar opposite of politics. A random sampling of hippies today would show about equal numbers of Buddhists and Hindus, and a few like Karen Stingle, 42, of Eugene, who practices a mixture of Native American, feminist and post-Christian spirituality "based on natural cycles and the Goddess tradition"; the rites take place in Indian sweat lodges, and the liturgy is part Sioux, part Hebrew.

The drugs are mostly gone, or so graying hippies claim. A few say they still smoke marijuana—although no longer before breakfast and at the movies—but few will admit to taking anything more powerful. But they don't denounce drugs, either. Stingle, who left a UCLA program in 1971 just short a doctorate in clincial psychology, says she took LSD often in the succeeding years. "Acid was worth it because I had so much to learn," she says. "It breaks down boundaries, but once you see, you don't need it anymore." A while ago she and some friends tried the mood enhancer ecstasy, and she found it interesting but unnecessary. "It made everyone warm and loving," she reports. "But we were all that way anyway, and afterward I was exhausted."

There is an epitaph for an era, all right. Sad but true: hippies are not what they used to be, any more than anyone else. Consider the fate of communes. Just as most outsiders suspected, one of the reasons hippies used to live in communes was to make it easier to have sex with each other. Precisely to escape that implication, when Karen Gruber rented a five-bedroom house in downtown

Boulder, Colo., as a commune for herself and four companions, she named it the May Day Collective. The philosophy of the May Day Collective is noble but not exactly galvanizing: to minimize their impact on the planet by sharing electricity, appliances, newspapers and the like. The house lacks even the most basic equipment of a traditional hippie commune, a stereo that could be heard in Denver. Two of the five members are bicycle repairmen, one is a philosophy professor at the University of Colorado and Gruber, 39, is an antinuclear activist and mediator of landlord-tenant disputes. Her idea of a good time is to visit ghetto neighborhoods or the offices of peace groups. "We sit around and read and talk to each other," she says.

Even outside of communes, though, hippies are still trying to live off the land, at least figuratively. The May Day Collective gathered most of its furniture on the street during the city's annual Spring Clean Up last year. In Oregon, Stingle gathers chickweed and sow thistle for her salads, and she lists about a dozen things she has done for money, including pruning orchards, sewing beads, teaching a class in dreams, gathering seaweed and "whatever else comes up." By definition, a hippie cannot have a traditional career in a straight business. If he works for a large organization at all, it is likely to be in some unexpected context, like Albert Fioretti, 46, who is a janitor for the University of Virginia in order to live close to his guru, Sre Swami Satchidananda Maharaj.

There is a concept in Buddhism called "right livelihood" that motivates most paleohippies, whether they are Buddhists themselves or not. It means finding work that is in harmony with one's values. Some hippie workplaces even make it a condition of employment, or very nearly: Whole Foods Market in Austin attaches a five-page statement of purpose to every employment application. "We recognize," it says in part, "that our success reaches far beyond the company by contributing to the quality of life renaissance occurring here on earth." For Ed Levin, who once spent a month in jail after a Dartmouth antiwar protest, right livelihood means building timber-frame houses after the fashion of the 18th century. "You can't get a lot of spiritual nourishment from sheetrock," he says. Peter Grogan, 38, found his right livelihood in garbage—his Eco-Cycle is a million-dollar recycling company in Boulder, Colo. Grogan, who has cut his once bushy curls and now wears a suit when calling on clients, thinks of social change as a balancing act and cites the Warren Zevon song "Lawyers, Guns and Money": "There has been no need for guns," he says, but much need for lawyers and money.

Right livelihood, it should be noted, is not necessarily synonymous with penury. Mirabai Bush found her right livelihood in a
stationery and notions business called Illuminations, manufacturing the rainbow decals that were ubiquitous on car windows in the
late 1970s. Today it is a four million dollar enterprise that employs
25 people—hired, Bush says, precisely because they seemed like
the type for whom their jobs would not be their whole life. Bush
has lived an unusually thorough and full hippie life from the time
she divorced her first husband, an Air Force officer, in 1966: spent
a couple of years smuggling draft dodgers into Canada; lived in a
tepee on a commune in British Columbia; got married during a
pilgrimage to India, where her guru renamed her (from Linda) to
honor a 16th-century queen who had "an erotic love for God." In
1973 she had a son, whom she gave a Hindu name; but, teased by
schoolmates, he asked to be called Owen, his middle name.
Mirabai moved back to live in Cambridge, Mass., and began the
silk-screening business that grew into Illuminations; she became
active in the Seva Foundation, which works to improve health and
sanitation in India.

Now Mirabai watches, pleased, as her 14-year-old son grows
up in a multiracial neighborhood, "beyond prejudice." She is
pleased, too, if a bit wistful, that while Owen and her friends' kids
"don't feel like they're Hindus, they're not freaked out by it." In her
business she is a living exemplar of righteous livelihood to the
myriad benighted bankers and lawyers in the silent counterculture. "I was at lunch with two lawyers downtown and we started
talking about what was important to us, and by the end of the
lunch this woman lawyer was crying. She was so grateful to know
someone else felt the way she did. There's just this huge segment
of the population that can't talk about it."

For many, right livelihood can be found only in living on the
land. One such is Jim Lato, locally famous in the '60s as the pro-
prietor of Chicago's leading head shop, Headland. "The shop got
more political [after 1968]," he recalls. "I thought we had to get out
of it politically and get ourselves together spiritually in a more
holistic sense." That meant becoming a farmer. He lived for a few
years on a Wisconsin commune, Karma Farm, which disbanded at
the end of the 1970s. Today he keeps bees on 40 acres near the
town of New Lisbon and spends time with his 24-year-old son,
Jim Jr., whom he describes as "a punker." The two share "an interesting kind of respect," Lato says. "It's not the same kind of differences that existed between me and my parents. We were worlds
apart. With our own kids, it's not like that. If I were his age now,

I'd probably be a punker. I can understand that," Lato sells his products to trendy Chicago markets and organic restaurants, and when he thinks about the Third World today, it reminds him less of heroic Viet Cong cadres and oppressed Bangladesh peasants than of cheap imported honey.

Others find their right livelihoods in unlikely places, such as the Wasserman Uniform Co. of Columbus, Ohio, which makes the heavy black shoes favored by postmen—and cops. Harvey Wasserman once stayed high for 10 straight days, smoking hashish on the roof of a hotel in Istanbul. From 1969 until 1984 he lived on a commune in Massachusetts, growing organic tomatoes and writing and agitating against nuclear power. When the commune dissolved, a victim both of couples who married and moved away and of suburbanization closing in, he moved back to Columbus to run the family business. He tried to observe a distinction between an entrepreneur, which is how he sees himself, and a capitalist. "An entrepreneur is someone who tries to create a business," he says. "All a capitalist seeks to do is acquire money." He has discovered, he says, that he is "a lot more comfortable selling uniforms than selling ideas."

Not all hippies have made a successful adjustment to the 1980s; some of those whose original impulse was to drop out are dropouts still. David Reardon, 41, is one of the last surviving original residents of Earth People's Park, 592 exceedingly untended acres in northern Vermont. Reardon lives with his girlfriend and her 15-year-old daughter in a one-room log cabin he built himself, without running water or electricity, except for a car battery powering a TV and the lights; he is insular, hardworking and a little bewildered by the kinds of people the commune now attracts. They are often wealthy kids up for a weekend of partying and drugs, or entrepreneur members pushing the commune to follow logging for profit, or alcoholics. "There's a group of guys that cater to each other's drinking," he says with distaste. "They get a keg once a month, blast the stereo up and party if the cops don't catch them. Then they punch each other out and leave."

But dreams die hard, especially those launched with industrial-strength hallucinogens. Far from giving up, Reardon plans to buy a goat to save on milk costs. "There's still magic in the woods," he says, and he is not alone in feeling its allure. Someday no one will believe there was a time when young men and women tried to stop a war with music and bring down a president with flowers, or that they could have sex with dozens of strangers and run the risk of nothing more serious than body lice. It is time to move on, but not yet time to forget. "The world is sliding toward the brink and going to hell in one direction," as Levin, the builder, says, "and rebuilding itself in another."

Notebook

1. Would you say that the hippie culture is dead? What about punk? Heavy metal? Why or why not? What makes a subculture "dead"?
2. Imagine yourself 20 years from now. What do you think will have changed about you? What do you think will stay the same? How do you think your current values or beliefs will influence the way you raise kids, or make a living? If you are a teenager now, do you think that in 20 years you'd advise a teenager you know to stay away from drugs or alcohol? Have premarital sex? What music do you listen to now that you think you'll still like in 20 years? Do you have any tattoos or piercings, and if so, do you think you'll still want them in 20 years?
3. Historic subcultures like the hippies were documented in their own time. Research some primary sources—texts written or produced during the subculture's time—on historic subcultures like the 60s counterculture, or the 1950s Beat generation, or on flappers from the 1920s. How was the subculture written about in its own era, and how does that compare to the way it's written about now?
4. The 1960s hippies were particularly well documented. The documentary film *Woodstock*, about the famous music festival, is a wonderful artifact of that time and culture, and is available on DVD. The opening scenes, in which hippies are interviewed before the concert starts, are especially interesting. For a different perspective, by those who had no choice about their participation in the subculture, read *Wild Child: Girlhoods in the Counterculture*, edited by Chelsea Cain.

Growing Up and Out of the Rave Scene
JOHANNA M. HOADLEY

Johanna Hoadley, a former raver, looks back on her time in the subculture with great fondness—and considers how she got into it and why she left it. Currently, Johanna Hoadley is the news producer for the San Jose Mercury News *web site,* MercuryNews.com, *in San*

Jose, California. A recent transplant to the San Francisco Bay Area. Hoadley studied abroad, backpacked in Australia and has traveled the world; she scuba dived in the Great Barrier Reef, enjoyed the culture of the Burning Man Festival and hiked into—and out of—the Grand Canyon to raise money for the Leukemia & Lymphoma Society. A graduate of Ohio University's E.W. Scripps School of Journalism, she enjoys writing when she has the chance.

◆

The beat explores the muscles, feeling low—the feet, the calves—a tingling touch of bliss.

—My diary, June 19, 1995

Thump. Thump. Thump. Thump.

Those are the first sounds that come to mind when I think back to my raver days. The music's bass reverberating off warehouse walls or echoing in rural fields was the heartbeat of every good party. I would dance for hours on end to techno, house, or jungle music. DJs and musicians like Dubtribe, Richie Hawton, Deee-Lite, Dieselboy, Rabbit in the Moon and others would keep the sweaty crowd on its feet from dusk until sunrise.

To this day, hearing just about any beat—whether it's at a club or background music in a TV ad—makes my head involuntarily bob.

IN THE BEGINNING

How I got into the rave scene is a little foggy for me. I didn't set out to "join" the community. There were no hazing or pledge activities. I don't think I even fully understood what it was when I went to my first rave in college. The only dancing I had done up till that point was to songs like AC/DC's "You Shook Me All Night Long" in the high school gymnasium or at the cheesy clubs on campus that freshmen could get into.

Raves' best promoters were their devotees. Virtually everyone I knew went to their first party because of a friend. I was no different. Friends of friends were going to raves. Then my friends were going. And then I went along to check it out. And the cycle continued.

To be honest, I wasn't hooked after my first party. I didn't really know how to dance to the music. And I had trouble keeping my eyes open after about 3 a.m. I actually remember thinking that I just didn't quite get it as I sat on the grungy floor of some warehouse in some city hours away from home. Why I bothered going to a second rave is still a mystery to me, but I'm glad I did. It was at my second party that I danced my heart out and never looked back.

THE COMMUNITY

Raves are, in the simplest terms, all-night dance parties. But for those of us who drove hundreds of miles on the weekends to go to the next big event, it felt like so much more. It was a community of smiling faces, hugs and dancing. Ravers were to me the 1990's equivalent of hippies—only on ecstasy. The kids, the music and the venues were a little more urban and gritty than those of a Grateful Dead show, but at the heart of it was the same sense of "family" love, sharing, and music. Everyone was your friend at a good party, even if you just met them for the first time. Perhaps I was a bit naïve, but I believed in that friendly community—and with enough believers it felt real.

Though raves were about the community for me, it would be lie to talk about the subculture without mentioning the drugs. The music made the vibe; for many the drugs enhanced it. Ecstasy, and to a lesser extent acid, psychedelic mushrooms and others, were easy to find at any given party if you wanted them. It's no wonder that ecstasy, named for the happy feeling it gave you, found its match in the rave community with its child-like, friendly vibe. And once you knew it was there, you could see its influence everywhere in the scene. Pacifiers were more than a fashion statement—they came in handy when the jaw-clenching side effect of ecstasy kicked in. And the toys in everyone's backpacks could entertain someone rolling on E for hours. Don't get me wrong, not all ravers took drugs, but drugs were certainly at every rave.

I know now that I was a weekend warrior in the rave community. I went for the music and friends. But my life was at a university hours away. And I always came back to that life; my whole group, for the most part, did. My friends and I graduated. Some went on to grad school. We all have respectable jobs. Some are even parents now. We believed in the community, but didn't get lost in the scene. The weekdays were about school; the weekends were about parties. I was oblivious—at least at first—to the rave scene's underbelly where the drug culture took its toll. There were those who lived for the parties and the drugs. And there were those who died because of it and made the evening news. There were the shady event promoters out to make a buck and the shady drug users who stole for their habits.

But that was only a part of the scene. I was involved because I loved to dance, I loved the music, and I loved the rave kids. I had found a place where I felt I belonged.

THE PARTIES

Memory is a funny thing. Over time the details fade and all that's left are brief snapshots—moments that you can't forget, even though the context of them is missing. My rave memories are much the same. The parties tend to all blur into one. I remember sleeping on gritty warehouse floors and dancing amid crowds of sweaty kids with the strobe lights flashing and the beats thumping. I remember getting close to the stage when my DJ friends were spinning. There were more than a few disgusting bathrooms and porta-pots. And I can't forget the early morning drives home with the sunshine and open windows helping to keep me awake until I could finally crawl into my own bed and sleep the day away.

But a few more specific rave moments remain in my mind, like the three-hour early morning performance of San Francisco's Dubtribe at the original "420" rave. Even though we were all exhausted from a night of dancing in a warehouse filled with industrial barrels of who-knows-what, when Dubtribe took the stage for an amazing set, the music, vibe and company all seemed to just click. It was a magical moment where I truly felt I had found my place. It makes me smile now just thinking about it.

And I can't forget "Coup D'Etat," a rave at Cleveland's Agora Theatre. It was the day after my 22nd birthday and I planned to celebrate. But the night started off all wrong when the club confiscated my favorite water bottle at the door (more money for the club if you have to buy your water). The well re-used Gatorade bottle covered with Sesame Street stickers was a one-of-a-kind piece of rave memorabilia that had traveled with me from party to party and seemed, at the time, a necessary part of my rave experience. It's funny to think on it now, but I can't forget how sad I was to see my bottle in the trash can-graveyard of beverage containers. Later in the night when Rabbit in the Moon took the stage, the bottle seemed a small price to pay to be where I was, with my friends, for my birthday.

Other memories are just brief fragments from the scene, like the random raver who gave me an Ohio University baseball cap when he found out that's where I went to school (I still have that hat). The sea of tents in an open field for the weekend-long "Family Affair." Sleeping on the ground at a park after another party waiting for a locksmith because someone locked my keys in the car. Sitting in a line on a warehouse floor, everyone giving and receiving massages. Or stashing fliers for upcoming raves picked up off the floor in my backpack. They are all brief, but vivid, memories.

THE BACKPACK: AN URBAN SURVIVAL KIT

Water: check

Toilet paper: check

Paper and pen: check

Toys: check

Glowsticks (optional): check

It reads like a child's summer camp checklist, but these were my backpack essentials before heading to a rave. The "kid" moniker we ravers gave ourselves certainly fit.

Water was the ultimate necessity. I learned very quickly that you couldn't count on rave promoters to provide potable water. The more underground venues, like abandoned warehouses, often didn't have running water at all—you were lucky to get porta-pots. The more "upscale" club-style venues would charge for it. And the fear of dehydration was very real. After one night of dancing without a water bottle, I felt like a marathon runner crossing the finish line without a drop of liquid along the race route—parched, hot and dizzy. I honestly thought I might be the one raver to make the news for something other than drugs, "Girl hospitalized for dehydration after night of dancing at rave." Luckily it didn't come to that, but it's safe to say I never forgot that water bottle again.

Toilet paper was a close second to water. I would often stash an entire roll in my backpack before heading out the door for the night. There's nothing worse than a porta-pot without paper. If I forgot it, the first stop of the night would be to the bathroom to nab some before it ran out. Friends in need would get carefully torn off and rationed squares; we had to have enough to last till morning.

The rest of my backpack stash was more for fun than survival.

Paper and pen came in handy to jot down the names of people I met along the way.

When tired feet and shins begged for some downtime off the dance floor, a few well-chosen toys could pass the time. They also made great gifts when you crossed paths with someone on ecstasy. You wouldn't believe how much joy a cheap McDonald's Happy Meal toy could provide someone rolling on E. The smiles were infectious.

And glowsticks came out on the dance floor, where one person could create a personal light show with the sticks in hand. A good dancer with glowsticks was living art, melding the body's movements to the music with the neon green lights to create a blur of intricate and beautiful patterns.

Beyond the backpack, the rave fashions could best be described as urban: low-rise baggy Jnco jeans with cuffs so huge your skate shoes would barely peek from beneath, extra-large T-shirts or baby tees for the gals, childish pigtails or sharply angled short haircuts, glittery makeup, body piercings, and tattoos.

ALL KIDS MUST GROW UP

Though I still fight my "grown-up" status to this day, the fact is I did grow up—and out—of the rave scene.

I hadn't consciously joined the rave scene and I didn't purposely lose touch with it either. I didn't wake up one day and just decide I'd had enough of the subculture. But as I got older and the scene evolved, the innocence of it seemed to disappear and with it my sense of belonging.

My friends and I graduated from college and went our separate ways. I continued to go to the occasional rave but it just never felt the same. The crowd was younger than ever, making me feel conspicuously an elder and an outsider. And the vibe seemed to have lost its hippie leanings, in favor of a more hardcore edge. At the same time, the venues were becoming less underground and the prices were rising to match.

There were a few pivotal moments toward the end of my rave days that made me rethink going to parties. I was coming to the sad realization that what I used to believe in was either gone or perhaps had only existed when an innocent mind ignored the negative side of the subculture. I remember, for example, seeing someone passed out on the floor of a party after taking the drug "Special K" (ketamine) and thinking to myself that he missed the point entirely. How could he enjoy the music if he was so high on a horse tranquilizer he couldn't even move?

The dancing had changed, too. I felt like an audience was scoping out the dance floor, interpreting the dancing as an invitation. I missed real, almost tribal, dancing, where I could get so wrapped up in the moment that everything melted away except for the *thump, thump, thump.* I longed for uninterrupted dancing where time stands still leaving just me and the music. I still miss that.

Mostly, I no longer felt a part of the community—and though I would go back in hopes of finding it again, it seemed to have moved on without me.

Then again, maybe I had moved on without it. Despite my best efforts to prevent it, I was growing up. Staying up all night on the weekends, when I had a full-time job during the week, was getting more and more difficult. And I was less willing to put up with a dingy bathroom without toilet paper. I was becoming jaded and no matter how much I wanted it to feel like it did in the beginning, I had lost my place in the community.

LOOKING BACK

The rave subculture is a part of me, even if I'm no longer a part of it. It's also a part of the mainstream world around us. Television ads use the "rave" music and scenes of young people dancing to sell their products. Old-school toy icons, like Hello Kitty and Care Bears, have taken over store shelves. The design-style of flyer art has influenced everything from magazine ads to product packaging. Some of the top rave DJs now spin in mainstream clubs. Teens everywhere are wearing those baby tees with low-slung (though arguably tighter) jeans. Even video arcades have welcomed the rave culture with the popular dance-to-win game "Dance Dance Revolution."

And all those raver buddies from college? They are all leading very different lives as university professors, journalists, club DJs, graphic designers and parents. We are definitely all a little older and more responsible these days. Yet, for the most part, we are as close as ever, some even closer. I guess you could say we all grew up and out of the rave culture together.

As for me, I still carry my urban survival skills with me to this day. If toilet paper is running low when I'm out at a club or restaurant, I put some in my pocket for later. I can sleep just about anywhere no matter how loud it is. And I still get a little panicked if it's hot and I don't have a water bottle.

More importantly, I strive to keep the community's ideals of sharing, giving and caring alive in my life. I learned the power of a smile and a hug, and hope I'll always be able to give them freely.

But the rave's biggest influence on my life, without a doubt, was an appreciation of the power of music. The right music at the right time can move me. It leaves an emotional imprint that transcends time with the push of the play button. It can carry away all my troubles, or help me deal with them. And in the end, it somehow makes my world feel just a little bit more complete.

I know the music of my life will change, but as long as I keep listening, I'll always be where I belong.

Notebook

1. How did being a part of the rave subculture help Joanne Hoadley form her adult identity? What have the members of the subculture you're studying learned from their subculture that they use in their "mainstream" life?
2. Hoadley calls herself a "weekend warrior": She participated in the rave culture on weekends, but always returned during the week to her "normal" life as a college student. How do you think that "weekend warrior" status might impact someone's ability to leave a subculture later? Talk about the varying degrees of participation possible in various subcultures you're studying.
3. As a group, talk about how you might rewrite this essay using a different rhetorical approach. How might it work as a news article, or an argumentative essay? What elements of the style would have to be changed?
4. Are raves still happening in your area? Has the rave scene morphed into something else? Tara McCall's book *This Is Not a Rave: In the Shadow of a Subculture* may provide more information if you can't seem to find any evidence of the culture around you at present.

Deadheads Yesterday and Today: An Audience Study
MELISSA MCCRAY PATTACINI

What happens when the reason for the subculture disappears suddenly? In this essay, Melissa McCray Pattacini looks at what the death of Grateful Dead leader and beloved subculture figure Jerry Garcia—and the subsequent end of the Dead's "long, strange trip" on tour—meant for legions of online Deadheads, loyal followers of the band who meet on the Internet. Pattacini worked on her graduate degree in American Studies at Trinity College and is the mother of three children.

———————————   ✦   ———————————

In the summer of 1995, following the death of Jerry Garcia, the Grateful Dead stopped touring. For thirty years, their concerts served as a gathering place for a diverse group of followers, nicknamed Deadheads. Coming from all walks of life, they exemplified the hippie-culture ideologies of peace, generosity, and sharing. The era of the three-season Grateful Dead tour has ended and the fans need to fill the apparent void left by its absence. This is a report of an Internet survey of Deadheads illustrating how they have compensated for this lack to different degrees and in a variety of ways. These include following other tours and bands, communicating on the Internet, and other creative pursuits. A great number have just gone on with their lives, better off for being touched by the music of the Dead.

Sometimes the light's all shining on me, other times I can barely see.
    Lately it occurs to me, what a long strange trip it's been.
                                    —Grateful Dead, *American Beauty*, 1970

In understanding the Deadheads and their current disposition, a closer examination must be made of their historical attachment to the Grateful Dead. The culture outside the concerts became a ritual, a homecoming, almost a religion to some. Others participated for the readily available psychedelic drugs and to experience a special freedom that seemed to originate in the music.

As Fred Goodman wrote in a 1995 essay in *Rolling Stone* magazine, Jerry and the boys "hosted rock & roll's best and longest-running party." The parties started in the winter of 1965, in the Haight-Ashbury section of San Francisco, an artists' colony recognized as the birthplace of the American hippie culture. The band garnered attention for playing at Ken Kesey's Acid Tests, where 200 people would show up at an Acid Test to experience LSD. The numbers multiplied due to the effect of the combination of music and drugs. As Rock Scully and David Dalton chronicle in their memoir, *Twenty Years on the Bus with Garcia and the Grateful Dead: Living with the Dead*, The Dead were forced out of smaller clubs by the burgeoning crowds, into open-air arenas and parks.

A 1971 Grateful Dead album jacket included the message: "DEAD FREAKS UNITE. Who are you? Where are you? How are you? Send us your name and address and we'll keep you informed." To the surprise of the group, thousands responded and were (and still are) kept in touch through newsletters, called Almanacs, and the Official Book of the Dead Heads, released in 1983. According to John Skow's *Time* magazine article "In California: The Dead Live On," in 1990, it was estimated that 500 to 1,000 hardcore followers traveled to every show. The overall number of fans in the early 1990s was "over 37,351, because that many attended an outdoor concert at Saratoga, NY."

A distinction should be made between a Deadhead and a tourhead. Any fan of the Grateful Dead can be termed a Deadhead (or Head). These people collect Grateful Dead music; some wear tie-dyed gear, while others wear suits and ties; some have a spaced-out, unclean look while others, maybe even those clad in the tie-dyed uniform, are squeaky clean. But they come from all walks of life: students, laborers, bikers, lawyers, sports figures, and some of the nation's most prominent politicians all declare themselves to be Deadheads. A Tourhead is a sub-category of fans. They trek from gig to gig, camping out in their cars, some living hand to mouth, others off of their parents' credit cards. According to Scott Sutherland's *New York Times* article "In the Deadheads' Footsteps," "Tourhead culture is one of the latest forms of what American studies scholars like to call communitas (Latin for fellowship)— that habit Americans have of celebrating their individualism with others just like themselves." This holds true of the early followers and of the younger fans who "got on the bus" in the late 1980s and early 1990s.

While unfathomable to many, the fervent quasi-religious fixation these fans experienced was, and still is, caused by numerous factors. In online interviews, some point to a feeling of alienation from mainstream organized religion. The concerts themselves provided a ritual to follow. Standing on a stage covered with Persian carpets, the band would play a few songs (granted some were as long as 18 minutes). These would flow into what is termed "Drums," free-flowing drum solos. A few more tunes would be spun, followed by "The Space," then some more music, another "Drums" break, then the end of the show. The band might play continually for four hours, sometimes longer. The set lists changed, and if there were three shows in the same town there would be three separate lists. Still, you could count on the ritual to be the same.

The drugs, coupled with the Dead's unique musical style, allowed some to commune with a higher power. This generally happened when Jerry Garcia and Bob Weir played their impromptu solos during a show. The Dead termed these interludes "Space." Space has been defined by M.D. Carnegie in an article called "Jerry's Kids" as "that quintessential bit of Deadness in every concert, when the group would abandon all pretense of musical structure and just sort of noodle around for a very long period of time . . . noodle noodle noodle noodle." From the perspective of one nondrug-using first-time concert-goer, this is remembered as "so weird, I mean, I had only been to standard concerts up to that point, I'm talking Huey Lewis and the News. All of a sudden the crowd would get really loud, 'cause they knew what was coming, then the guys would just start jamming and the whole place would just, well, sway together." These experimental jam sessions, coupled with hallucinogenics, allowed for some "really beautiful people" to "make some type of magical contact with the heavens, the creator and a few deities that I'm unfamiliar with." Drugs were the way to reach a higher plane. As Richard Folkers theorizes in a *U.S. News & World Report* article in 1995 called "The Band for the Eternally Young," for many it was the way to escape the suburban life that lay behind and ahead of them.

Certainly, the most sensational aspect of a Dead show took place in the parking lot or area surrounding the venue. The parks where the fans camped out resembled colorful street fairs. Many of the hardcore followers would subsidize their tour by selling tie-dyed T-shirts, beaded necklaces, and "magic" cookies or brownies. Drugs were ever-present in the barter economy. A case or six-pack of beer could be traded for food, space to sleep in a motel room, or a hit of acid.

As one online devotee noted, "Drums, bongos would be playing at you from different directions, people dancing . . . kids walking around saying 'I need a miracle, miracle me' which was like a code for needing a ticket into the show." The Dead tried to discourage this "Miracling" by using mail-order ticket sales. In the late 1980s the tour's tone and fans began to change. The tour in 1995, in which ticketless groups physically crashed down gates, was the bottom of a spiral that had been winding its way down for some time. As reported in a 1994 *Rolling Stone* article by Neil Strauss, "The Acid Test: Deadheads Face Hard Time in LSD Crackdown," the band sat down and wrote their fans an open letter with these messages: If you do not have a ticket, do not come to the show. If you are looking for drugs, you will be an easy target for arrest.

In light of the 1995 tour, the band was feeling the change and strain from the difference in their fans. In a 1972 interview in *Rolling Stone*, Garcia said: "You wonder where these people are coming from, but they're self-invented. We didn't invent them, and we didn't invent our original audience. In a way, this whole process has kind of invented us." But by the 90s it was no longer the hippies with their quasi-political causes talking philosophy over a joint. It was changing into divided factions, old school vs. new, with an increasing number coming only to get a hit of the nitrous oxide being sold in the parking lot, as *Rolling Stone* reported in 1990.

While the Dead have stopped traveling, many of the Tourheads have not. Tourheads primarily consist of younger Deadheads. Among the most notable bands they have latched onto are Phish and the Furthur Fest Bands. Of these, Phish has had the most press aimed at trying to pass the torch of the Grateful Dead on to their scene, Mikal Gilmore wrote in "Life After Garcia" in a 1995 issue of *Rolling Stone*. While the Deadhead attachment remains, for the most part, cool, as a once unified "communitas" they are now scattered into tiny factions: there is no whole entity left to physically identify with any one group.

Online questionnaire opinions tell of the feelings toward the various styles and musical groups. "Phish is musically talented and innovative—not focused on a mentality of kindness; that informs their life as were the Dead—and thus a bit empty by comparison." While all who have heard Phish attest to their musical capabilities, common reactions to their concerts include, "Going to Phish makes me feel old (I'm 30) because of the young following they attract" and "Their music seems to attract more of the jocky, punky element that really began to be a serious pain in the ass the last few years the Dead were around."

The comparison to the Dead "just may be the silliest damned thing anybody has ever attempted. [Phish has] a completely different approach to music, outside of the open-ended jamming that both groups draw from." The sentiments of many who have forgone traveling are summed up as follows: "Have seen Phish a couple of times. I admire their unique talent and their energy and enthusiasm. But I'm not willing to follow them around the country."

With most Deadheads unwilling to follow a new band across the country, more support for the Furthur Fest (Furthur was the name given to the bus used during Ken Kesey's legendary Acid Tests that featured the emerging Dead) would be expected.

Remaining members of the Dead Bob Weir, Mickey Hart, and Bruce Hornsby along with their new bands, have grouped together to try to fill in the summer months left empty by the end of the Grateful Dead tour. In a *Boston Globe* interview in 1996, Gary Susman quoted Hart as saying, "Musicians gotta play, Deadheads gotta dance. Considering they never heard the songs before, the fans are on their feet all night. They're getting it. It's all a little strange at first, but after a few minutes they get into the groove and go for a ride. They depend on the succession of the notes. It's a habit for them. It's a healing process for me too to get out and play again. It felt good to get back in the familiar groove. It was like revisiting an old lover, like good sex with an old girlfriend."

After two years, fans looking to re-create the Dead scene appear disappointed: "Furthur is an evolving reincarnation of various band members' new musical efforts. Last year one could still detect the spaces left in the music that Jerry used to fill." Still others acknowledge there is no going back: "Furthur Fest is a nice try. I admire the other bands that participate, however it can't replace the Dead. They are fun shows, and I went last year and will go again this year because I love live music and there will be bands that I like. But I won't go thinking that the Grateful Dead will be playing. I will go to see some old friends that I haven't met yet and hear some familiar music played just a bit differently than I'm used to."

Much of the lack of interest has been attributed to the tour creators' intentions. When ticket sales weren't as brisk as anticipated, headline acts such as the Black Crowes were added to the bill. Said one online fan, "[T]he promoters are trying to reach beyond those who want to see acts with some connection to the Dead and get anyone with a credit card to show up. The problem with the last few years of the Dead tour WAS that everyone with a credit card was showing up."

Many of the older fans still have a lingering mixed reaction to the "newbies" (fans new to the bus, new to the culture). Many see the experience of following the group as the equivalent of running away to join the circus. There is freedom in the utopian vision of the hippies—it wasn't all just peace, love, and kindness. But it seems that as new fans got on the bus, these visions changed forever. The parking lots during the last concert tour are most brutally described by an online fan as "a haven for overindulged white kids who were looking to rebel against their parents, but not rebel so far as to never be able to return at the first sign of trouble." While older Deadheads feel some responsibility to be guides for the youths recently attracted to the scene, a large portion are turned off by the new attitudes they embody.

Economically, the Grateful Dead supported both big and small business enterprises. Official Grateful Dead Merchandising has been going strong since the early 1990s. They sell an assortment of memorabilia ranging from commemorative T-shirts and books to tie-dyed socks and golf club covers.

Smaller in scale were the vendors (fans) outside the concerts peddling their homemade wares in the carnival-like atmosphere. It was a traveling craft show. But the popularity of the 1987 album *In the Dark* produced an organized outdoor vendor scene, which, in large part, killed off the craft market. At this point commercial success changed the scene by attracting large groups of younger fans. Previously, Heads could count on a relatively safe and laid-back atmosphere in which to experience the show in any manner they wanted.

In the last few tours, references were made to groups of families called "the Wrecking Crew" or "the Five Families." (It is common to refer to an immediate group of Deadhead friends as "family.") The main focus of these loosely knit groups was selling beer, burritos, and (nitrous oxide-filled) balloons. Most Heads gave them a wide berth. These groups staked out territory at each venue for selling their wares and it was rumored they carried guns. There was some suspicion that they were involved with the government or with the police as informants. As one fan told me, "They'd get picked up by the cops, you'd see it at one show, and they would be back out the next day, which was weird." There was little respect for the clique aspect of these groups.

What has happened to these people now that the tour has ended? According to one Deadhead: "My beliefs are that those in it for economic interests followed their interests . . . economics." The biggest commodity outside the stadiums was drugs. The dealers have just moved on: "I have seen several friends who are still surviving quite nicely in their old trade, even though the venue has changed. I think there are enough other bands and tour attractions to keep the entrepreneurs active for quite some time. Trust me, if they have to sell stuff at a Metallica concert, they will."

While the band continues to sell and put out CD sets from their archives (available through the Grateful Dead Almanac), an amazing aspect of the Dead is the availability of their music free of charge. It has the largest trading market of its kind, fully sanctioned and encouraged by the band itself. Each concert arena was set up in different sections. There was a spinners section, where those who danced by spinning in circles could have a large area for unrestricted movement. There were the ticketed seat areas (which it appears nobody really sat in for a whole show). Last, there was the tapers area.

The taper section was partitioned for the "bootleggers" to set up their tape decks and microphones to get the best sound. Anyone with a tapers ticket could record the show and make copies for the Heads who requested them. They could be seen as a branch on a tree (with the band as the trunk). The tapes they dubbed for others became leaves. With the ready access to the Internet, the tape trade has been bustling. A blank tape is sent to a "branch," who then sends back your "leaf." Thus, the quality of the tapes being disseminated is assured, at least as far as keeping the music at a second generation of copying. No money changes hands in this process, just tapes. These collections range from the modest to the extensive; one interviewee said "I've only got about 200 tapes, I mean you should see my friend Jeff, he has like 7 times as many."

Admirably, this truly is about "getting the music out there." To mention or believe in a large-scale for-profit "bootleg tape industry" is to seriously offend any true Deadhead and show yourself to be an outsider. In one online interview I was taken to task on this issue. The interviewee pointed out the need to define ("humanize") myself within the context of the Deadheads. They needed to know that I was not an intruder and was genuinely interested for academic, as well as personal, reasons.

After Jerry Garcia's death, Deadhead scholar Rebecca Adams noted, "Deadheads, some belonging to on-line communities and others not, found solace on the Internet. This was particularly important for those isolated from local communities of Deadheads." They can be found at the official website of the Grateful Dead (http://grateful.dead.net). Deadbase (http://www.deadbase.com) has hundreds of personal Deadhead home pages.

Through the Internet, Deadheads gather in much the same way they did outside a concert. They catch up on the years, months, or days since they were last together. Tape trading is a favorite pastime at the tape site. Heads visit Deadnet Central, which has bulletin board files for questions. This includes the Robert Hunter Journal site, with anecdotal stories about the lyricist's life and his plans for the future.

Many Deadheads bought computers specifically to keep in touch with each other, either when they stopped touring or after the tour ceased. Gary Susman noted in a 1996 article in the *Boston Globe*, "Part of touring for me was meeting fellow Deadheads from around the country. I've been able to meet many of those people on-line and even in person from time to time. I am a 'bus driver' (chat room supervisor) in the AOL Dead Forum, and this allows me to not only be in touch with other long-time heads, but to teach the kind and peace-loving nature of us to the newbies." In the electronic age, instead of "being there," the traditions and shared experiences are sent pulsing along the wires.

The Deadheads are in touch with each other in a more mainstream way than when the band was touring. Their cyberspace connectedness is something even those "people over thirty," whom they were cautioned not to trust, can understand. Not to trivialize the importance of this phenomenon, this need to stay in touch could be seen by an outsider as the equivalent of writing letters to friends made at summer camp. It is a need to catch up and to reaffirm that they experienced something special together.

The end of the tour and dispersion of the group has elicited a variety of responses from within the Deadheads community. They are an articulate group and have much to say on what the "end of the era" has meant. This response sums it up best:

> It's meant childhood's end for people ranging all the way up into their sixties. . . . It's also been a new BEGINNING in many ways for many of us, because there's no longer the Dead for us to be entertained by, so we have to now do the entertaining. . . . All the creative seeds that were sown in each of us during our time with the Dead are just now beginning to burst into bloom. People are starting to take the energy they put into going to shows and surviving on tour into the gifts that they themselves possess. I think you're going to see a lot of artists of all types popping up in the public eye in the next decade or so who will be attributing a lot of their inspiration to the Dead. I mean, you already see that to a certain extent, but it'll be continuing to happen, I think.

In the past two years, there has been a noticeable upswing in Grateful Dead-related works. There are "I was there with the Dead" biographical books. There has been tremendous activity in submissions for Dead tribute magazines such as *Dupree's* and *Relix*. An important touchstone has been David Gans's Grateful Dead Hour, a nationally syndicated radio show (started in 1985) plays the music and discusses various concerts. The most notable artistic works can be found on the Internet. They range from animated home pages to photo and art galleries. Each is trying to bring the Dead to life. As far as the Deadheads are concerned, the ideas live on, the music continues to play, and the Dead are alive.

Notebook

1. Deadheads, as is noted in this essay, spend a lot of time documenting their own subculture through magazines, tapes, websites, art, and so on. How do other subcultures document themselves? Why is it important for a subculture to document itself?

2. Jerry Garcia's death is the major reason the Deadhead culture has begun to fade and transform itself, although Melissa McCray Pattacini's article cites other reasons as well. What reasons account for the collapse of other subcultures? Do you see any subcultures fading away right now? Do you know of any new ones developing? What current events or moods might spawn a subculture in the near future?

3. Pattacini shows how Deadheads use the Internet to keep part of their subculture alive. This book includes many other essays about subcultures whose members gather online. Why do you think these members still gather? How do you think the Internet has changed the nature of subcultures overall?

4. Part of the inspiration for this textbook/subcultures reader came from another textbook/subculture reader, called *Deadhead Social Science: You Ain't Gonna Learn What You Don't Want to Know*, edited by Rebecca G. Adams and Robert Sardiello. Unlike this book, it is exclusively about the subculture of Deadheads, and all the essays take a social science approach. Like this book, though, it contains writing by students. Check out the book and see what you think. Do those social science approaches give you any ideas about ways you can write about your subculture?

Too Dirty to Be a Hobo?
John Lennon

In this essay, we see what happens when the older members of a subculture—in this case, hobos—clash with the younger generation over what the subculture means, both to the members themselves and the outsiders who enjoy its spectacle. John Lennon is currently an assistant professor at St. John's University. When not working on his book on hobos and their creative politics of resistance, John can be found looking for the next train going in one direction or another.

━━━━━━━━ ✦ ━━━━━━━━

Every August, a strange phenomenon happens in the small town of Britt, Iowa. A large number of hobos converge on the small town, set up camp on the grass next to the railroad tracks and, sharing food and drinks, reacquaint themselves with friends and former traveling companions, as well as the townspeople who (for the most part) welcome them "home" every year. Like migrating birds, the hobos seem to appear from nowhere but always arrive on time. It's a time for Britt residents to open their town to these men and women whose lifestyle is very much contrary to the accepted codes of behavior for this family-oriented, blue-collar town of 2,500.

The National Hobo Convention is a celebration as well as a memorializing of the hobo: history lessons are taught to the uninitiated through songs and stories, rules of jungle (camp) etiquette are passed out along with the beer, campfire philosophy is expounded, and townsfolk and hobos mingle along Main Street. During the festivities, men and women with such descriptive monikers as Texas Madman, Roadkill, Adman, Frog, Derail, and Lady Nightingale can be found riding on the Hobo float waving and throwing candy at locals, ordering the hobo breakfast (there is a vegetarian version!) in the Hobo House Restaurant, and answering the questions of inquiring tourists outside of the Hobo Museum, discussing their views of life on the Iron Road. The mood is festive, albeit surreal. In a country that shuns the homeless and, for the most part, refuses to see the hundred of thousands who are living on U.S. streets daily, Britt residents donate land and resources to these wanderers and make them celebrities for a three-day party that attracts thousands of people to the town each year. As Papa Smurf said of the 100th year anniversary of the convention in Britt in 2000, "The whole thing is a bit of a carnival."

The convention began as a type of joke in 1900, when (as the legend goes) three Chicago hobos hoping to celebrate the beginning of the century with a convention were looking for a town that could appreciate and publicize an annual hobo gathering. And while the convention was more of a town fair (complete with "wild" sack races and "exciting" tours of the grain elevator), newspapers from around the country who had been hoodwinked into covering the event reported on it with sobriety. Thirty-three years later, the townspeople of Britt, trying to find an event that would bring revenue to their hard-hit Depression town, decided to resurrect the Hobo National Convention. And almost every year since, Britt has held the most popular and well attended Hobo celebration in the United States and, for that matter, the world.

But who gets included under this term hobo? Or to put it another way, when town revenue is at stake, what particular type of hobo do the tourists and townspeople of Britt want to commemorate?

The hobo subculture that is celebrated each year mainly existed in the United States in the late 19th and early part of the 20th century, consisting of mostly single, white, migratory workers who owned no property, belonged to no religious organization, and who had both the ability and desire to keep moving. While memorialized now by Britt, in the past, they were not greeted with open arms. Even though they were needed for labor and were thus essential to local economies, their lifestyle was antithesis to the larger, stable culture. They were, after all, homeless and therefore seen by many as unstable and morally bankrupt. Suddenly appearing in town, usually dirty, often hungry, they were an unpredictable subculture that was both wanted (when crops needed to be harvested) and shunned (as soon as their usefulness ran out). And since the townspeople owned property and therefore had rights under the law, they could dictate what would happen to the hobos who had no property and very little political voice.

To remain free as well as survive, then, hobos needed to avoid the authorities. Relying on presented opportunities (for example, an open boxcar and a policeman looking in the opposite direction), the hobo hid in the bowels of the train, hoping that he could avoid detection in "hot" (unwelcoming) towns. Most hobo autobiographies (and there are many) refer to this moment of "catching out" as the location of their subcultural power: by using their physical and mental skills in life-threatening situations, they *proactively* become invisible on the moving train.

This power, however, disappears when the hobo is spotted climbing down from his train, dirty, tired, and hungry after many miles of a bumpy ride. Entering a town looking for work and also free "lumps" (food) by banging on the back doors of houses, he suddenly became visible and his obvious out-of-placeness was deemed potentially dangerous. The invisibility that sheltered him while riding the trains disappeared when walking through towns—the hobo's outward appearances spoke of poverty, of immorality, and of a particular type of freedom that caused anxiety in the larger communities. The subculture can resist the rules (both moral and legal) of the mainstream culture by remaining invisible—but as soon as they become seen in the straight community, the bodies of the hobo are once again placed securely under the rules and regulations of the stronger one.

While invisible on the trains and in the fields as indistinguishable hired hands, there was a forced recognition between the subculture/culture when they met on town property because the hobo was both a physical and symbolic threat to many in the privileged cultures. During the early part of the twentieth century, the hobo "problem" was discussed in the classroom to the barroom, from the Sunday pulpit to the campaign stump, resulting in a myriad of vagrancy laws that were written and rewritten to "cure" the society of this "evil." Whether a person wanted to save the soul of the dirty hobo or seek vigilante "justice," the hobo was a figure that—especially in times of economic crisis—needed to be dealt with.

By the second part of the 20th century, the hobo "menace" was no longer a viable problem. As the numbers of the hobo dwindled, due to a myriad of economic and cultural reasons, and the perceived threat of the hobo lessened, his popularity grew. With no fear of the corrupting and subversive threat of a homeless man knocking on the backdoor of a home, the culture began to celebrate certain culturally acceptable traits that the hobo embodies. The harsh reality of the hobo life succumbed to a glorified narrowing of the term and the hobo figure now celebrated by Britt is either the quirky, eccentric freedom-loving caricature or the hard-living but morally upright individualistic member of society. Either way, though, the more deviant and resistive politics of the hobo is downplayed or completely sanitized. The "authentic" hobo is seen by the majority of the mainstream community (and some older hobos) as mostly dead, and with his supposed death, the revisionist memorializing has begun.

But revising history is a tricky business. Contemporary hobos are testament to the evolving nature of the term, and receive the scorn of those both within and outside the subculture who have a stake in keeping this term aligned with culturally acceptable ideas and values. The most prominent space for this struggle over the term is on the national stage of the Hobo Convention.

For the past thirty plus years, one man has made it his mission to be a part of each of these conventions and to inform the general public about the history of the hobo—Steam Train Maury Graham. While others make it their cause to make the term Hobo known—Ben Reitman, Jeff Davis, William Howe, to name a few—it is Steam Train who has been the most positively interviewed and most favorably publicized 'bo. Well into his eighties now and in poor health, he is still a force in the jungle of the Hobo Convention. With a long white beard that makes him look like a hard-luck Santa Claus and a beautifully carved walking staff, rumors of his whereabouts run throughout the jungle at any given moment. Driven around Britt's town streets and the jungle in a golf-cart that looks very much like a discount version of the "Pope Mobile," he gets out and slowly walks to each campsite, shaking hands and telling stories to everyone he meets.

Steam Train, who has written two books in order to "set the record straight" on the history of hobos—*Tales of the Iron Road: My Life as King of the Hobos* and *A History of the Hoboes, Tramps, and Other Vagabonds*—has been the key figure in making the term hobo safe by endearing himself to both townspeople and hobos alike. Mary Paniccia Carden, in her article "The Hobo as National Hero," from the journal *a/b: Autobiographical Studies*, points to this feature as the basis for his success since he is able to write himself into paradigms of American identity while at the same time stressing his difference from the mainstream culture.

This move to place the hobo figure within the accepted paradigms of US cultural history is apparent when analyzing the way that the author recounts his life in *Tales of the Iron Road*. As a young man of 14, and using the advice of older 'bos who had dubbed him "Idaho," Maury Graham traveled during his summer vacations, receiving an education and a taste for the road. And for the next few years, he split his time between hoboing and going to high school, until 1936, when he began his first complete year as a full time hobo. And like a man who discovered God, Graham found the path to "true happiness and total freedom."

But Graham succumbed to a temptation that the road could not supply him—a wife. In 1938, Graham married Wanda Matty and he realized that, "[i]n taking unto myself a wife I had forsaken my life as a hobo" (120) and decided to "settle down" and take a job in construction. Except for a brief tour of duty in the military, Graham remained in his home in Toledo, Ohio with his wife and children; he abandoned his brotherhood of the road and settled into a middle-class lifestyle for the next twenty five or so years.

The urge to ride the trains never left him, however, and by 1968, Graham once again decided to hit the Iron Road. Without telling his wife that he was going, he decided to "answer that call" of the road and hopped freights for many years until he went back to Toledo to live with Matty in the fall of 1980.

If Steam Train just traveled the Iron Road anonymously, he could have been easily an inconsequential figure in hobo lore—an eccentric 'bo who could cook a mean Mulligan Stew in various jungles around the country. But what has differentiated him from many other hobos is that he loves the spotlight. And he was extremely successful at getting his face in the news; a likeable older man, Steam Train could spin a good yarn about a now safe, forgotten subculture and its positive link to American history. But it was the Hobo National Convention that allowed Steam Train to find the right platform to help solidify his particular definition of the term. When Steam Train went to his first convention in 1971, he was not impressed by what he saw. The King of that year was sleeping in an abandoned jail that was in disrepair and most of the hobos were drinking heavily in the local bars. But what did impress Steam Train were the large crowds who "were genuinely interested in hobos" and he was determined to show these people "what the hobo life was *really* like." For Graham, then, it was possible to replicate an "authentic" hobo experience among a tourist crowd of— depending on the year—between 5,000 and 20,000. Encouraged by the large numbers, he began campaigning to become the King of the Hobos and the next year, running on a platform to visit Veterans hospitals across the country, Steam Train won the coveted title. Instead of being outside the dominant culture and due to his illegal nature, in opposition to it, Steam Train would actually become an (unpaid) extension of the "normative" culture.

Steam Train was as good as his word, making 34,000 bedside visits that year and in a chapter entitled, "The Reign of Steam Train," he tells of his travels of visiting many veterans in hospitals where television cameras and the ubiquitous microphone were also in evidence. During this year, he also made himself a regular event on newscasts, a guest of honor for the premier of the most famous of hobo movies, *Emperor of the North* (1973), and even spent a day in Congress urging the passage of a bill to provide extra funds to hire more railroad police and increase yard security.

Virtually all hobo autobiographies—including Steam Train's— inevitably write of bad, sadistic bulls who viciously attack hobos when they were caught. Now, as King of the Hobos, Steam Train was trying to increase the police presence because he felt that there were too many young, dangerous railriders who were present in the yards and the older 'bos (who, like the younger riders, were also illegal bodies in the train yards) were in danger of being attacked. Instead of trying to avoid the law and remain invisible, Steam Train, dressed in his colorful hobo attire and waving his hands in Congress, was adamantly forcing himself to be seen. And, even more tellingly, he was being allowed to do so.

So while Steam Train might represent one particular type of hobo, he has, in fact, become The Hobo—the one whom all newspaper reporters talk to when they are doing a piece on the Convention. And this definition is the recognized one in communities outside of the hobo subculture. Sitting in a local bar in Britt during the August festivities, I talked with many locals about their feelings about the convention and hobos in general. Every person I talked to expressed the same sentiment—the hobos of the present are "fake" and "bums" compared to the "real" hobos like Steam Train or some of the older men. The middle-aged daughter of the owner of a bar who had been serving beers to hobos for the past 20 years (she also works part time in the Hobo Museum on Main Street) stated that the real hobos were "gentlemen" and "respectful" and "hard-working" but the days of "authentic" 'bos were over.

And there seems to be a lot at stake for both those inside and outside the subculture in keeping this narrow definition of the hobo as the *only* definition. But there is something too sanitized about this version of the hobo. By staying so clearly in the harsh light of the public gaze, the Hobo Convention has whitewashed the subcultural identity politics. The hobo has stopped being primarily defined in opposition to the dominant culture and instead has become an accepted figure—one that is attempting to define itself both inside *and* outside of the dominant cultural ideologies.

But there are still railriders, many of whom call themselves (or are called by others) "Krustiez" or "Gutterpunks," to differentiate themselves from hobos, who are not so interested in being accepted by the mainstream culture and relish their resisting stance. Sarah George in her documentary *Catching Out* (2002) has an intimate look at present day railriders, some of whom have a very combative attitude towards Britt and its confining atmosphere while maintaining a deep respect for the lifestyle. Lee, whose credentials include being an environmental activist, a fulltime squatter, and author of the hobo 'zine *There's Something About a Train*, speaks of the uniqueness of hopping a train and the close community that centers around the idea of play, "I really love the deep conversation that happens on a train or happens waiting in a yard. . . . Dancing in the freight yards. Dancing on the boxcars. As you are zooming through the deserts waving at passerbys and waving at the little kids who pay attention to trains . . . I really cherish that, the hobo philosopher archetype."

All of the current railriders interviewed in George's documentary speak of a desire to connect to the long history of the hobo in this country. When I was in Britt, I witnessed this respect countless times as well. Part of the time I spent with Malachi, a traveler who lived on the road with his dogs and made his living by singing

Tom Waits songs on curbs for change. Tattooed and dirty, he didn't seem to fit in with the older hobos, many of whom had much pride in the way they looked; however, he was deferential to them and listened quietly to their stories only adding input about the present day situation when asked. When RedBird Express, that year's Hobo King, made mention of him in a ceremony around the main jungle fire, Malachi was clearly affected by this inclusive gesture.

Others, however, while respectful of their hobo elders, are not as worried about upsetting either the older 'bos or the townspeople in their mannerisms and actions. They feel that the Hobo convention belongs to them as well and they are not content to just listen to stories of the days that are "done and been." Rather, they see themselves as laying claim to the term because they are the only ones currently putting their physical bodies in danger by hopping trains. And it is during these moments when they do exert their voices and through their appearance separate themselves from the "authentic" hobos that the tension over who can be considered a "hobo" becomes an obvious site of contention.

In the late nineties, Britt town officials became concerned that the appearance of these new riders were causing a disturbance among the town and could possibly disrupt the marketing capability of the event. Marie Steenlage, then director of the Britt Chamber of Commerce, summing up some of the different possible options to keep a "family atmosphere" in the hobo convention, suggested using wristbands to differentiate "real" hobos from "fakes." In other words, Steenlage and others wanted to control the meaning of the word hobo and define it in terms that they felt were suitable to them. They would then own this word and could dictate that only those whom the town had physically "tagged" could be considered a hobo and permitted to sleep in the hobo jungle and ride on the hobo float during the parade. Multiple facial piercings or too many rips in their worn-out jeans and the town could then decide that a person didn't fit the criteria of the hobo and were thus only unwanted and illegal vagrants.

While the town did not issue arm bands, they did begin to crack down on the new riders, beefing up security within the town as well as within the jungle itself. With increased police presence and newer train riders making their presence felt in the jungle, the tensions came to a boiling point in the 1999 convention. After reading about these incidents in a variety of hobo 'zines and listservs as well as talking to a number of hobos who were present in Britt that year, there are two main instances that will help shed light on the power dynamics that are in play in the Convention: one that shows both older and younger hobos using their visibility and status as hobos for leverage against the town and another that shows how the town, anxious over the increased visibility, re-asserted its dominance and exerted its power over *all* the hobos. The first instance has to do with an event that has been affection-ately referred to in hobo circles as "The Liberation of the Boxcar."

The hobo jungle is actually a small park located at the edge of Britt and a few feet away from the train tracks that intersect this town. In the middle of the jungle is an old, rusted boxcar that was put there by town officials for tourists to be able to reenact hop-ping trains. But while they figured the boxcar would be used for these symbolic purposes, the younger riders, many of whom do not carry tents that the retired 'bos pack in the back of their vans, used the boxcar for a much more practical reason: to sleep. In 1999, however, wanting to discourage these new "gutterpunks" from participating in the convention, the police closed and padlocked the boxcar. The hobos, after all, were *guests* on town property and had to follow its rules. Their action, however, imme-diately caused a response among the hobos that crossed genera-tional lines.

After a discussion with the mayor and the police to reopen the boxcar did not produce immediate results, the *BLF* (Boxcar Liberation Front) broke the padlock in the middle of the night, opened the boxcar, and slept inside. When ordered to get out, a few remained and Lee staged an act of peaceful resistance and was arrested. Through his arrest, Lee forced the police to ac-knowledge their actions: they were padlocking the quintessential symbol of hobo travel—the boxcar—and making the object a pseudo-museum piece that could be looked at as a historical arti-fact but not used by the "stars" of the convention—the rail riders themselves—for the practical use of sleeping.

Lee was not the only one involved and town officials, not wanting to create a public relations disaster that might have an effect on the amount of income generated by the town, relented and allowed the car to remain open for the three days during the convention. Hearing this story told many times from both older hobos as well as a few of the current railriders, it was quite ap-parent to me the pride they felt in resisting the authority for the hobo cause. It was their convention and the town was making money off their lifestyles and they therefore demanded some au-tonomy in the jungle (regardless of who owned the property). The liberators were an eclectic group: a female librarian who travels the rails on weekends, a fulltime 'bo who has been hopping freights since he was a teenager, a squatter who lives most of the year in a house he built in the woods, and a professor of a community college who is an "amateur 'bo" and collects and publishes hobo lore. It was an interesting and telling moment as those who were subordinated made their stand and actively fought back, reclaiming the box-car that they felt belonged to them. Of course, many of the hobos are members of the "straight" community. If only young, full time 'bos had appropriated the car, would the police have relented so easily? When younger railriders exert their identity—during the election that took place in the center of town, no less—the consuming "normative" power relations were quickly reinstated.

The culmination of the festival and the largest single draw of the convention is the crowning of the King and Queen Hobo for the following year. In itself, the crowning is ridiculous: a man and woman, who represent an illegal, homeless subculture are raised to the inflated title of King and Queen. The "election" takes place in the town square: after a parade, an auction that raises money for the Hobo Foundation, and a feast of Mulligan Stew cooked by town volunteers (in previous years, it was the hobos who would cook it), a large crowd gathers on the square's lawn. After some preliminaries by the town officials, a few words by the ex-incumbent King and Queen and multiple tributes and bestowing of honorary titles to various hobos, the election of the hobo begins.

The hobo's campaign speeches range from the comic to the serious. When I was present at the Convention, one hobo who had obviously been drinking for awhile made ludicrous campaign promises that were unrealistic (as well as misogynistic); a female Hobo, on the other hand, told the crowd that God filled her with love and as Queen, she would continue to spread love to everyone she met. The new royalty were crowned with tin cans.

The crowning can be seen strictly as a joke; the audience gathered on the lawn were clearly having a good time listening to the speeches. But there are elements of seriousness as well. The town is bestowing an amount of cultural and political capital on a subculture that is in conflict philosophically and practically to the authority and traditions of the town. To elect a King and Queen Hobo therefore must remain a joke—and the threat of the hobo must not be a viable one. Firecracker, running for Queen in the 1999 election, tore away the veneer of fun of this election and showed the seriousness that is involved when a subculture forces itself to be recognized.

On the wall of the Hobo Museum, there is a picture of a woman standing on the platform in the gazebo, holding a "Railroad Crossing" sign (a large X) over her head on which is written GIRLS. Surrounded by older hobos, the young energetic woman seems to be out of place; sporting dreadlocks, she is wearing army-issue camouflage pants and a tattered shirt that reveals underarm hair. The photo tells of the female hobo and her modern day traveling—something that is given very little attention in the overtly masculinized literature about the 'bo. This woman is Firecracker.

It was explained to me by many hobos who present at the event that it was obvious that Firecracker won the most applause in the election. Her feminist speech that included song and dance steps, culminating with the raising of the sign (it was this moment that is captured on the wall of the museum). Her attitude, dress, and mannerisms spoke loudly about her political affiliations: she was a feminist, an anarchist, and she was proud of both.

And while she received the most response from the crowd, her speech was not well received by the older members of the community as well as some older hobos. Citing that her speech might be a bad influence on the local girls in the crowd, there was a "recount" of the vote and the title of Queen was bestowed on someone who was deemed a more appropriate role model. While this caused some uproar among the younger trainriders and was even reported in the Mason City newspaper as "an election irregularity," the town's decision stood.

This belies the anxiety and battle over the word hobo. While the town enjoys (and makes money off of) the notoriety of older male hobos like Steam Train, who make good copy bouncing children on their knees, a young woman with dreadlocks, spouting feminist propaganda cannot be allowed to speak so freely in the middle of the town square.

What would have happened if the hobos refused to accept the town's decision and stopped the election, refusing to leave the gazebo until it was acknowledged that Firecracker was, in fact, Queen? What if more "gutter-punks" were present at the convention and, refusing to capitulate to the town, were joined by the older hobos who fought for their fellow train riders? What type of media coverage would that have drawn and consequently, how would that have affected the amount of income generated by the town in the upcoming Conventions with the threat of anarchists running wild around downtown? And while it may seem as if the questions are moot, it is crucial to understand because it shows the tension involved on the borderland areas where subcultures/cultures meet and the political play that is involved to keep the hegemonic forces in control.

Notebook

1. In this essay, we witness two controversial events—the "taking back" of the boxcar and the election of Queen Firecracker—that seem to signify turning points in the life of the railriding subculture. In a similar way, many people talk about how murder of a concert-goer by Hell's Angels bodyguards at the Altamont music festival was the "end of an era" for the hippies. Are there moments in your own life that signified the "end of an era," or a transformation? What moment or event seems to be most important to the subculture you're studying?

2. John Lennon shows how the historic hobo culture—which relied on both trains and migrant work in order to exist—has died out as the economic factors that created them have died out. What other subcultures can you think of that have died out due to changes in technology or the market?

3. "Too Dirty to Be a Hobo?" looks at how the gutterpunk subculture grew out of the declining hobo subculure. Can you find another example of a subculture that rose from the ashes of an earlier one? See if you can locate members of these two subcultures and interview them. How do the members of the older subculture feel about the newer one?

4. How would you characterize Lennon's view on the hobo subculture? How does his style allow you to sense his own opinions on the controversies he describes? What details from this essay support your characterization? Take a look at a section from Steam Train Maury Graham's autobiography *Tales of the Iron Road: My Life as King of the Hobos*. How does the style of the book, and the author's voice, work to present the subculture? Are there any similarities between the style of that book and the style of this essay?

A Straightedger's Journey
ROBERT T. WOOD

In this personal interview, a straightedger (and icon in that subculture) thinks about why he left the subculture he loved—and why he became part of the subculture he belongs to now. Robert Wood is an Associate Professor of Sociology at the University of Lethbridge in Alberta, Canada. He has been studying contemporary subcultures for over ten years. In addition to publishing his research on theories of schism among subcultural groups, Dr. Wood has conducted several studies of the straightedge youth subculture as well as the nonracist skinhead subculture.

✦

INTRODUCTION

I conducted the following interview with Porcell in January of 2000, as part of a study of the American straightedge youth subculture, which branched out from the American punk-rock subculture in the early 1980s. Straightedge individuals are known for their active rejection of drugs, alcohol, and promiscuous sex; many also endorse vegetarian and vegan lifestyles.

At the time of my initial study, I was interested in many different facets of straightedge, but particularly in people's experiences of forming and maintaining a straightedge identity. I conducted a number of interviews with straightedgers in order to understand how they came to identify themselves as straightedge, and to understand how they experienced that identity over time. Many people described their transition into straightedge identity as a sort of journey, saying that the straightedge concept resonated profoundly with their perceptions and life experiences. Indeed, many of these people first experienced the straightedge concept as a sort of epiphany; for them, it suddenly clarified and articulated their perceptions of the social world and helped them to make sense of themselves and their lives. However, as I talked in more depth with longer-term straightedgers, I quickly realized that their perceptions of straightedge and their relationship to it often changed over time. For some people, for example, displaying external straightedge symbols (such as the "X" on the back of a hand) and collecting straightedge cultural artifacts (such as straightedge music recordings) became far less important as the years passed. Others explained how the militancy of their commitment to a straightedge lifestyle declined, over time, and how their tolerance of non-straightedgers increased. Still others explained how they began to distance themselves from the subculture, eventually transitioning out of a straightedge identity emtirely.

I was led to explore a very interesting question. How can a subculture be so profoundly meaningful to a person at one point in her or his life and then later assume such a low priority, or such a different meaning, that the person nearly abandons it altogether?

In the following interview, Porcell sheds some light on this question. Those who are familiar with straightedge might already know Porcell by reputation. He was active in the subculture during its early years and was a member of several very influential straight-edge rock bands, including Gorilla Biscuits, Judge, Project X, and Youth of Today. He is also currently a member of a well-known Krishna Conscious hardcore band, called Shelter.

The Interview

BECOMING STRAIGHTEDGE

Rob: When was it that you first heard about straightedge and how was it that you came to be involved in it?

Porcell: I was into hardcore probably since about 1980, when I was just a little 12 year old kid. I was into progressive living. You know, making the world a better place, and making yourself a better person. I heard about straightedge bands like 7 Seconds and Minor Threat, and I was like "wow, this is something smart, this something positive, this is something progressive." These bands sang about hope, against racism, against the whole consumer culture. They really had such a big impact on me.

Rob: So, when did you first know that you were a straightedger? Was there a time when you said "OK, I am straightedge, and here's why?"

Porcell: You know, I went to a kind of straight-laced upper middle class suburban high school, and pretty much the only kind of activities that you would do on the weekend was go to a party, get drunk, or smoke pot. I was on the football team, so it was even more engrained. [So] there was a period of time from when I was like 16 to 17, when I was really into straightedge, but once in a while I would go to a party and get drunk. I was never really like the party animal type guy. I went through my phase of that, but then I remember there was a point where it was just like, "Straightedge is the way I want to live my life. I am not going to cave into peer pressure. Plus, if I am going to be in a band singing about this, then I am really going to have to make a commitment." There was a point where the rest of the guys would try to get me to drink, and I would be like, "Hey listen, I don't drink anymore, leave me alone."

Rob: When did you join your first straightedge band?

Porcell: Me and Ray, the singer for Youth of Today, were in a band called Violent Children. We were just 15-year-old kids messing around. But we were influenced by bands like Minor Threat, and Youth Brigade, and 7Seconds, who really had a lot to say and a lot of criticisms on the way that American life is set up. We wanted to be in band with a positive message that could actually impact kids, like these other bands that impacted us. So, we broke up Violent Children and started Youth of Today. And we came out and we were very vocal. We were very straightedge. We put big black Xs on our hands. This was before there was a whole straightedge movement. There was a few straightedge bands, [but] they didn't really necessarily champion straightedge. Even Minor Threat: I think Ian was probably the only one that didn't drink in the band. It was sort of a more personal thing to him. There was also SS Decontrol: one guitar player was straightedge. He wrote all the lyrics, but the singer who was singing the songs wasn't even straightedge. So there wasn't really a band that fully embraced it.

Rob: So, you perceived yourselves as a fully straightedge unit?

Porcell: And that was what we actually set out to do. And at the time in the scene, the punk scene, there wasn't a straightedge niche. It was a very drug oriented scene. We got serious about the band and we moved to New York City. My early memories of going to CBGBs [a famous venue for alternative music in New York City], you're walking into the bathroom, and there's six guys in there sniffing glue, and everyone is rocked out of their mind. People are just passing out in the corner. It was pretty horrible. That reinforced in me that [drugs are] a destructive thing, and [doing drugs] is horrible and has nothing to do with punk rock, or supposedly trying to go out and make a change in the world. . . . I was like, "this is ridiculous!" I was thinking, "how is this the alternative?" My whole life, on the weekend you go to a party and people would get drunk and they get in fights. Then you have the punk scene, which is supposed to be this big alternative, and what happens? People go to shows, and they get drunk, and they get in fights. It was white-bread suburban life in leather jackets and spike bracelets. It was ridiculous.

DISAFFILIATING FROM STRAIGHTEDGE

While Porcell's commitment to straightedge was fueled in part by his active role in the straightedge music scene, it is ironically the music scene that ultimately prompts him to distance himself from a straightedge identity. Porcell never relinquishes his straightedge identity entirely, but negative experiences in the straightedge scene cause him to seriously question the meaning of straightedge and his own relationship to it.

Porcell: [Project X] had this one song, "straightedge revenge," and the lyrics were: "I am as straight as the line that you sniff up your nose, I am as hard as the booze that you swill down your throat, I am as bad as the shit you breathe into your lungs, and I'll fuck you up as fast as a pill on your tongue." And, I mean, whatever, at the time, that's the way I felt. But, then, as we went on, I saw what a negative reaction this had on kids. The kids were becoming arrogant and they were beating people up that weren't straightedge. I was in this other band, Judge, and we were one of the prototypes of the whole hardline thing. The last tour we ever went on, in America, was completely disheartening, because there were just so many fights at every show. A kid with an X on his hand would come up to me after the show and start telling me how he just beat the crap out of some guy that had a beer in his hand. As if I was gonna be like, "Yeah, that's really cool, man." As if he was impressing me or something. At the end of the tour, me and the singer, we had a little meeting about it. We were just like, "We're gonna break up, this isn't worth it." It's such a horrible thing to know that you could have impacted a person in such a negative way. We just called it quits. I felt bad because I felt like I was actually promoting [fights] with records like that. It was another testament to me about how, when you get on stage, and say something, people are going to take it to heart. For me, becoming straightedge meant I was trying to become a better person, and if I get caught up in all that then it is actually going against what I originally set out to do.

Porcell further explains that his growing discontent with straightedge stemmed partly from his perceptions of a lack of commitment to the straightedge ideal among his older straightedge peers. These experiences, along with his perceptions of growing violence among younger straightedgers, caused Porcell to seriously

*question whether straightedge was the sort of vehicle for personal
and social change that he once perceived it to be.*

Porcell: All the straightedge kids grew up, and they started going
to college, and they grew their hair out, and they just start
drinking again. I was just really getting sort of introspective
about why I was straightedge in the first place. And, you
know, then you see these other straightedge kids, and they're
assholes, and they're beating people up. And, then, there's
other people that drink, but they seem pretty cool. So, what
actually is the goal? Is the goal to become straightedge or is
the goal to become a better person?

TRANSITION TO KRISHNA CONSCIOUSNESS

*In time, such experiences and reflections prompted Porcell to explore
alternatives to straightedge. In the following interview excerpt,
Porcell explains how the lifestyle similarities between straightedge
and Krishna Consciousness made his transition to the Krishna
Consciousness Movement a seemingly natural progression.*

Porcell: I had known about Krishna Consciousness because after
Youth of Today broke up, the singer actually became like a
[Krishna] monk and he moved into a temple. So I always
knew about it and always kind of respected it. I believed that
money was not the all and all goal of life, and I believed that
consumerism and materialism were bad things, and I was a
vegetarian. All these things sort of coincided with Krishna
Consciousness, so I always had a respect for it. Also, I was
always idealistic but I always didn't live up perfectly to my
ideals. I remember I worked at a health food store, and I used
to steal all this food from it. You just take something off the
shelf, you don't pay for it, and you eat it. And, I was like, "this
is terrible." Here I am, in a band, singing "make a change,
make a change, make a change," and I am finding it difficult
to even make a change in myself. And that's when I realized
it's not enough just to scream, "make a change." You have to
learn how to do that. Krishna Consciousness is called the
science of self-realization. It's like a process where you can see
the results manifesting in your life. So, when I first started
getting into it, going to the temple, and trying to live a Krishna
Conscious lifestyle, I noticed that things in my life were
changing. Things that were a struggle for me to give up before

were just kind of naturally falling away, which is part of the whole process. So, to me it was just like a natural progression from straightedge.

Rob: And so what really changed in your life then? What did becoming Krishna Conscious mean for you in terms of your lifestyle?

Porcell: I moved into a temple in 1992. For me, at the time, I was really burnt out on the hardcore scene. I was playing with Gorilla Biscuits at the time, a big straightedge band, but no one in the band was straightedge. They were straightedge early on, but they were getting older, and none of them were straightedge anymore. And I was just like, "Y'know, this whole movement isn't really changing people." I was like, "I want to try something that's actually going to make some lasting changes." To become a devotee of course you don't have to move into a temple. You can take the slow boat. For a lot people that might be a better way because it's a lot easier than making major life changes. But, at the time, I was ready and I just quit the hardcore scene. I quit my job, quit my apartment, and I moved to a Krishna Conscious cow protection farm in Pennsylvania. And I shaved my head, I lived like a monk, I woke up at 4 o'clock in the morning. I was farming and protecting cows all day long. It was a pretty amazing experience.

Rob: In what sense was it amazing?

Porcell: It was amazing because it was such a spiritual lifestyle. Waking up at 4 o'clock in the morning, chanting in those early morning hours and going through a whole morning program, and studying all these Vedic literatures. Such a higher lifestyle than I was used to living, you know, waking up at noon and watching TV and stuff life that. The farm was great. We were growing all our own food there. We were taking care of all kinds of animals. And, I really felt like now I am living a lifestyle that's conducive with everything that I think and believe.

I remember that the band Shelter was still going, and they were monks living in a temple. The whole band was now monks, and Ray was singing. Their guitar player, Vic, left to start this other Krishna Conscious band, called 108. So they didn't have a guitar player. They had no idea that I had moved into a temple. I mean, I hadn't been in contact with Ray for about a year. They were in India at the time that I moved into a temple. They all came back, and they were like, "Oh my God, here we are back from India, we really want to get this band going, we have no guitar player." They looked for guitar players for months, and finally one straightedge kid came up to them and was like, "Hey, I don't understand it, why don't you get Porcell to play guitar? He's a Krishna now, he's living on that farm. He's probably just not doing much. You should get him." And they were like, "Porcell's a Krishna living on a farm?" They couldn't believe it. So, one day, I got this call from Ray, and Ray was like, "This is great, I can't believe it. I finally tracked you down, and you're a devotee now. We need a guitar player. This is Krishna's arrangement, you gotta join the band." And I was like, "Ray, forget about it, I'm not going back to the hardcore scene. I'm not gonna travel around in a van and deal with all this crap."

And then there was a big revelation to me, because I was reading the Bhagavad Gita. I was really studying it and I was starting to understand it. The Bhagavad Gita takes place on a battlefield. And Krishna is talking to this other warrior, Arjuna. Arjuna wants to be a spiritual person. He wants to do the right thing; he wants to be dharmic. And therefore he decides he shouldn't fight in the war because it's a bad thing. And, the whole Bhagavad Gita is about Krishna trying to tell him that he should fight in the war. It's sort of like a parable that you can apply to your own life. The conclusion of it is that it's not *what* you do, it's *how* you do it that's important. You can do anything in a spiritual way, even fighting in a war.

And so when I started understanding the Bhagavad Gita, I was understanding that, by nature, I'm a musician. I always loved music. Ever since I was 10 years old I was listening to music all day long. I loved playing it, and I was in successful bands. It's not that I have to give that up to become Krishna Conscious, and live on a farm, and try to be a farmer, which really wasn't my nature at all. When you do something that's against your nature, you can do it for awhile, but you can't really do it in the long term. And so I was like, "Okay, I'm gonna try to be a musician again, but this time I really want to do it in a spiritual and righteous way, and I want to try to give a message to people that will have a lasting impression on their life." And that's when I decided to join Shelter, finally. I've never had any regrets since.

I do believe that everyone ultimately is spiritual by nature, and unless they develop that side of themselves, they're never going to be happy, and they're always going to be searching for material happiness, like fame, money, and sense gratification. You can see people knocking themselves out trying to get these things. I mean, so many people think, "If only I can be famous then I'll be happy." Then you have people like Kurt Cobain, who's the most famous musician in the world and blows his head off with a shotgun.

I remember that after Youth of Today, I moved out to California because Revelation Records moved out there. I mean, it was sort of like a big fish in a small pond type thing, but amongst the hardcore scene I had fame. And, I remember I moved out there, and the day that I moved out there, the whole straightedge scene from Huntington Beach, and the surrounding areas, they had this big party for me. They all gave me gifts. It was like the weirdest day. There were instantly kids who were practically worshipping me because I was some straightedge idol to them or something. I was working for Revelation Records. I barely worked like two hours a day. I had tons of money because I had just put out six records, and I was getting royalty checks from them every three months, so I didn't even have to work. I was going to the beach everyday. I had a motorcycle. I had a beautiful girlfriend. I remember one day just being on the beach and being like, "I have such a good material situation that practically every kid in the hardcore scene in southern California is envious of me." And I was like, "I'm not happy. I feel so shallow and incomplete. This is horrible." Just from what little connection with Krishna Consciousness that I had, I realized that what's missing in this equation is spirituality. I have this whole side to myself that I am just ignoring, and of course I am going to feel incomplete.

RECONCILING TWO IDENTITIES

Rob: You mentioned that you see yourself still as straightedge. How do you reconcile your straightedge identity with your identity as a Krishna devotee?

Porcell: I just see them as parallels. I mean, I see every devotee as straightedge. I mean, what is straightedge? We don't drink, we don't eat meat, and we don't take any intoxications of any kind.

Rob: Do you think that's enough, Porcell, to actually make a change? The whole theme around straightedge seems to be about making a change. From your perspective, is being straightedge enough to actually make that change?

Porcell: From my own personal experience, and seeing people around me, I definitely don't think it's enough. I personally witnessed, first hand, the whole straightedge rise and the straightedge fall. And, you know, when it was the coolest thing in the scene to be straightedge and have an X on your hand, I would say 99% of those kids aren't straightedge anymore.

Rob: From your perspective, are there a lot of straightedgers who find meaning in Krishna Consciousness? Is it common for straightedge individuals to make that transition?

Porcell: When Shelter was going on, from like 1992 to maybe like 1995, there was a real Krishna-core trend in straightedge. Every kid would have the neck beads and they'd have the bead bag and they'd be chanting before the shows. What can you say? A lot of people get into things for superficial reasons. It just becomes a trend like any other thing. But I know a lot of kids that got into it seriously. It seems to be that the people from back in the [early] days who managed to stay straightedge, I'd say most of them are devotees.

To me, it's sort of like the culmination of what straightedge really should be. What is the purpose of straightedge? The purpose of straightedge is not to put something in your head that's going to screw you up and make you think unclearly. Okay, once you've cleared your head, now what? Now what are you gonna think about? Being straightedge is not an all in all, it's just a means to an end.

CONCLUSION

For Porcell, maintaining a straightedge identity has been journey over time, during which his identity has endured numerous transitions and changes. Like Porcell, many people don't simply drop in or drop out of a subculture or a subcultural identity. Instead, (un)identifying or (dis)affiliating with a subculture can be a highly nuanced process that unfolds in numerous directions over years. Rather than a condition that is either present or absent, subcultural identity and subcultural affiliation are processes that ebb, flow, wane, dissipate, and possibly even rejuvenate at various times in the individual's life. Thus, if future researchers want to properly understand the experience and process of dropping in and dropping out, then these complexities are best kept at the forefront of any future investigation of people's journeys into, and out of, contemporary subcultures.

Notebook

1. Wood notes that through his research on the straightedge subculture, he began to wonder, "How can a subculture be so profoundly meaningful to a person at one point in her or his life and then later assume such a low priority, or such a different meaning, that the person nearly abandons it altogether?" Was there ever something in your life that was extremely meaningful that you later abandoned? Can you chart the progression? Why did it happen, and how?

2. What, if anything, did you know about straightedge before reading this interview? What did you know about Krishna? How have your opinions changed, if at all, on these subcultures from reading Porcell's account? Some people consider the Krishna movement, and other similarly non-culturally-mainstream religious sects, a cult. In what ways are religious sects, or cults, subcultures, according to the definitions put forward in this book? In what way is something like Krishna similar, or different, than something like Wicca?

3. The punk subculture has spawned many subsets, and here, Porcell discusses the overlap between straightedge and Krishna consciousness. What other subcultures can you think of that overlap? For more on the history of punk and its subgenres, read *Punk Rock, So What?: The Cultural Legacy of Punk*, by Roger Sabin.

4. The essays for this chapter were the hardest to find: Not much has been written on dropping out of subcultures. Why do you think this is? What do you think can be learned about a subculture from the members who leave it?

CREDITS